ST. PAUL

A STUDY IN SOCIAL AND RELIGIOUS HISTORY

BY

ADOLF DEISSMANN

D. THEOL. (MARBURG), D.D. OF ABERDEEN, ST. ANDREWS, AND MANCHESTER
PROFESSOR OF NEW TESTAMENT EXEGESIS IN THE UNIVERSITY OF BERLIN
AUTHOR OF 'LIGHT FROM THE ANCIENT EAST'

TRANSLATED BY

LIONEL R. M. STRACHAN, M.A.

ENGLISH LECTURER IN THE UNIVERSITY OF HEIDELBERG
FORMERLY SCHOLAR OF ST. JOHN'S COLLEGE, OXFORD

περὶ ψυχῶν ἀνθρώπων τὸ ἔργον.

Wipf and Stock Publishers
199 West 8th Avenue, Suite 3
Eugene, Oregon 97401

St. Paul
A Study in Social and Religious History
By Deissmann, Adolf
ISBN: 1-59244-471-7
Publication date 1/15/2004
Previously published by Hodder and Stoughton, 1912

ST. PAUL: A STUDY IN SOCIAL AND RELIGIOUS HISTORY

THE GALLIO INSCRIPTION AT DELPHI.

UNIVERSITATI

SANCTI ANDREAE

APUD SCOTOS

SACRUM

PREFACE

An Anatolian St. Paul, a man of the ancients, a *homo novus*, rising from the mass of the insignificant many, heeded by no man of letters among his pagan contemporaries, yet destined to be a leading personality in the world's history; a *homo religiosus*, at once a classic of mysticism and a most practical man of affairs; a prophet and dreamer, crucified to the world in Christ, yet for ever memorable as a citizen of the world and traveller in it, and still moulding the world at the present moment—such is the man whose outlines I have been seeking to portray. After long years devoted to the study of the ancient records of St. Paul and their modern interpreters it was my rare good fortune to find a new teacher to supplement those to whom I shall always look up with gratitude, the old teachers at home. This new teacher is in no sense academic: paper and paragraphs are unknown to her; all that she teaches she dispenses with generous hand in the bright sunshine and open air—she is in fact the world of the South and East, the world of St. Paul. If the western stranger approach the mistress but reverently beneath the olive-trees, she will gladly, and with a mother's joy, speak to him of her great son.

Two journeys to the East, in 1906 and 1909, enabled me to realise the long-cherished hope of seeing with my own eyes the places where the primitive gospel was preached and St. Paul's life-work was done. With some small exceptions I visited all the places of importance in the primitive history of Christianity, and I think I may say that I gained a general impression of the structure of the Pauline world which to me personally has increased in value and effect from year to year. There is no need to labour the point; the advantages of such journeys to the student can only be ascertained by actual trial. If the traveller goes in a teachable spirit, and leaves at home all conceit of his own superior civilisation, he will learn to see things in their true relief and to view them from the proper distance. He sees what light and shade are, and the meaning of heights and depths. His appreciation of simplicity and wild spontaneous growth, and of things not yet harmonised and conventionalised, becomes keener; wondrous problems of classification and division suggest themselves; the extremes of contrast between the modern book-culture of the West and the ancient non-literary culture of Anatolia become tangible. Ill fares it, on the other hand, with our painful inheritance from the scholar's study—the microscopic ingenuity, inexorable, and overweening in its ignorance of the world, which rules straight lines with wooden ruler and cuts out boldly with scissors of steel. Even Doctor Bahrdt,[1] return-

[1] [Karl Friedrich Bahrdt (1741–1792), a notorious Professor of Theology at Giessen, whose 'New Revelations of God, in Epistolary and Narrative Form,' an attempted modernisation of the New Testament, was satirised by Goethe in a 'Prologue' (1774), in which occurs the couplet:

> 'So müsst ihr werden, wie unser einer,
> Geputzt, gestutzt, glatt—'s gilt sonst keiner.'

—Tr.]

ing to Giessen, would not again say to the Four Evangelists:

> 'Become like one of ourselves, I implore you,
> Spruce, dapper, sleek—or they'll ignore you.'

Summing up the effect of my travels upon myself, I may say that the good germs of an historical appreciation of St. Paul, which I owed to my teachers and my own studies, underwent new growth in the apostle's own field and beneath the rays of his sun, but that many rank shoots that had sprung up in the shade of the school walls withered under the same beams. Never for one moment, however, have I experienced the 'disappointment' which has come to be characteristic of the newspaper writer of letters from abroad. The New Testament and the prophets whose souls are vibrant in the Sacred Book have become greater to me than before.

Therefore beside the Paul who has been turned into a western scholastic philosopher, beside the aristocratised, conventionalised, and modernised Paul now suffering his eighth imprisonment in the paper bondage of 'Paulinism,' I would fain set the Paul whom I think to have seen at Tarsus, Jerusalem, and Damascus, in Antioch, Lycaonia, Galatia, Ephesus, and Corinth, and whose words became alive to me at night on the decks of Levant shipping, and to the sound of birds of passage winging their flight towards the Taurus—alive in their passionate emotion, the force of their popular appeal and their prophetic depth. I mean Paul the Jew who in the days of the Caesars breathed the air of the Mediterranean and ate the bread which he had earned by the labour of his own hands; the missionary whose dark shadow fell on the glittering marble pavement of the great city in the blinding glare of noon; the mystic devotee of Christ who, so far as he can be comprehended historically at all, will be understood not as the incarnation of a system but as a living complex of inner polarities which refuse to be parcelled out—contending forces the strain of which he once alluded to himself in writing to the saints at Philippi [1]:

'I am in a strait betwixt the two.'

I have a word to add concerning what I regard as an important conception strongly emphasised in the following pages. The whole development of early Christianity—to which Adolf Harnack has lately applied the term 'double gospel,' *i.e.*, the gospel of Jesus and the gospel of Jesus the Christ —appears to me as an advance from the gospel of Jesus to the cult of Jesus Christ, that cult deriving its sustenance and its lines of direction from the gospel of Jesus and the mystic contemplation of Christ. This view, which regards the apostles as devotees of a cult (not, of course, to be confused with an established religion), seems to me to do greater justice to the essential nature of Primitive Christianity than any other that has been formulated. No other excludes altogether the possibility of mistaking the development of Primitive Christianity for something in the main doctrinal. The emphasis which I have laid on the development of the gospel into the cult is nothing 'recent' on my part, as William Benjamin Smith [2] seems to assume (meaning, I suppose, subsequent to the publication of his

[1] Phil. i. 23, *συνέχομαι ἐκ τῶν δύο.*

[2] *Der Vorchristliche Jesus*, second edition, Jena, 1911, p. xxvii.

'Prehistoric Jesus'). It goes back many years, and will even be found in my writings before the appearance of Smith's book, the hypotheses and propositions in which, by the way, do not commend themselves to me.

My sketch of St. Paul is founded on eight lectures which I delivered in German by invitation of the Olaus Petri Trustees at the University of Upsala in March, 1910, and which were immediately published in a Swedish translation.[1] For the German edition the text has been newly revised and greatly enlarged, yet so that the whole should still remain a 'sketch.' There is therefore no attempt at a discussion of recent literature on St. Paul, to which I am, in spite of many differences of opinion, greatly indebted. . . .

As regards the map of 'The World as Known to St. Paul' prepared according to my design, and appended to this work, information will be found in the book (see Index, s.v. 'Map') and on the map itself.

ADOLF DEISSMANN.

BERLIN-WILMERSDORF,
19 *July*, 1911.

[1] *Paulus. En kultur- och religionshistorisk skiss*, Stockholm, 1910. Fragments of the German original appeared by the editor's desire in the *Internationale Wochenschrift* for 1910 and 1911.

TRANSLATOR'S NOTE

My thanks are due to Professor Deissmann for reading the proofs and answering a multitude of questions; to my sister, Miss C. E. Strachan, B.A., for supplying the needful references to English translations of certain books quoted; and to Mr. Hans Baedeker, of the well-known Leipzig firm, for the loan of guide-books and the kind offer of further assistance when I was at work upon the map.

For the English edition two small features have been added to the map, viz. the Osmanieh railway, as mentioned at p. 30, and the railway in Cyprus, which had been accidentally omitted. The explanatory matter in the lower left-hand corner has been translated, and the spelling of the modern names in the upper corner has been brought into harmony with English usage. It being obviously impossible to re-spell the names on the map itself, the squares have been numbered and an index compiled which will, it is hoped, afford all necessary help to a reader accustomed only to English spelling and measurements in English feet. In many cases the modern names of ancient towns are not given on the map, but as far as possible they have been supplied in the index. For these additions, and indeed for the whole index to the map, I am alone responsible. A work that was of the greatest service to me was

Murray's 'Handbook for Travellers in Asia Minor' (1895, with supplement dated 1907), by Sir C. W. Wilson.

The index of places, persons, and subjects is also my independent work. While differing not inconsiderably from the author's own index, it is, I believe, quite as extensive, and I hope more useful to an English reader than a mere adaptation of the German index would have been.

As the inscription facing p. 246 has come out none too clearly, it may be as well to point out that the last capital in each of the lines 1 and 10, the last three in line 7, and also the first Τ and second Π in line 3, are meant to be dotted, at least in part.

L. R. M. S.

HEIDELBERG,
September, 1912.

CONTENTS

CHAPTER VIII

CHAPTER IX

APPENDIX I

APPENDIX II

APPENDIX III

INDICES

ILLUSTRATIONS

THE PROBLEM AND THE SOURCES

CHAPTER I

THE PROBLEM AND THE SOURCES

Two names contain in themselves the primitive history of Christianity: the names of Jesus and St. Paul.

Jesus and St. Paul—the two figures do not stand side by side as first and second. From the broadest historical point of view Jesus appears as the One, and St. Paul as first after the One, or—in more Pauline phraseology—as first in the One.

Consciousness of His own personality—this is the living force in Jesus from which proceeds that soul-stirring movement which has continued at work among mankind throughout the centuries down to the present day. This consciousness is self-supported; Jesus stands out in history linking heaven and earth together, but stands in lonely majesty and might.

St. Paul needs some foundation. What St. Paul is, he is in Christ.[1]

But compare St. Paul with the others. Then St. Paul is spiritually the Great Power of the apostolic age: he laboured more,[2] and not only laboured more, but created more than all the others.

Therefore the others recede behind him, and

[1] Phil. iv. 13, R.V. [2] 1 Cor. xv. 10.

therefore the historian, surveying the beginnings of Christianity, sees St. Paul as first after Jesus.

Visible though it be to a great distance, the historic personality of Jesus is not easy for research to grasp; the personal interval is too immense, and the hieroglyphics of the gospels have not yet all been deciphered.

St. Paul stands nearer, and is more easily accessible to us.

Even St. Paul is considered by many to-day to be darksome as well as great. The darkness, however, is largely due to the bad lamps in our studies, and the modern condemnations of the apostle as an obscurantist who corrupted the simple gospel of the Nazarene with harsh and difficult dogmas, are the dregs of doctrinaire study of St. Paul, mostly in the tired brains of gifted amateurs.

But if we place the man of Tarsus in the sunlight of his Anatolian home and the clear air of the ancient Mediterranean world, among the simple folk of his social stratum, that which pained our eyes like a book of faint and faded pencil sketches becomes suddenly plastic, alive with light and shade like some mighty relief of ancient date.

Not that we can completely restore this relief. We shall only gain fragments; but they will be important fragments, essential fragments, from which we can recover, at least hypothetically, the proportions and lines of the whole, when we have learnt to look on fragments not as scraps but as integral parts.

That really and properly is the task of the modern student of St. Paul: to come back from the paper St. Paul of our western libraries, Germanised, dogmatised, modernised, to the historic St. Paul; to penetrate through the 'Paulinism' of our New Testament theologies to the St. Paul of ancient reality.

The work accomplished by the nineteenth century on St. Paul is both by its thoroughness and the magnitude of its production one of the most imposing achievements in the scientific study of religion. Considered as a whole, however, it is very strongly influenced by interest in St. Paul the 'theologian' and St. Paul's 'theology.' Together with enormous discussion of literary questions, especially the authenticity of St. Paul's letters and the relation of the Acts of the Apostles to those letters, it is chiefly the so-called 'System of the Pauline theology' or 'Paulinism' that three generations have wrestled over.[1]

With this doctrinaire interest, however, the study of St. Paul has gone farther and farther astray. One factor, which certainly is not wanting in St. Paul, but which is by no means the historically character-

[1] An important scientific parallel to the doctrinaire study of St. Paul is the doctrinaire study of Plato during the nineteenth century; cf. Paul Wendland, *Die Aufgaben der platonischen Forschung*, Nachrichten der K. Gesellschaft der Wissenschaften zu Göttingen, Geschäftliche Mitteilungen 1910, 2. Heft: 'It may now be confidently said that the comprehensive exposition of the system, however indispensable it may be on didactic grounds, is, from the purely scientific point of view, a wrongly stated and therefore insoluble problem' (p. 97). . . . 'A system can be worked out with certainty only in the case of thinkers who have employed the form of the systematic didactic treatise. The same problem must fail, or is only approximately soluble, in the case of Plato, St. Paul, Luther (p. 98), and Goethe; their writings are not calculated for systematic exposition' (p. 99). There follows a polemical protest against Zeller's presentment of Plato.

istic one, the factor of theological reflection, has been placed in the foreground, and the real characteristic of the man, the prophetic force of his religious experience and the energy of his practical piety, only too often underestimated. The doctrinaire study of St. Paul has left moreover one great riddle unsolved: the open question how far the 'Paulinism' of its discovering was the seat of those vital forces which were bound to have a missionary effect because they carried away the simple folk of the ancient Mediterranean world. I am afraid the people of Iconium, Thessalonica, Corinth would all have been overtaken by the fate of Eutychus of Troas[1] if they had been obliged to listen to the Christological, hamartiological, and eschatological paragraphs of modern 'Paulinism.'

What is best in St. Paul belongs not to theology, but to religion.

It is true, St. Paul was the pupil of theologians, and learnt how to employ theological methods; he employs them, indeed, as a Christian missionary. But we must not for this reason rank the tent-maker of Tarsus along with Origen, Thomas Aquinas and Schleiermacher. His place is with Amos, the herdman of Tekoa, and Tersteegen, the ribbon-weaver of Mülheim. St. Paul the theologian looks backward towards Rabbinism. As a religious genius St. Paul's outlook is forward into a future of universal history.

St. Paul is essentially a hero of piety first and foremost. That which is theological is secondary with him. The naïve is stronger with him than the

[1] Acts xx. 9 ff. The excellent Eutychus, whose name is a warning to all who slumber in church, was certainly one of the extremely few people who managed to go to sleep in the presence of St. Paul.

premeditated, the mystic stronger than the dogmatic; Christ means for him more than Christology, God more than the doctrine of God. He is far more a man of prayer and witness, a confessor and prophet, than a learned exegetist and brooding dogmatist.

To show that this is so, is, I consider, the object of this sketch. There is to be no question of a profound study of the manifold problems of the external incidents of St. Paul's biography; in particular, the discussion of chronology [1] and questions of literary criticism must give way before the main object, viz., an estimate of the man from the point of view of social and religious history.

When the problem is thus set, the question of sources appears a comparatively simple one.

In the wider sense of the word, the sources for an estimate of St. Paul on the basis of social and religious history are the records of the ancient Mediterranean world in the age of the great religious change, especially the authentic records recovered for us in such abundance by recent discoveries among inscriptions and papyri—records of the middle and lower classes,[2] the social environment of St. Paul.

In the narrower sense the sources are the Primitive Christian texts, chiefly the original letters of St. Paul, and with them St. Luke's Acts of the Apostles, but including everything else on which reflections of the personality of St. Paul are discernible. I am thinking especially of the Johannine writings,

[1] Just one fundamental problem of chronology is treated in Appendix I.

[2] Cf. my book, *Light from the Ancient East:* the New Testament illustrated by recently discovered texts of the Graeco-Roman World, second edition (London: Hodder and Stoughton), 1911.

charged as they are with the warm life-blood of Pauline devotion to Christ. St. John is the oldest and greatest interpreter of St. Paul.

The question of sources, so far as it applies specially to the letters left us by St. Paul, has become complicated, not from any intrinsic cause, but owing to an ingenious *circulus vitiosus* in which Pauline study has often moved. The personality of St. Paul having been lifted from the naïve to the premeditated, from the religious to the theological, his letters were also transferred from the non-literary to the literary category, and with the aid of these letters, now made literature, a further attempt was made to exhibit the apostle as a literary man and a dogmatist.

The letters of St. Paul therefore share with their writer the fate of having been frequently misjudged. I am not referring to exegetical blunders in details, I mean misunderstood as a whole. Their intimate, peculiar character—their soul—has been misunderstood. They have been regarded as treatises, as pamphlets in letter form, or at any rate as literary productions, as the theological works of the Primitive Christian dogmatist.

This momentous misunderstanding, by which the letters of St. Paul are rooted up and laid in the herbarium, is to some extent excused by the fact that in the age of St. Paul the letter was really employed in the regions of literary culture as a form of literary production.[1] The literary letter, which we propose to denote by the technical term 'epistle,' to distinguish it from the real letter, was throughout the later period of antiquity one of the most popular

[1] For what follows cf. 'Prolegomena to the Biblical Letters and Epistles' in my *Bible Studies*, 2nd ed., Edinburgh, 1903, pp. 1–59. (A new German edition of *Bibelstudien* is about to appear.)

forms of literary art. We find the epistle not only among the Greeks and Romans, but also among the Hellenistic Jews; it was afterwards freely used by the Christian *literati* of the ancient church, and to this day it plays a great part in our modern literatures. But its most intrinsic characteristics make it something different from a letter, and if we wish to do historical justice to the letters of St. Paul we must seek to comprehend them as non-literary letters distinct from the literary epistles.

What is a letter? And what is an epistle?

A letter serves the purposes of conversation between two persons separated from one another. It is an 'I' speaking to a 'you.' Individual and personal, intended only for the addressee or addressees, it is not calculated for publicity, and is indeed protected from publicity by good manners and by the law as a private and secret document. A real letter is non-literary, like a receipt or a lease. It concerns only the one who has written it and the one who is to open it, and it is of no consequence whether the addressee intended is a single person, or a family, or any other circle of persons. Its contents are as manifold as life itself. A letter can be trifling, vulgar, passionate, kind, trivial, dull, and it may be the reflection of a human fate or a domestic tragedy, moving the souls of the writer and the receiver mountain-high or to abysmal depths.

An epistle is different. It is a literary artistic form, like the drama, the epigram, the dialogue. The epistle shares with the letter only the external form of a letter; for the rest it is the opposite of a real letter. It aims at interesting and influencing some public or other, if not the public. Publicistic in its essential character, it makes use of the personal only in order to keep up the illusion of a letter. If the letter is a secret, the epistle is cried in the market. It does not go abroad, like the letter, on a single sheet of papyrus, but it is reproduced at once at the beginning by the slaves of the bookseller in the great city: it is to be bought, read, and discussed in Alexandria, in Ephesus, Athens, Rome.

The epistle is distinguished from the letter just as the historical drama from a piece of real history, or as a Platonic dialogue from a confidential conversation, or the conventional biography of a saint from the accounts in which eye-witnesses tell their co-religionists by word of mouth, halting with excitement, how the martyrdom took place. In a word, epistle and letter are distinguished from one another like art and nature, like the conventionalised and the natural growth, like the premeditated and the naïve.

There are, it is true, midway between letter and epistle certain changeable varieties, letter-like epistles and epistolary letters, that is to say lively epistles lightly dashed off, and unnatural, tortured letters without simplicity and originality. But these intermediate species cannot do away with the fact and the importance of the difference between letter and epistle. And this question in particular remains to be settled: To which of the two groups are the letters of St. Paul to be assigned?

An ample amount of material for comparison here offers from the ancient world. Real non-literary letters, by Epicurus and Cicero for example, have been preserved to us, but besides these we possess in hundreds of originals, written on papyrus and on earthenware potsherds by unknown Egyptian men and women of the Hellenistic and Roman periods, private letters in the original handwriting.[1] Their letter-like nature is at once perfectly obvious, and their formal peculiarities in the matter of address, praescript, religious wishes at the beginning, formulae of greeting, and other details belonging to a letter, have given us quite a new insight into the ancient letter.

On the other hand we have numerous literary letters in the prose epistles, *e.g.*, of Lysias, Aristotle, Seneca, and in the poetical epistles of Horace and Ovid, and it is of special importance with regard to the problem of our sources, that already before St. Paul the epistle had made its way as a form into the literature of Hellenistic Judaism, as shown for example by the Epistle of Aristeas, treating of the origin of the Septuagint, and by a pamphlet against the worship of idols styling itself an Epistle of 'Jeremiah.'

It would therefore be in itself not at all impossible that St. Paul might have written epistles and ought therefore to be ranked with the men of literature—the more so because in the New Testament there are besides the letters of St. Paul other texts which look like letters, and which are certainly to be described as literary epistles, the clearest example perhaps being the Epistle of St. James.

And yet, when once the significance of the distinction between non-literary and literary production has been seen and acknowledged, there can be no doubt as to the non-literary letter-like

[1] Cf. the selection in *Light from the Ancient East*, pp. 147–217, and the literature there (p. 147, n. 2), to which is now added G. Milligan, *Selections from the Greek Papyri*, Cambridge, 1910; Mitteis and Wilcken, *Papyruskunde*, Leipzig, 1912.

character of St. Paul's letters. A mere comparison of the formalities in the letters of St. Paul with the corresponding details in contemporary papyrus letters shows us clearly the non-literary character of the Pauline texts. Most particularly, however, in the course of an exact commentary on the letters themselves it is seen, more clearly in the case of one, not quite so strikingly in the case of another, but unmistakably nevertheless, that these texts were the outcome of a definite epistolary situation, not to be repeated, and, being calculated solely for this single situation, are not the products of literary art, but of actual life, documents of the primitive apostolic cure of souls confidentially exercised between man and man, relics of the apostle's missionary work among his churches, 'survivals' in the sense of the technical language employed by the historical method.[1] St. Paul wrote these letters, or, in many cases,[2] spoke them to the pen of a companion in the midst of the storm and stress of his wandering life, which was so rich in deeply moving experiences; and then he sent them, a single copy in each case, by trusty messengers to the place of their destination, over sea and over land, from Ephesus to Corinth, from Corinth to Rome and to Ephesus, without the great world or even Christendom as a whole immediately knowing anything of their existence.

That a portion of these confidential letters should be still extant after centuries, St. Paul cannot have

[1] For this view cf. a forthcoming work of mine, *Das Neue Testament als das historische Dokument des Urchristentums*.

[2] 2 Thess. iii. 17; Gal. vi. 11; Col. iv. 18; 1 Cor. xvi. 21; 2 Cor. x. 1 (?); Rom. xvi. 22. Either the writer is named, or Paul emphasises the fact that he has added the conclusion of the letter with his own hand.

intended, nor did it ever occur to him that they would be. His ardent faith never reckoned with centuries to come. Spanning apostolic Christendom like a sultry sky fraught with thunder was the hope that the present age of the world was hastening towards its end, and the new world of the Kingdom of God drawing nigh. A hope like this does not thirst for earthly fame as an author, it aspires longingly to the new, the heavenly.

St. Paul laboured to help prepare the way for this new era, and the letters that he sent out are subservient directly or indirectly to this purpose. Their subject is always some problem connected with souls or with the church in a definite and peculiar position. The letters are simply a substitute for spoken intercourse, and it is of great importance in their exegesis to imagine them as spoken (*i.e.* dictated) and to try to restore the modulation of the living and by no means bookish words; to discover, that is, where St. Paul is smiling, where he is angry, where (to the horror of his later Atticist commentators) he falls halting into anacolutha, or where prophetic fervour lends wings to his words. St. Paul sets out to comfort, admonish, chasten, strengthen; he defends himself against his adversaries, settles doubtful questions, speaks of his experiences and intentions, adds greetings and messages of greeting, generally without anxiety as to arrangement of his matter, passing unconstrainedly from one thing to another, often indeed jumping, and the longer letters show clearly the often abrupt change of mood while he was dictating.

Some of these letters were no doubt early lost. The Corinthians, for instance, suffered letters of

St. Paul to disappear,[1] for which we would to-day gladly give the entire polemical literature of our theological journalists, and that is sure to have been the fate of other letters of St. Paul, even in early times.

Nevertheless, after the death of the apostle, when people began to collect and copy the sheets from his hand that were scattered among the churches, it was still possible to rescue more than a dozen of Paul's letters, some of them lengthy, and gradually this collection, although non-literary in origin, acquired literary importance. It even became part of the canonical corpus of the sacred writings of Christendom, and thus the letters of St. Paul have come into our possession bearing the venerable distinction of canonical dignity. It is as though old jewels in a precious setting were placed in our hand; the setting is so rich that we are somewhat distracted from the stones themselves. But take the setting away, and then the diamonds will blaze in their own fire and sparkle more brilliantly than before.

The non-literary conception takes nothing essential from the letters of St. Paul, it rather restores to them their original glow. And whoever sees this sacred fire glowing in the precious relics sees also that they are genuine stones. Dust-covered, and distorted with doctrinaire additions, several of the letters of St. Paul seemed not to be Pauline; and many a scholar, made suspicious by the great contrasts in their spiritual contents, has given up some of them as not genuine.

[1] The letters of St. Paul mentioned in 1 Cor. v. 9 ff. and 2 Cor. ii. 3 f., vii. 8 ff., the contents of which it is possible partially to reconstruct. A letter from the Corinthians to St. Paul (1 Cor. vii. 1) is also lost.

If the non-literary character of St. Paul's letters be energetically thought out, and if they are continually compared with undoubtedly genuine familiar letters of other great men, most of the objections that have been made to the authenticity of individual letters of St. Paul will have nothing left to stand on.

The delusion is still current in certain circles that the scientific distinction of a Bible scholar may be estimated in the form of a percentage according to the proportion of his verdicts of spuriousness. It is as though the fame of Bentley had made many have recourse to false standards; and the extant letters of St. Paul have been innocently obliged to endure again a fair share of the martyrdom suffered by the historic St. Paul[1]:—

> 'Thrice was I beaten with rods, once was I stoned, thrice I suffered shipwreck.'

Applicable perhaps to literary epistles, the commonplace interrogation-marks employed in the study are not illuminating in the case of non-literary letters: I am thinking especially of St. Paul's Second to the Thessalonians and what is called his letter to the Ephesians. There is really no trouble except with the letters to Timothy and Titus, and even there the difficulties are perhaps not quite so great as many of our specialists assume. That which in these letters seems conventionalised, stereotyped, non-letter-like, is partly perhaps an inheritance, taken over by St. Paul and only slightly adapted to his purposes, from the communal experience of Hellenistic Judaism, and

[1] 2 Cor. xi. 23 ff.

partly, it may be, post-Pauline interpolation. As these letters, however, do not supply so very much characteristic material for the task before us—a delineation of St. Paul from the point of view of religious and social history—I conclude that there is no need for me to go at any length into the problem of their authenticity[1] while speaking of the question of sources. It is a problem, moreover, on which my mind is not yet definitely made up.

Other difficulties, such, for example, as those presented by the letters written in prison, may perhaps be made easier by a revision of the old ways of putting questions. To name but one such case, it is very well possible that the prison-letters are to be assigned partly to an imprisonment of the apostle at Ephesus.[2]

The chief evidence for the essential authenticity of the letters of St. Paul that have come down to us, is the circumstance, defiant of all inventive power, that in each of these letters the same man of character is mirrored, each time in a new light, and with new expression, or even with a great change of expression within the same letter. It is not the unchanging cold marble bust of Paulinism that we see every time; but it is, I think, always the living man, Paul, whom we hear speaking and see gesticulating, here playful, gentle as a father, and tenderly coaxing so as to win the hearts of the infatuated children — there thundering and

[1] In the following pages I shall quote them only where they confirm the impressions gathered from the certainly genuine letters, or in illustration of typical facts in the world of St. Paul.

[2] Cf. *Light from the Ancient East*, p. 229; M. Albertz, Theologische Studien und Kritiken, 1910, p. 551 ff.; and Benjamin W. Robinson, Journal of Biblical Literature, vol. 29, part ii. (1910), p. 181 ff.

lightening with the passionate wrath of a Luther, with cutting irony and bitter sarcasm on his lips. Another time his eye is radiant with the experience of a seer, and his mouth overflows with acknowledgments of grace experienced; or he loses himself in the tortuous paths of a religious problem, and his soul trembles under a heavy trouble, or he draws forth from David's harp a gracious psalm of gratitude. It is always the same Paul, though the posture is constantly changing, and even where apparent contradictions can be observed it is the same Paul, the man whose nature contained such polar extremes that we might apply to them the words of the poet[1]:—

> '. . . no book excogitate am I,
> But man, made up of contrariety.'

The inmost, the most intimate character of St. Paul's letters is easiest apprehended if we begin with the letter to Philemon. It is the shortest and probably also the most letter-like letter of St. Paul, written on a single sheet of papyrus like plenty of other contemporary Greek letters from Egypt. The doctrinaire and literary theory fails completely in this case. It is a sin not only against historical judgment, but against human taste, to have described this delightful document as a tractate on the position of Christianity towards slavery. That is turning men into abstractions and making a confidential little letter into a book: Paul becomes

[1] Conrad Ferdinand Meyer (1825–1898), 'Huttens letzte Tage' (1871), xxvi:—

> '. . . ich bin kein ausgeklügelt Buch,
> Ich bin ein Mensch mit seinem Widerspruch.'

impersonal as 'Christianity,' the slave Onesimus is transformed into 'slavery.' And really the whole thing is so extremely simple. A slave named Onesimus has run away from Philemon, a Christian living at Colossae, in the interior of Western Asia Minor. He hoped no doubt to be able to hide himself in the great seaport of Ephesus, which was accessible in a few days' journey,[1] but he was probably arrested[2] there and in prison became acquainted with St. Paul, who, I believe, was then also a prisoner at Ephesus. St. Paul converted the man to the gospel and sent the runaway (for whom perhaps he had become a surety to the prison authorities) back to his master. The little letter that he gave him to take with him prays that the poor good-for-nothing[3] may find pardon and a kind reception. This letter is like an instantaneous photograph of pastoral direction in Primitive Christian times; all the charm of a unique personality is shed over these few lines of St. Paul's: Christian feeling is combined with Greek delicacy and the tact of a man of the world. Though a

[1] At the present day it would be possible, on horseback and then with the railway, to get from Colossae to Ephesus in a single day in case of need. At any rate in 1909 I did the journey from Ephesus to Laodicea, which is near Colossae, and back again in two days (13 and 15 March).

[2] Runaway slaves were probably not infrequently pursued with warrants, and the authorities had to try to arrest them. In the Paris Papyrus No. 10 we still possess an original warrant for the arrest of two runaway slaves in the Ptolemaic period (Notices et extraits 18, 2, pp. 177 ff.); a high reward is offered for the capture of the fugitives, who were to be reported to the authorities as soon as their whereabouts were discovered.

[3] So says St. Paul (Philemon 11, 'unprofitable,' A.V., R.V.), punning on the name Onesimus, which means 'profitable.'

prisoner, St. Paul writes with perfect calmness;[1] a blissful good-humour beams from his eye, he opens the treasures of his confidence, appeals to brotherly love and love of the Saviour, and knows that these powers are irresistible. Yet there is not a trace of triviality in the treatment of a subject that in itself is trivial, not a word is without its significance, a strong and yet elastic soul is revealing itself to the trusted friend.

A similar mood gave rise to the little letter contained in the sixteenth chapter of Romans. In all probability this was originally not an organic part of the letter to the Romans but a special letter from the apostle to his gathering of Christians at Ephesus, recommending to them the Christian woman Phoebe. Here too St. Paul speaks in a thoroughly letter-like way to people in whom he confides. Like several papyrus letters of that age, this letter contains hardly anything but greetings to individuals, but every greeting is given a personal tone, and the whole is full of allusions to work in common and suffering in common. St. Paul the great martyr and the great labourer shows himself in

[1] Read, for the sake of the contrast, the plaintive, whining letters (Flinders Petrie Papyri III. No. 35 *a* and *b* and 36 *a*) written from prison by captive Egyptians in the Ptolemaic period —highly interesting parallels to St. Paul's prison-letters. Intercourse with the outside world was certainly easier for prisoners in those days than it is in our country. Cf. the smuggled letters (called 'slums' by modern gaol-birds) offering bribes at p. 48 n. below, also Matt. xi. 2, xxv. 36, and prisons in Anatolia at the present day. A visit to the great prison at Konieh (Iconium) on 6 March, 1909, showed me with palpable clearness the lively intercourse that goes on through the barred gate between the prisoners and their relatives who have come in from the country to see them.

this page of writing, Paul with his knowledge of men, the living centre of his circle. In one place glowing indignation against corrupters of the gospel breaks in, and at the end we hear a full chord from the harp of Paul the psalmist.

First and Second Thessalonians are also thoroughly letter-like. First Thessalonians, indeed, is full of moving personal reminiscences. The two may be said to exhibit the average type of the Pauline letters, written on the whole with a certain degree of calm, in spite of polemical remarks.

Sacred indignation altogether dictates the beginning of the letter to the Galatians. No wonder this letter, with its lightnings and thunderbolts, was especially fascinating to the great German reformer. St. Paul is obliged to justify himself before the Galatian Christians, deep in the heart of Anatolia, against malicious calumniators who sought to rob him of the confidence of these young converts by casting doubts on his apostolic mission and branding his Christianity apart from the law as apostasy. He does not, however, write a dogmatic treatise, but a fiery letter of self-defence, in which afterwards he also strikes other notes. With all the ardour of his soul he pleads with the Galatians for the old love. The character-portrait of the apostle is most clearly defined in the most various directions.

Much calmer than Galatians is the beginning of First Corinthians. St. Paul speaks his mind about a number of weak points in the Corinthian church, and so the letter shows us the depths of the writer's wisdom as a shepherd of souls. Here, too, there is no lack of sharp controversy, biting irony, and prophetic indignation, but on the whole St. Paul is more reserved; he spares the church where he can, and deems it worthy of the deepest and most splendid personal confessions. Amidst the wild uproar of parties at Corinth, amidst the noise of wrangling over the denarius and of quarrelling between advanced Christians and the weaker brethren in the cosmopolitan city of Roman Hellenism, he introduces a sublime figure, powerful, noble, and chaste enough to be worthy of a Phidias, and Agape, that is Love, reveals the uttermost mystery of the nature of God and of His Son, and binds together the sons of God in one great brotherhood. And afterwards St. Paul makes passionate and affecting confession of Christ, bears witness to his hope of eternity, and converses in charming alternation of small things with great concerning his plans and his troubles.

Perhaps the most personal of the longer letters of St. Paul is the Second to the Corinthians. Regarded as a whole it is also the least known to us, for the very reason that it is so entirely letter-like, so entirely a personal confession, full of allusions that we can no longer understand in their entirety. St. Paul is deeply affected at the outset, for God had once more graciously delivered him from fearful peril that threatened his life. The beginning of this letter breathes therefore an unspeakable thankfulness; but this mood is succeeded by others, especially by one of sharp antagonism against Christians with a hankering after the law, who at Corinth as elsewhere had scattered their seed of calumny. Again, as in writing to the Galatians, St. Paul allows his Corinthian brethren to look deeply into his life, in its inner as well as its outward aspects, and chapters xi. and xii. especially are documents of unreplaceable value for the apostle's history.

The least personal letter of St. Paul's of any length is the one to the Romans. But that also is a real letter, not an epistle. There are parts in it, certainly, which might find a place in an epistle, and it might here and there be called an epistolary letter. But all the same it is a letter, and not a book, and the saying, popular with many German students of St. Paul, that it is a compendium of Paulinism, and that the apostle has here laid down his dogmatic and ethical system, is, to say the least, very liable to be misunderstood. St. Paul wished, certainly, to instruct the Roman Christians, and he did so partly with the resources of contemporary theology. But he does not contemplate as his readers the literary public of his time, nor even Christendom in general; he addresses himself to a handful of people resident in the more modest quarters of Rome, of whose existence the public knew practically nothing. It can hardly be that the apostle sent copies of the letter to the gatherings of Christians at Ephesus, Antioch, and Jerusalem; he sent his written message only to Rome. The fact that these pages are not so markedly enlivened by personal phraseology as most of the other Pauline letters is explained by the circumstances under which the letter was written: St. Paul was writing to a church with which he was not yet personally acquainted. The decreased prominence of personal detail is no evidence that the letter to the Romans is epistolary and literary in character; it is the natural consequence of the letter-like and non-literary situation underlying it.

The situation was similar at the time of writing the letter ('To the Ephesians'), contemporary with the one to Philemon, which was sent up the valley of the Lycus to Colossae and Laodicea. These churches also were not yet known to St. Paul from personal intercourse, and so the personal element is less prominent than the impersonal. The peculiar solemnity of the language is striking—a gravity of tone suggestive now of liturgical worship and now of meditation, and moreover not unknown in certain parts of other letters of St. Paul's. As regards the contents, the detailed development of the mysticism centring round Christ, which is usually only hinted at, because taken for granted as something known, is unmistakable. A large portion of the critical difficulties caused by the contents of these letters disappears when St. Paul has become known to us from the undoubtedly 'genuine' letters as the great mystic where Christ is concerned.

On the other hand, the letter to the Philippians is thoroughly letter-like and most markedly personal, being addressed to a church with which the apostle was particularly well acquainted, and which had given the prisoner a great proof of affection. St. Paul returns thanks for this, and his words seem to quiver with personal notes that are peculiarly affecting and could not be invented, so that we realise in all its freshness the personality of this man of many contrasts.

Thus each of St. Paul's letters is a portrait of St. Paul, and therein lies the unique value of St. Paul's letters as materials for an historical account of their writer. There is probably not a single Christian of any importance in later times from whom we have received such absolutely honest materials to enable us to realise what his inner life was like. Even the Confessions of St. Augustine, owing to their literary appeal to the public, cannot bear comparison with St. Paul's letters. And there are probably only extremely few men of the Roman imperial period whom we can study so exactly as we can St. Paul by means of his letters.

It is quite obvious that a man who, as a contemporary and as an occasional travelling companion of St. Paul, describes the apostle from outside as it were, could not attain that faithfulness of portraiture which St. Paul unconsciously attained when he drew himself in his letters. How colourless is the picture of Bismarck drawn by Moritz Busch, as he appeared in the great war, compared with Bismarck's picture of himself in the letters he wrote from France to his wife! But St. Luke's representation of St. Paul in the Acts of the Apostles is nevertheless indispensable in supplementing the letters of St. Paul; it may be corrected occasionally in some details by the letters, but in many others it rests on good tradition.[1] In opposition to the thesis that St. Luke consciously distorted the statements in St. Paul's letters in favour of a movement for union which sought to mediate between conflicting parties in the apostolic age, I assert most emphatically that St. Luke was not even acquainted with the letters of St. Paul that we possess. When St. Luke wrote they had not yet been collected and published. What St. Luke knows of St. Paul he knows from other sources. Some things no doubt he heard told by St. Paul himself, for instance the striking story of the escape from

[1] Adolf Harnack's recent studies of St. Luke betoken a healthy reaction against the severely inquisitorial method.

Damascus in a basket,[1] which the apostle no doubt laughingly related on various occasions with variations in the details. Other things—and those his best—come from St. Luke's own observation, narrated by him in the first person plural, in the regular style of ancient voyagers.[2] And it is his great merit to have shown us especially Paul the practical man, Paul the traveller, making his way through the ancient Mediterranean world and preaching to that world the living Christ.

This Mediterranean world, which is the world of St. Paul, because he was born in it and spent his life for it, we must now try to picture to ourselves.

[1] Acts ix. 24 f. It is tolerably certain that St. Luke did not get this story from 2 Cor. xi. 32 f., for in that case, with his fondness for potentates, he would certainly not have forgotten the ethnarch of King Aretas.

[2] Cf. for instance the narrative of King Ptolemy Euergetes I., told in the first person plural, concerning his voyage to Cilicia and Syria, which has been discovered in the valuable Flinders Petrie Papyri III. No. 144. Further details in the forthcoming publication announced on p. 12 n. 1 above.

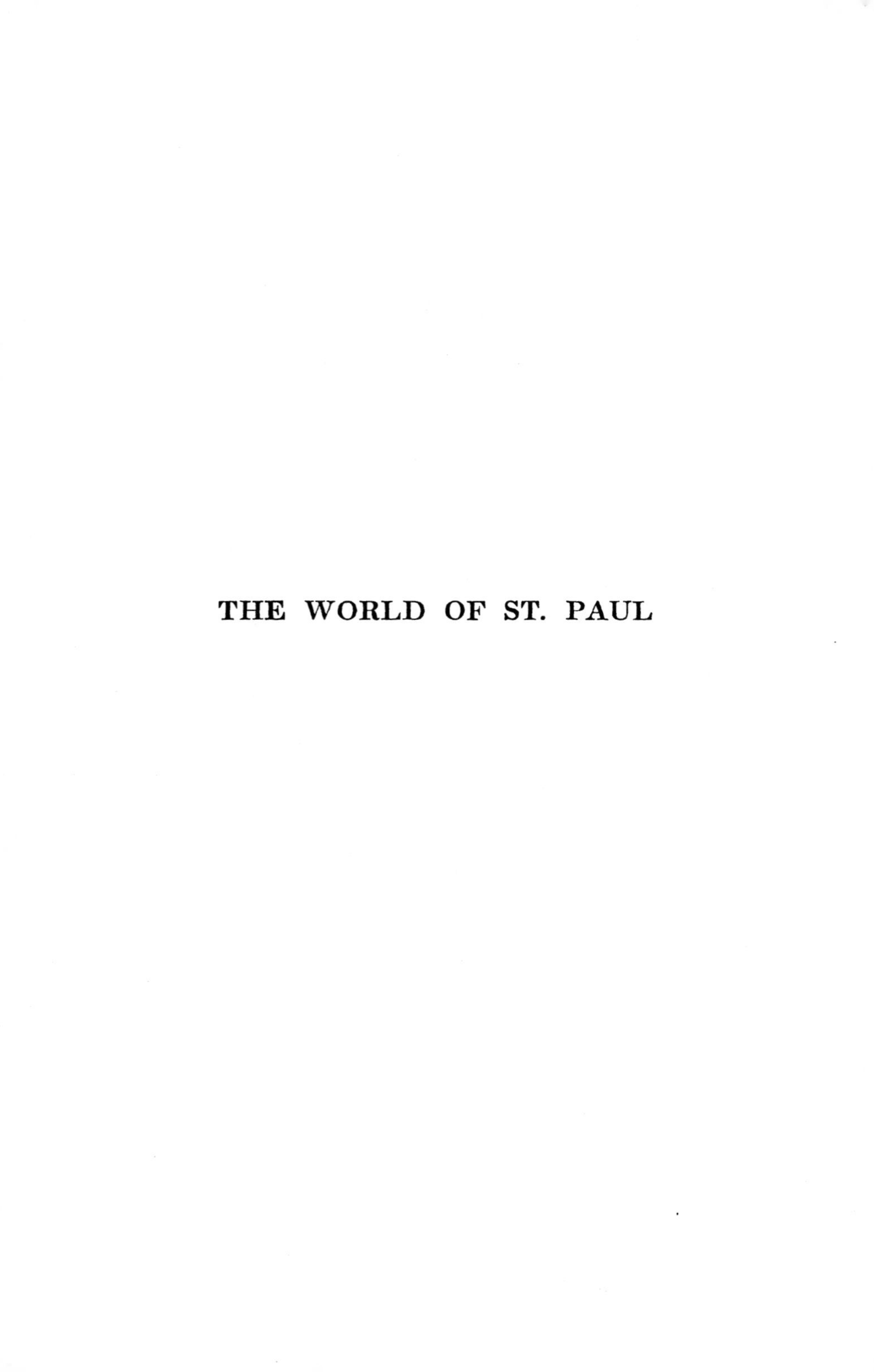

THE WORLD OF ST. PAUL

CHAPTER II

THE WORLD OF ST. PAUL

SAILING southward on the Russian pilgrims' steamer from Smyrna along the west coast of Asia Minor,[1] you are carried quickly past the silent shore of Ephesus and the naked rocks of Samos, through the island world of the Sporades, and in four-and-twenty hours arrive at Rhodes. And if you then steer eastward, after a voyage of barely thirty-six hours along the south coast of Asia Minor you can drop anchor in the roadstead of the Cilician port of Mersina.

The glorious landscape spread out before us while the boats from the harbour are rowing out to take us ashore, is unforgettable. The bright light of the Anatolian morning sun trembles on the waves and

[1] For the following pages cf. my map. We made this voyage on the Russian steamer 'Korniloff,' bound from Odessa with pilgrims to Palestine, 16 to 19 March, 1909. We took lodgings in Mersina and visited Soli-Pompeiopolis and (on two occasions, 20 and 21 March) Tarsus. The following observations were for the most part made then; a few Anatolian details are from my journey of 1906. On the pilgrims' ships, where one is no doubt often the only 'educated' person among hundreds of Siberian and Russian peasants, members of the eastern Jewish proletariat, Armenians, Turks, and Arabians, you learn ten times more about the modern (and ancient) popular life of the East than you do on the big Levant steamers, which even on the waves of the Mediterranean do not let us escape from the cage of our European civilisation.

flashes on the high-lifted oars of the gaily-dressed Turkish boatmen. The distant houses of Mersina stand out in blinding whiteness, and we see the minarets and cupolas of the places of worship, while the flags of the European consulates and the Turkish authorities flutter merrily in the breeze. At the east end of the town white clouds of steam are rising, and the whistle of a locomotive comes to us across the waves. Mersina is the starting-point of the line, now owned by the Anatolian Railway, which runs through the broad, fertile plain of Cilicia to Adana.[1]

And then behind the town this Cilician plain stretches away, green and luxuriant, into the distance, here and there enlivened by gently rolling hills crowned with ruins, until it is brought up by the massive outliers of the Cilician Taurus, whose peaks, soaring defiantly to heaven, cut the horizon into quaint jagged forms. The contours of this mighty mountain chain are so wildly thrown about that it is not easy to follow them, and as our eye rests on the sunny snow of the summits, we find ourselves dreaming, though with but a faint conception, of the primeval catastrophes and the aeons of work by the elements that formed this landscape before human hand ploughed the field or tended the loom, and before human knee bowed to the powers of the upper world.

Far away in the east the ridge of the Syrian Amanus mountains, coming from the south, meets the Taurus, and it is a strangely moving experience

[1] See the map, which also shows the course of the other projected lines.—Another railway, which was proposed in March, 1911, from Osmanieh (between Castabala and Issus) to Alexandretta (Alexandria), has been marked on the map for the English edition.

on deck in the evening, after sunset, to watch the Amanus chain and, all in a wonderful Alpine glow, the snowy peaks of the Taurus looking down upon us across plain and sea, while an Arab singer trolls forth his passionate songs of farewell to a company of young people embarking.

If you come from the interior of Asia Minor and from the west coast and enter the Cilician plain in March, you seem to have skipped over some weeks, so far advanced are the days of spring. The fig-trees that were putting forth their first bright green tips at Ephesus and in the valley of the Maeander, have here got big leaves that shine deliciously in the sun; the asphodel, which blooms luxuriantly even in April in the plain of Troy and on the mounds of ruins at Ephesus, is fading in the fields of Soli-Pompeiopolis, a ruined city on the sea near Mersina; and the anemones which delighted us in the valley of the Maeander and near Ephesus in their first glory of colour, bloom as early as January in the Cilician plain. The poplar of Asia Minor with its slender, silvery stem, forming in sisterly rivalry with the minarets the characteristic emblem of Anatolia in town and village, is here farther advanced, much farther than in Konieh or Angora; and on the grey old columns of Pompeiopolis the luxuriant blossom of the Judas-tree glows a deep red. Snow hardly ever falls in the plain, and all through the winter the garden supplies the household with its green produce.

Later on the cornfields and cotton-plantations bear heavy crops of great luxuriance, but then the fields swelter under a heat that is indescribable, and the fever rages up and down the country. When in March, 1909, after some time spent in following the missionary routes of St. Paul in the interior and on the west coast of Asia Minor, we travelled by the Adana Railway through the magnificent wheat districts of the plain on our way to St. Paul's city of Tarsus, we little imagined that millions of grains in those ears of corn would never reach the threshing-floor. A few weeks afterwards there broke out in that sultry Cilician plain a fever that decimated the population as far as Antioch in Syria worse than the most terrible malaria—the religious and national fanaticism of Mohammedans goaded on to murder, to whose fury thousands of Armenian Christians fell victims. And while the surging waves of the rivers Cydnus and Sarus, then swollen by the spring, bore the bodies of the slaughtered by hundreds to the sea, and the soil of Cilicia once more drank daily the blood of Christian martyrs, out in the fields the corn rotted on the stem or was trampled down and burnt by the blind fury of the persecutor.

More peaceful pictures presented themselves to us on our journey, and we were all unconscious that the sultry burning heat of that plain brooding upon the soul of the people for centuries and centuries has accumulated passions which, when the spark comes, go off in fire and sword, in 'threatening and slaughter.' [1]

Our thoughts on that occasion [2] in the broad plain were strangely stirred by a spectacle rarely seen, far more truly a fragment of the world of St. Paul than was the first building we afterwards entered in his native city—that being the railway station with its bilingual inscription, in Turkish and European characters, TARSUS! High up in the air were enor-

[1] Acts ix. 1, *ὁ δὲ Σαῦλος ἔτι ἐμπνέων ἀπειλῆς καὶ φόνου.*

[2] 20 March, 1909.

mous columns of storks, advancing from the direction of the sea. They were the storks of Asia Minor and Europe on their way northwards from Africa in the south. They had come through the Nile valley and the valley of the Jordan by way of Antioch in Syria (a few days later,[1] near Antioch, we observed a large and greedy synod of storks, and at the Beilan Pass a part of the route taken by this crowd); they had then probably flown over the gulf of Alexandretta, and were now making ready for the flight over the Taurus, some detachments of them provisioning in the broad wet fields, others manœuvring splendidly in the air, other legions again already sailing away in a calm, steady course to the passes of the Taurus.

Who was it that showed the birds this road, which is the road of the great kings of the East, the road of Alexander and the Caesars, the road of the Crusaders and the Mohammedan armies? Was the human road made to follow the immemorial track of the birds of passage? Did we not hear in the rustle of wings over the lonely Cilician plain the eternal rhythm of travel? And afterwards, where the pavement of an old Roman road runs through an Antiochian wheatfield beside the modern road, did we not find the footprints of a Cilician who roamed the world long ages ago, who went from Syria in the south northwards over the Taurus and from Asia Minor in the east towards Europe in the west over land and sea?

The feeling that the plain of Cilicia has been a site of international intercourse since time immemorial becomes much clearer still in St. Paul's city of Tarsus. Little of ancient Tarsus remains above

[1] 25 March, 1909.

ground, but when the natives dig for ancient worked stones on the site of the old city wall near 'St. Paul's Gate' they find terracotta and coins of the time of St. Paul. And above all, the geographical situation for international intercourse is genuinely the same as in the age of the great religious change. Just as to-day the two Islamic civilisations, Turkish and Arabian, meet in the plain of Cilicia, so also in former times the country was the threshold of two civilisations, the bridge between two worlds.

From the highest point of the modern city, perhaps the castle hill of ancient Tarsus, you look out on all sides over the wide plain, and turning to the south you have on your left, behind the blue heights of Amanus and behind where the shimmering vapour hides the last outliers of the other Syrian ridges, the world of Semiticism. Behind you and on your right there stretches in still greater majesty, as seen from Tarsus, the never-ending chain of the Taurus with the famous pass, so momentous in the world's history, known as the Cilician Gates, and behind them lies the world of Romano-Hellenistic civilisation. Anything coming from Syria and the Jordan and bound for Ephesus and Corinth must pass through these gates, or else cross the waves of the Mediterranean by the western shore. Through these gates went the swordblades of Damascus and the balm of Jericho, through these gates went the Logos, which had become Man in Galilee and then again Spirit for the whole world.

Two young Anatolians who had received their education in the excellent St. Paul's Institute founded by the Americans at Tarsus, acted as our guides in their native city. As we sat at table with them in a little inn, one of them wishing to say something complimentary to me praised our German philosophy. 'You have Kant!' he said, with pride in his own knowledge. I answered him, not in conventional phrase, but because I was full of the presence that had become living to me in the lonely Cilician plain, as I looked up at the crowds of travelling birds, and on the castle-hill of Tarsus in sight of the Syrian and Cilician passes: 'You have St. Paul!'

And certainly it is so. That Tarsus has its St. Paul, and that St. Paul came from Tarsus, is no mere accident. The apostle of the nations comes from a classical seat of international intercourse, and his home itself was to him from childhood a microcosmos, in which the forces of the great ancient cosmos of the Mediterranean world were all represented.

The Mediterranean world the world of St. Paul! Any one who wants to understand this world,[1] the world that St. Paul himself once defined[2] as stretching from Jerusalem in the east to Illyricum, Rome, and Spain in the west, in the north of which dwell the Scythian[3] and the Barbarians,[4] while in the south rises the marvellous Mount Sinai in Arabia,[5] must

[1] As regards geography in the widest sense we are indebted for the best information to the great works on the Mediterranean by the late Theobald Fischer and Alfred Philippson; as regards the ancient topography of the world of St. Paul we are similarly indebted to the works of Sir W. M. Ramsay. Admirably suited as an introduction is T. Fischer's masterly sketch, 'The Mediterranean Sea and adjoining Lands,' in K. Baedeker's *Mediterranean* (first English edition), Leipzig, 1911, pp. xxvi–xxxvi.

[2] Rom. xv. 19–24.

[3] Col. iii. 11.

[4] Col. iii. 11; 1 Cor. xiv. 11; Rom. i. 14.

[5] Gal. iv. 25.

not start with the preconceived idea that it falls into two distinct halves, one Semitic, the other Graeco-Roman. We must rather start from the fact of the relatively great unity at least of the coast civilisation in this world.

St. Paul knows a large part of the interior of Asia Minor, and the list given in the Second to Corinthians of the hardships he had endured on his journeys 'in perils in the wilderness' and 'in cold'[1] reflects in the main no doubt experiences in the interior of Asia Minor. The changes of the weather especially are often very abrupt there at the different altitudes.[2] On one day in March, 1909, towards evening at the top of a Phrygian pass we had a violent snowstorm, and the next day at noon we were passing pink-blossoming peach gardens, just as on the journey through the Gotthard from Göschenen to Airolo the transition from winter to smiling spring takes place within half an hour. The 'perils of robbers'[3] no doubt also point rather to the interior of Asia Minor.[4]

[1] 2 Cor. xi. 26 f.

[2] The journeys of St. Paul should not be studied without some attempt being made to realise the various heights of the places he passed through. See the map at the end of the book, where the heights are given in metres (1 metre = 3·28 feet English). Tarsus, Ephesus, Corinth have no elevation worth mentioning, Antioch in Syria is only 262 feet above sea-level, Jerusalem, however, 2587 feet, Damascus 2266, Antioch in Pisidia 3936, Iconium 3368, Lystra about 4034, and these facts are at least as interesting to me as the question about the addressees of 'Galatians.'

[3] 2 Cor. xi. 26.

[4] At the present day it is true even the coast region of Western Asia Minor, which was then so flourishing, is to some extent dangerous, especially for the native traveller. See the descriptions by Alfred Philippson, *Reisen und Forschungen im*

The contrast between the interior of Asia Minor and the coastal regions of the world known to St. Paul[1] must be taken into consideration if we are to judge rightly of the area in which Primitive Christianity expanded. In the interior plateau scarcity of rain and the cold winters of the steppe; in the west an ample winter rainfall and a regular Mediterranean climate, with Mediterranean vegetation. The interior 'an isolated plateau of almost Central Asiatic character,' Western Asia Minor (and the neighbouring coasts) 'Aegean country with contours as varied as in Greece and close mutual connexion between the sea and the scenery and history.' But at the same time an 'easy and extensive contact' between the two regions was possible.

Any one who has seen successively Angora and Ephesus, or Konieh and Tarsus, has the contrast and yet the close contact between the two regions present with indelible clearness before his eyes.

Now though the red lines of St. Paul's pathways run for hundreds of miles through the 'upper country'[2] of the mountainous interior of Asia Minor, they more often adapt themselves in double or treble parallels to the roads of the coast region and

westlichen Kleinasien, I. Heft (Petermann's Mitteilungen, Ergänzungsheft No. 167), Gotha, 1910, pp. 6 ff.—The neighbourhood of Miletus one evening in April, 1906, when we had lost our way and were riding after sunset through the swamps of the Maeander, and next day when we were at Didyma in the house of a Greek who had just been shot dead by robbers, afforded us a drastic commentary on the 'perils of rivers, perils of robbers,' 2 Cor. xi. 26.

[1] My remarks here are based on the concise statement of this contrast given by the best authority at the present time, Alfred Philippson, *Reisen und Forschungen im westlichen Kleinasien*, I. p. 20.

[2] Acts xix. 1, τὰ ἀνωτερικὰ μέρη.

the mariners' routes:[1] in the main the world of the apostle is to be sought where the sea-breeze blows. The coast world of Cilicia, Syria, Palestine, Cyprus, Western Asia Minor, Achaia, and also of the distant west, is the world of St. Paul.

The heart of the Pauline world, however, is undoubtedly the wonderful district which we might call Aegean; Ephesus, Troas, Philippi, Thessalonica, Corinth, Ephesus—this circle witnessed the greatest work of St. Paul. The fact is shown most clearly by the circumstance that almost the whole of St. Paul's letters that have been preserved in the New Testament were written for or else in the Aegean district.

The world of St. Paul is a cosmos—in the truest sense a world. Affording from high-towering lordly peaks endless prospects of green luxuriant plains and sunlit sea, and here as also in wild gorges and rustling groves provoking an awesome recognition of divinity, it enabled to grow up in the light and air a race of open-souled men who were able to interpret voices from heaven and the riddles of Hades. Become the mother of navigation and international commerce, thanks to the ample extent of coastline with innumerable safe inlets, thanks also to the islands which serve as piers to the bridge from east to west, she made wanderers of the boldest and best of the men collected in her ancient cities—heroes, artists and merchants, students and singers and prophets—and enabled that civilisation to be created on which we all stand to-day.

If any one, not being a specialist in geography, wished to characterise this Mediterranean world, which is the world of St. Paul, by a single concrete

[1] See the map.

formula, he might call it the world of the olive-tree, and with this formula he would also be keeping within the range of the observations that we know St. Paul to have made, for in writing to the Romans he himself, of course with a quite different application, compares the heathen world to a wild olive-tree.[1]

The world of St. Paul the world of the olive-tree! The modern traveller from the Teutonic north who fares southward remains at first for some time in his own world; the printing on the railway tickets changes a little, the newspapers at the stations become different, the North German and South German guards relieve each other, but one is not aware of a boundary of civilisation. You are asleep when you enter Switzerland or France, and in the morning you are not sure at once whether you are still in Baden or in Alsace or already over the border. But then there comes a moment which transfers us from the north to the south as it were with a single jerk. That is the instant when, on the road to Genoa somewhere about the Lake of Lugano, or, if Marseilles is the goal, in the Rhône valley south of Valence and north of Avignon, you see the first olive-tree. Many a man who at home as a boy had cut himself willow whistles at Easter, has been mistaken in this first olive-tree at a distance and thought it to be an old willow-tree, owing to the deceptive resemblance of the gnarled stem and silver-grey leafage. Others like to see in the orange-tree, laden with golden fruit, the typical tree of the south and east. But this will not apply to ancient times; the orange-tree is relatively of later importation. Nor is the fig-tree, which thrives

[1] Rom. xi. 17 ff.

even in Heidelberg and in Norderney and Heligoland, the characteristic tree of the Mediterranean world. Much rather that first olive-tree of Lugano or Avignon, with its gnarled growth and its air of gloom, is the south, and is the Levant.

This tree's ancestors distilled blessing upon the nations: in the eye of history an enormous amount of humanising culture stands crowned with the olive-branch. The tree of Homer, the tree of Sophocles, the living symbol of the unity of the Mediterranean coast-world, the olive-tree is also the tree of the Bible, of the Old as well as of the New Testament, and in the names 'Mount of Olives' and 'Gethsemane' (that is 'oil-press') as also in the titles and names 'Messiah,' 'Christ' ('the anointed'), the influence of the olive-tree extends to the deepest associations and most sublime words of our sacred tradition. Without provision of olives, moreover, the world-wide journeyings of St. Paul would be inconceivable; on his voyages especially the fruit of the olive-tree must have played the same part as it does still to-day on the Levantine steamers and sailing ships, particularly for the sailors and deck passengers. A handful of olives, a piece of bread, a drink of water—the Levantine requires nothing more.

The world of St. Paul the world of the olive-tree! There exists a map of the distribution of the olive-tree in the Mediterranean area.[1] Seldom have I learnt so much from a map as from this.

[1] In Theobald Fischer, *Der Ölbaum. Seine geographische Verbreitung, seine wirtschaftliche und kulturhistorische Bedeutung* (Petermann's Mitteilungen, Ergänzungsheft No. 147), Gotha, 1904. In my map of the world as known to St. Paul the olive zone according to Fischer is shown by a green tint.

When I first looked at it without having noticed its title it seemed to me like a map to illustrate the Jewish or Primitive Christian Dispersion. As a matter of fact the zone of the olive-tree coincides almost exactly with the region throughout which scattered Jews were living in the Roman imperial period.[1] Really we might name the Jews of the Dispersion in the same way as one of the many synagogues in the ancient capital of the empire was called: 'Synagogue of the Olive Tree.'[2] And then there is St. Paul's comparison of the Jews to an olive-tree.[3] But the zone of the olive-tree, if we leave out Tunis, Algiers, and Morocco, also coincides almost exactly with the map of St. Paul's missionary work; especially striking is the almost complete absence of the olive-tree in Egypt, where traces of Pauline journeys are entirely wanting. It may be accidental, but still it is very remarkable that almost all the important places in the history of St. Paul lie within the olive zone: Tarsus, Jerusalem, Damascus, Antioch, Cyprus, Ephesus, Philippi, Thessalonica, Athens, Corinth, Illyricum, Rome (Spain).

This world of St. Paul is relatively uniform, in the first place in respect to the climatic and other external conditions determining its civilisation. The contrast of vegetation that we have seen between Cilicia and Ephesus or between Antioch and Corinth does not weigh so very heavily in the

[1] See the ring of about 143 cities (marked blue in my map) encircling the Mediterranean basin, in which Jewish residents are found in the imperial period.

[2] Συναγωγὴ Ἐλαίας, *Corpus Inscriptionum Graecarum*, No. 9904.

[3] Rom. xi. 17 ff.

opposite scale. In the whole of this great civilised world the possibilities of life, especially for a poor man, were everywhere very similar, as regards food and drink, clothing, lodging, and labour.

And politically a uniform stamp had been impressed upon this and upon the still greater extent of the whole ancient world by the Imperium Romanum. Alexander and his successors, the Diadochi, had of course done an enormous work of preparation. The centuries of world-wide political history before St. Paul, from Philip and his son down to the Caesars, are clearly reflected in many of the Greek names of cities which re-echo through the accounts that have come down to us of St. Paul: *Antioch* in Syria and *Antioch* in Pisidia, *Seleucia* in Syria and *Attalia* in Pamphylia, *Laodicea* in Phrygia and (*Alexandria*) *Troas* in Mysia, *Philippi* and *Thessalonica* in Macedonia, *Nicopolis* in Epirus, *Ptolemais*, *Caesarea* (*Stratonis*) and *Antipatris* in the coastal region of Syria and Palestine—each of these names is a monument of the political history which had worked towards unifying the world of St. Paul.

The importance of this world-wide political unity for the coming world-wide religion has long been recognised. When you are at Angora (Ancyra), the capital of ancient Galatia, which St. Paul must probably have touched at, as you stand before the walls of the temple of Augustus[1] you have before you in a somewhat remote quarter of St. Paul's world classical contemporary testimony to that world-wide political unity, testimony which St. Paul himself may once have read—the Latin and Greek text here preserved of the summary which

[1] 3 March, 1909.

the Emperor Augustus himself wrote of the events of his reign.

Though this Monumentum Ancyranum is written in two languages, we must not conclude from it that in the world of St. Paul Latin was then as much an international language as Greek. Among the people of the great cities especially, to whom St. Paul in his world made his appeal, Greek was the language of intercourse, as is most clearly shown by his letter in Greek to the Christians of Rome.[1] Greek had penetrated far into Syria and Palestine; the great cities, St. Paul's own peculiar field of work, were particularly exposed to strong Hellenistic influence, both in language and in general culture. In Palestine it is true the living language of the country, which St. Paul also spoke,[2] was Aramaic; but at Antioch in Syria Hellenism made itself felt all the more strongly, and the greatest difficulty that a missionary elsewhere has, the difficulty of conquering the language and with it the psyche of the heathen, hardly existed for St. Paul in his world. As he was to the Jews a Jew[3] from his childhood up, so he was also to the Hellenist a Hellenist, because he had inhaled the language and soul of Hellenism with the air of Tarsus.

Finally, the world of St. Paul is uniform in respect of a broad undercurrent of religious convictions and expressions common to the people everywhere. The naïve conception of the sky and the universe with the earth as its centre is common to everybody in east and west. Everyone knows the difference between here and above, knows that the divine comes

[1] The Greek inscriptions of Roman Jews in the catacombs also point to the same fact.

[2] Acts xxi. 40. [3] 1 Cor. ix. 20 f.

down on earth from heaven, and that the human must rise from earth to heaven. Throughout the whole of St. Paul's world, from east to west and from west to east, run traditions, thousands of years old, of visible manifestations of the deity, of the deceit and wickedness of daemons, of divine strength taking the form of man and compelling the powers of darkness. And throughout this world of St. Paul we see a mighty wandering of pilgrims desirous to wash away their sins at the great shrines and to be delivered of their need. The Jew of the western Dispersion travelling to Jerusalem meets perhaps on the very same ship a pilgrim to Ephesus and a sick man striving to get to Asclepius of Epidaurus, and each of them extols the miracles of his god with believing ardour.

Such is the world of St. Paul, lapped by the same wave, blessed by the same sun, and when viewed from within, not a chaos of alien bodies artificially forced together, but an organism of relatively great solidity.

The reason why people have so often failed to recognise the compactness of the Mediterranean civilisation, lies in doctrinairism the like of which we not infrequently observe, especially in the study of St. Paul. The culture of the world of St. Paul has been far too much identified with its book-culture. And no doubt, if you compare the Graeco-Roman literature of the first century of the Roman Empire with the oldest records of Jewish rabbinical learning of the time of St. Paul, you become aware of a strong contrast, a contrast not only in methods of literary production, but principally in the condition of soul revealed. Compare at the present day —the analogy is perhaps not too bold—the oration of a teacher of Islam in a mosque at Damascus with the lecture notebook of a modern Italian historian, and here too you have two worlds with a yawning gulf between. But then compare an artisan or a street hawker of Damascus with his colleague of Naples, and you have before you men of essentially identical soul-structure.

In the study of antiquity the mistake has long been made of deducing our conception of the ancient world from ancient literature. The literature is only a part of the ancient world, and, being itself preserved only in a fragmentary condition, it reflects merely fragments of the culture of the ancient upper classes.

So too the picture of the world of St. Paul was formerly drawn almost exclusively with the aid of literary sources, and an extremely gloomy background it became, on the whole, against which the bright phenomenon of infant Christianity stood out all the more luminously. That it was a degenerate, morally corrupt, and as regards religion a bankrupt world into which the Gospel came—this has been learnt and taught by many because, besides being unconsciously influenced by the polemical superlatives of the Fathers of the Church, they had heard nothing but the loud, penetrating voices of denial, despair, mockery, and unbridled pursuit of pleasure. As the other voices were silent, it was no doubt supposed that they had never spoken. And St. Paul himself seemed especially lavish with the gloomy colours in painting the seamy side of the world of his day, when in his letter to the Romans [1] and elsewhere [2] he described the depravity

[1] Rom. i. 24 ff.

[2] Cf. especially the oft-recurring lists of vices.

of his surroundings with all the emphasis of a preacher of repentance.

But the simple truth has been forgotten that neither an isolated phenomenon nor a cultural complex can be described by a single formula. The world of St. Paul has its deep shadows, that is perfectly well understood; but it also has its abundant light, and this ought to be equally well understood. In the same letter to the Romans which depicts the seamy side of a life of unregulated instincts in the great city there are formulated the tremendous words about the law written in the hearts and living in the conscience of the Gentiles which have no law.[1]

And now, thanks especially to the great archaeological discoveries of the nineteenth century, we have recovered portions of the world of St. Paul which enable us to set the light alongside of the shadow. The excavations in Asia Minor and Greece have brought to light vast remains of the great cities of St. Paul's world, the most imposing being Ephesus, disclosed to us by British and Austrian workers, and the cities of Pergamum and Miletus, together with the great seat of worship at Didyma, which German scholars have restored to us. But besides this the non-literary texts on stone, papyrus, and broken pieces of pottery which now grace our museums in their thousands, have made once more audible the voices of non-literary persons of the world of St. Paul which had apparently become for ever dumb. In letters, wills, bills of marriage and divorcement, accounts and receipts, records of judicial proceedings, votive dedications, epitaphs, and confessions of sins,

[1] Rom. ii. 14 f., . . . *τὸ ἔργον τοῦ νόμου γραπτὸν ἐν ταῖς καρδίαις αὐτῶν.*

these people appear before us, laughing and scolding, loving and mean, malicious and kindly.

The chief importance of these new finds seems to me to lie in the fact that, besides affording highly valuable materials to the student of language, law, and civilisation, they show us living persons with the greatest truth to nature, since they are entirely without literary pose and altogether in the workaday clothes of their calling. That the records most interesting as human documents should come from Egypt is a consequence of the climate of that wonderful country. Papyrus sheets could not have lain in the earth for two thousand years in Asia; in Egypt that was possible. But we are certainly entitled to regard the psychical and other facts that result from those human relics of Graeco-Roman Egypt as for the most part typical of the world of St. Paul.

The examination of these non-literary texts for the light thrown by their contents on the souls of the writers is still in its beginnings; but it can already be said that the traditional picture of the ancient world as morally and religiously degenerate has been proved by these very texts to be a distortion.

They do indeed furnish contributions to the darker side of St. Paul's world; we have for instance among the papyri proofs of unchastity,[1] bribery,[2] robbery,

[1] Quite a number of papyri throw light on the subject of prostitution, which is reflected in repeated warnings in the letters of St. Paul.

[2] Cf. the bill of complaint against Egyptian officials of the imperial period who had suffered themselves to be bribed, Pap. Class. Philol. I. No. 5 (Archiv für Papyrusforschung, 4, p. 174), and the edict of the Praefect of Egypt, Tiberius Julius Alexander, 68 A.D., censuring cases of bribery of officials (Archiv, *loc. cit.*).

violence and theft,[1] the exposure of children,[2] and unbridled impudence,[3] and unfortunately it cannot be said that these proofs leave off in the Christian period of Egypt.[4] But nevertheless the bright colours that present themselves to us are on the whole more abundant. The family life of the middle and lower classes appears here in a light that is by no means only unfavourable; but above all a strong religious emotion and marked religious aptitude show themselves in these people, and here the numerous religious inscriptions are extraordinarily instructive. The world of St. Paul was certainly not bankrupt of religion; the blending of deities and the migration of gods from east to west and from west to east has long been recognised as a sign of strong religious excitement. In his speech on Mars' Hill at Athens St. Paul testifies of the Athenians that they were very religious,[5] and we need not hesitate to

There are even preserved several letters of the 2nd cent. B.C. in which a certain Peteyris (most probably a prisoner) tries 'by promises of baksheesh,' as Wilcken appropriately remarks, to obtain his freedom; he promises first five, and then fifteen talents of copper (Archiv für Papyrusforschung, 2, p. 578 f.). The much discussed passage in Acts xxii. 28 is probably to be understood from this point of view: Claudius Lysias refers with complacency to the great expenses for bribery that had preceded his acquisition of the citizenship. It is no use objecting solemnly that the citizenship was not purchasable. Cf. also Acts xxiv. 26.

[1] Cf. the innumerable bills of complaint in the papyri.

[2] Cf. Oxyrhynchus Papyri, No. 744 (17 June, 1 B.C.), *Light from the Ancient East*, pp. 154 ff., and Berliner Griechische Urkunden, No. 1104 (Alexandria, 8 B.C.).

[3] Cf. the letter from the bad boy Theon to his father Theon, Oxyrhynchus Papyri, No. 119 (2nd or 3rd cent. A.D.), *Light from the Ancient East*, p. 187 ff.

[4] Cf. for example the anything but happy Christian marriage reflected in Oxyrhynchus Papyri, No. 903 (4th cent. A.D.).

[5] Acts xvii. 22, κατὰ πάντα ὡς δεισιδαιμονεστέρους ὑμᾶς θεωρῶ.

apply this verdict generally to the world at large as St. Paul knew it. So too from the point of view of the history of religion we may adopt the fruit of St. Paul's intuition which he so admirably expressed by saying that the age in which Jesus Christ was sent was the age of fulfilment (pleroma),[1] the divinely appointed normal period for the arrival of salvation. How important within the complete religious network of the world of St. Paul the Hellenistic Jews of the Dispersion were in particular, requires only to be hinted: a glance at our map shows immediately the significance of the scattered Jewish communities.

From all that has been said it follows that the world of St. Paul can be reconstructed to-day with more ample materials than were available to previous generations of scholars, who had in the main only literary sources to work from. Now it is possible at least to inquire concerning that portion of his world from which St. Paul himself sprang—I mean the social stratum in which he moved.

The earlier students of Paulinism, with their one-sided zeal for presenting the 'doctrine' of St. Paul in orderly paragraphs like so many anatomical preparations, lifeless and undated, had no concern with the problem of St. Paul's social standing. Not until the younger generation was called upon to deal with the gigantic spectre of the present day social problem was an interest aroused and gradually deepened in the social affairs of the past. And I am convinced with many others that the problem of the social position of St. Paul is an important special aspect of our subject, 'the world of St. Paul.'

[1] Gal. iv. 4, *ὅτε δὲ ἦλθεν τὸ πλήρωμα τοῦ χρόνου, ἐξαπέστειλεν ὁ θεὸς τὸν υἱὸν αὐτοῦ.*

In order to understand a man completely it is of great importance to know the social class from which he sprang and with which he has associated himself. This does not mean that the man is simply a product of his surroundings, which can therefore be calculated out mechanically. A genius and a babbler may have their home in a palace as well as in a cottage. The truly individual part of a man, particularly of a great man, is a mystery that cannot be unveiled even when we know all about the man's milieu.

When, however, we admit that it is impossible to analyse the ultimate content of a personality by studying his environment, then we are in a position to appreciate with an open mind what the study of a milieu is really able to accomplish. If it cannot show us the very heart of a man, it can teach us to understand the lines and horny ridges of his hand and this or that interesting feature of his countenance. We should be sorry indeed not to have been told that Jesus came from an artisan's home in country surroundings, and that Luther was the son of a miner and the grandson of a peasant. Let us therefore follow the traces that point to the social class to which St. Paul belonged.

It appears to me certain that Paul of Tarsus, although his native town was a seat of high Greek culture, did not come from the literary upper class, but from the artisan non-literary classes, and that he remained with them. The inconspicuous remark in the Acts of the Apostles,[1] that St. Paul was a tentmaker and worked as such at Corinth, is here of extraordinarily great importance. We must not think of Paul the tentmaker as a scholarly writer of books who by way of recreation after his brainwork took his

[1] Acts xviii. 3, ἦσαν γὰρ σκηνοποιοὶ τῇ τέχνῃ.

place for an hour or two at the loom as an amateur; nor must we, as though the artisan missionary were a disgrace to our now elegant Christianity, disfigure him with the appellation of 'tent manufacturer.' He was much rather a plain and simple man whose trade was the economic foundation of his existence.

There are in his letters several proudly uttered confessions which show that as a missionary St. Paul earned his whole living by the work of his hands.[1] The man who worked 'night and day,'[2] who himself did not 'eat bread for nought at any man's hand,'[3] roundly upbraids the pious sluggards of Thessalonica.[4] The great significance of the idea of reward or wages in St. Paul becomes more intelligible when we have grasped that this popular imagery would come most naturally to a man who worked for wages, to whom the reward was not of grace but of right.[5] The figure of the house or tent 'not made with hands' which we shall one day receive from God[6] is doubly moving in the mouth of a maker of tents. The apostle's 'large letters'[7] are best explained as the clumsy, awkward writing of a workman's hand deformed by toil, and hence a light falls on the fact already mentioned, that St. Paul dictated his letters by preference; writing was probably not particularly easy to him, and possibly he dictated

[1] 1 Thess. ii. 9; 2 Thess. iii. 8; 1 Cor. iv. 12, and the whole of chapter ix.

[2] 1 Thess. ii. 9; 2 Thess. iii. 8.

[3] The R.V. translation of 2 Thess. iii. 8, *οὐδὲ δωρεὰν ἄρτον ἐφάγομεν παρά τινος.*

[4] 2 Thess. iii. 10 f.

[5] Rom. iv. 4.

[6] 2 Cor. v. 1, *οἰκίαν ἀχειροποίητον.*

[7] Gal. vi. 11, *ἴδετε πηλίκοις ὑμῖν γράμμασιν ἔγραψα τῇ ἐμῇ χειρί.*

many a passage in his letters while he was actually at his work.

In the East the ancient trades have no doubt survived to the present day with many of their characteristic features. The observations which can be made, for example, in the interior of Anatolia and Syria are highly instructive. On seeing in a side passage of the bazaar at Damascus a dyer reaching into the dye-bath with his blue naked arms, you remember that you have seen exactly the same dyer's shop somewhere or other before—yes, at Pompeii, where almost two thousand years ago the fellow-craftsmen of this dyer stood at the same dye-bath and drew out the same woollen yarn from the dye with the same blue arms. So, too, the old weaver whom we saw at Tarsus[1] near 'St. Paul's Gate,' weaving a coarse material on his wretchedly primitive loom, conveyed to us at least some notion of what a weaver's workshop looked like in ancient times. It may be that the melancholy beat of this ancient loom will not be heard much longer in Cilicia: English machinery of a quite different technical epoch has long been humming in the big modern cotton-mill at Tarsus, and those whose business it is to study the primitive forms of human industry had better hasten with their apparatus to record the manual dexterity and the proper rhythm required in the ancient handicraft still practised in the East.

It would be a mistake, however, to speak of St. Paul the artisan as a 'proletarian' in the sense which the word usually bears with us. The mere fact that he was born a Roman citizen[2] shows that his family cannot have been in poor circumstances.

[1] 21 March, 1909. [2] Acts xxii. 28.

As a freeborn man he was socially above the slaves who were so numerous in his churches. Moreover, the language of the apostle enables us to come to a better understanding on this point.

A close examination of the vocabulary of St. Paul's letters [1] has shown that St. Paul does not write literary Greek; and this observation confirms our thesis that his place of origin and the place he is historically entitled to occupy are situated somewhere below the literary upper class. But in spite of all the strong popular element in his vocabulary and the clear predominance of the colloquial tone, his Greek is not really vulgar to the degree that finds expression in many of the contemporary papyri. On the ground of his language St. Paul would be rather assigned to an elevated class. It is no doubt extremely difficult to solve the general problem of how classes were divided in ancient times; and in our attempt to establish the social class to which St. Paul belonged we are conscious that we are only groping our way forward. But any one who at all realises the problem will perceive that we have drawn a relatively certain line by placing St. Paul below the literary upper class and above the purely proletarian lowest classes.

If we ask in conclusion to which side the apostle more inclines from the intermediate position which he thus occupies, the answer must be that the whole structure of the man, his sympathies, and the conditions of his life, unite him much more with the middle and lower classes than with the upper class. He was not a man who had risen. Nor did he, as a missionary working chiefly among the non-literary masses of the

[1] Theodor Nägeli, *Der Wortschatz des Apostels Paulus*, Göttingen, 1905.

great cities, descend patronisingly into a world that was strange to him; no, he remained in the social world that was his own.

We will now look at such features of his human personality as are recoverable. We shall see that St. Paul, though related by birth and character to the non-literary classes of his world, does not disappear in the swarm of insignificant human beings; he towers high above the masses of that epoch as a leading personality.

ST. PAUL THE MAN

CHAPTER III

ST. PAUL THE MAN

CONCERNING the outward appearance of St. Paul the man no certain information has come down to us. We are like the Christians of Colossae and Laodicea, who had not seen his face in the flesh.[1] His Jewish origin, of which he was proud,[2] was no doubt visible to the people of Ephesus and Corinth when they looked at him. And the Paul of the letters that have been preserved to us is a man who had perhaps already passed the fiftieth year of his life; he calls himself once 'Paul the aged.'[3] An ancient account of his appearance in an apocryphal book[4] represents him as a by no means imposing figure, and when we think of the numerous confessions of bodily weakness which run through his letters,[5] we may be disposed to believe the account correct in the main fact, namely, that St. Paul was not distinguished by external advantages of feature or stature.

There are no portraits or busts of St. Paul—that goes without saying: who was to have thought in that age of preserving his features for posterity,

1 Col. ii. 1, ὅσοι οὐχ ἑόρακαν τὸ πρόσωπόν μου ἐν σαρκί.

2 2 Cor. xi. 22; Phil. iii. 5; Rom. xi. 1.

3 Philemon 9, ὡς Παῦλος πρεσβύτης.

4 Acts of Paul iii.

5 2 Cor. xii. 9; xiii. 4, etc.

when no one had ever immortalised the countenance of the Master Himself? Even if the ancient Jewish shyness of pictures had not stood in the way, the whole spirit of the Primitive Christian age was far too much dominated by the coming new aeon for any one to have been able to think of the interest which future earthly generations might feel in the external features of the Saviour and His apostles. Nor were the artists in marble and in colour who made all the portraits of the Caesars and imperial ladies or of generals and leading literary men, any more likely to crowd round St. Paul. Who in the official world took any notice of the obscure itinerant preacher?

The cult of Christ was in the time of St. Paul the secret affair of poor unknown persons in the great cities of the Mediterranean coasts. When St. Paul writes on one occasion that the faith of a Christian church is known 'throughout the whole world,'[1] he is employing a pleasant hyperbole[2] in the ancient manner and means the microcosm of the Christian 'world,'[3] not the great official world, just as the pagan inscription on the tomb of an otherwise unknown Egyptian woman, named Seratūs, and her relative boasts that their sobriety was known 'to the whole world,'[4] or as a Christian letter of later date says of a certain (bishop?) John, that his fame

[1] Rom. i. 8, *ἐν ὅλῳ τῷ κόσμῳ*; cf. Col. i. 6; 1 Thess. i. 8.

[2] It is the hyperbole of hatred when we find St. Paul's missionary efforts accused of setting the whole world in a turmoil, Acts xvii. 6; xxiv. 5.—The popular hyperbole of 'all the world' should also not be pressed in Luke ii. 1 and Acts xi. 28.

[3] Cf. 1 Thess. i. 8 with 2 Thess. i. 4.

[4] Archiv für Papyrusforschung, 5, p. 169, *ὧν καὶ ἡ σωφροσύνη κατὰ τὸν κόσμον λελάληται.*

extends through the whole world.[1] And though St. Paul once, as reported by St. Luke,[2] points out that the facts of his Christian life were 'not done in a corner,' these pregnant words of the apologist do not contradict our position, that the new cult and its leading personalities were at first practically unknown to the great world, and that consequently we can find neither in contemporary literature nor in contemporary art any reflection of St. Paul the man.

We must therefore content ourselves with what St. Paul himself says[3]: he bore the image of Adam, who was created out of the earth; after this earthly image, however, he would bear the image of the second Adam, the image of Jesus Christ, the Lord transfigured to spiritual glory.

Therefore when we confront St. Paul we see that his face is human, the face of Adam, on which stands written all the divided fate of Adam's sons: they are 'the image of God,'[4] and yet subject to sin and death.[5]

It is unfortunately not superfluous to call emphatic attention to the true humanity of St. Paul. The traditional view has but too often made of him a parchment saint unacquainted with the world, or else suffered the man to disappear behind the system. One of the most satisfactory advances made in the study of St. Paul is that in recent years greater interest has been taken in St. Paul the man, whereas even Ferdinand Christian Baur, in

[1] Archiv für Papyrusforschung, 4, p. 558.

[2] Acts xxvi. 26, *οὐ γάρ ἐστιν ἐν γωνίᾳ πεπραγμένον τοῦτο.*

[3] 1 Cor. xv. 49, *καὶ καθὼς ἐφορέσαμεν τὴν εἰκόνα τοῦ χοϊκοῦ, φορέσωμεν καὶ τὴν εἰκόνα τοῦ ἐπουρανίου.*

[4] 1 Cor. xi. 7.

[5] Rom. v. 12 ff.; 1 Cor. xv. 22.

his (for its time) classical book on 'St. Paul,'[1] had touched 'on certain features of the apostle's character' only in a supplementary chapter at the end.

The letters, viewed as confidential non-literary utterances, have much to tell us of St. Paul the man. Every letter of St. Paul is, as we have seen, a picture of St. Paul; in several letters we have a rapid succession of instantaneous pictures of the man unconsciously left us by himself, the words bearing the impress not only of his soul but even of the frowns and smiles on his face.

We shall not indeed be able to reconstruct him completely, in spite of this excellent evidence from his own pen. That lies in the nature of historical research, which, so far as it is concerned with men, must always come to a stop at a certain point, because that mystery begins which even the most consummate and delicate psychological skill cannot wholly unveil.

Nevertheless a large and essential part of St. Paul the man is accessible to us. And the result of even a rapid study of the personal confessions in his letters is this one deep impression: the man of whom these are fragments is a great man, an extraordinary man of most extraordinary endowments. A remark that applies purely to a point of style would make that clear, even to those who in discerning human greatness are apt to let considerations of form predominate: the power which St. Paul commands, and commands easily, of giving plastic form to his thoughts with the genius of

[1] *Paulus, der Apostel Jesu Christi.* Zweite Auflage (besorgt von Eduard Zeller), Leipzig, 1866 f. English translation, vol. i. by A. P., vol. ii. by Rev. A. Menzies, Lond. & Edinb., 1873, 1875.

a Heraclitus is proof of the spontaneous freshness of his creative nature.

> 'The letter killeth, but the spirit giveth life,'

—the man who had written only this monumental line[1] would have been for its sake immortal.

> 'The Jews ask for signs, the Greeks seek after wisdom,'[2]
> 'the kingdom of God is not in word, but in power,'[3]
> 'knowledge (the Gnosis) puffeth up, but love edifieth,'[4]
> 'we know in part,'[5]
> 'the Spirit searcheth all things, yea, the deep things of God.'[6]

—a hundred times there come such sparks and flashes in the letters, which yet were not calculated for the applause of literary salons but were sent quietly and unassumingly to unknown persons, to help them in their need by the power from above. Everywhere we find not the meditated artificiality of the rhetorician, counting the rhythm of his sentences, but the natural radiation of hidden greatness. Suppose for a moment that all these monumental sayings had been handed down to us not in their context in the letters, but in fragments scattered up and down the literature of a thousand years of antiquity, like the sayings of Heraclitus of Ephesus—the editor who for the first time

[1] 2 Cor. iii. 6, *τὸ γὰρ γράμμα ἀποκτέννει, τὸ δὲ πνεῦμα ζωοποιεῖ.*

[2] 1 Cor. i. 22, *Ἰουδαῖοι σημεῖα αἰτοῦσιν καὶ Ἕλληνες σοφίαν ζητοῦσιν.*

[3] 1 Cor. iv. 20, *οὐ γὰρ ἐν λόγῳ ἡ βασιλεία τοῦ θεοῦ, ἀλλ' ἐν δυνάμει.*

[4] 1 Cor. viii. 1, *ἡ γνῶσις φυσιοῖ, ἡ δὲ ἀγάπη οἰκοδομεῖ.*

[5] 1 Cor. xiii. 9, *ἐκ μέρους γὰρ γινώσκομεν.*

[6] 1 Cor. ii. 10, *τὸ γὰρ πνεῦμα πάντα ἐραυνᾷ, καὶ τὰ βάθη τοῦ θεοῦ.*

brought them together would be showing us fragments of a hero.

The human greatness of St. Paul is revealed, however, still more by the great polar contradictions observable in his nature. St. Paul had room in his personality for opposing principles which would irretrievably have shattered a small man, and which overwhelm the small-minded student of St. Paul with such countless problems that he is obliged to unburden himself with pamphlets and books on the spuriousness of the Pauline Epistles and their interpolations. The opposing principles did not shatter St. Paul; they set up in him the high tension which found an outlet in the energy he expended on the great work of his life.

The most obvious of the great contrasts is that which existed between his ailing body and his physical powers of work. His poor body was weak and ill; he speaks of it himself as a fragile 'earthen vessel,'[1] or, being a tentmaker, compares it with a light tent-house that has no permanency.[2] In writing to the Galatians he mentions a violent attack of illness, and it seems to have been an illness accompanied by symptoms of a revolting nature.[3] Best known of all, however, is his allusion to a severe chronic complaint with occasional attacks that were extremely painful. He calls this complaint[4]

> 'a thorn in the flesh,
> a messenger of Satan to buffet me,'

---

[1] 2 Cor. iv. 7, ἐν ὀστρακίνοις σκεύεσιν.
[2] 2 Cor. v. 1. [3] Gal. iv. 13, 14.
[4] 2 Cor. xii. 7, σκόλοψ τῇ σαρκί, ἄγγελος Σατανᾶ, ἵνα με κολαφίζῃ.

and we cannot say for certain what special disease these symptoms point to. Various conjectures have often been attempted, but none are adequately convincing; St. Paul's own scanty hints admonish us to caution. We only know of the prayer thrice sent up in his despair to the Saviour for healing,[1] cries for help which remained apparently unheard, and yet found really a divine hearing[2]:—

> 'My grace is sufficient for thee: for strength is made perfect in weakness.'

Strength in weakness! Therein lies the contradiction that we mean: this frail body is covered with the scars remaining from much maltreatment. It has undergone stoning; five times it has received from the Jewish ecclesiastical courts the terrible punishment of thirty-nine lashes, and three times the chastisement with rods that the state inflicted.[3] What that means we may learn from our own prison officials who have been present at the disciplinary punishment of refractory convicts. Often at the fifth blow the blood begins to flow, and at the twentieth the man's back is a torn mass of bleeding wounds. A tractate in the Mishna called Makkoth contains instructions for the overseer of the synagogue, who was to perform the scourging 'with all his strength,' while one of the judges read aloud passages from the Bible. By no means every culprit had the physical strength to endure the thirty-nine—some died under the hand of the overseer—so they 'assessed' the delinquent beforehand, *e.g.*, to be able to endure,

[1] 2 Cor. xii. 8.

[2] 2 Cor. xii. 9, ἀρκεῖ σοι ἡ χάρις μου· ἡ γὰρ δύναμις ἐν ἀσθενείᾳ τελεῖται.

[3] 2 Cor. xi. 23 ff.

say, only eighteen lashes. The paragraphs of the whole tractate [1] are a thrilling commentary on that simple line in the second letter to the Corinthians.

To all this must be added privations of hunger and frost, thirst, heat, and shipwreck, and the martyrdom of frequent arrest. He may often have experienced in his own person what he observed in the case of his companion Timothy,[2] and what we may often experience in the East to-day—that the drink of water found at last by the traveller who is perishing with thirst contains the hidden germs of disease. St. Paul can jest occasionally [3]—

> 'in everything and in all things have I learned the secret both to be filled and to be hungry'

—but the enumeration of his sufferings (not really monotonous, if it seems to be) in the second letter to the Corinthians [4] speaks clearly enough. It reflects the climatic hardships to which the man of weak health was exposed, and also all the cruelty of the fanaticism that rages like a consuming fire through the religious history of the East from the slaughter of Baal's priesthood to the stoning of St. Stephen, and from the butcheries of Jews at Alexandria under Caligula to the massacres of Christians at Adana, Tarsus, and Antioch in the year 1909.

[1] Now conveniently accessible in the small editions by Hermann L. Strack, Leipzig, 1910, and Gustav Hölscher, Tübingen, 1910.

[2] 1 Tim. v. 23.

[3] R.V. of Phil. iv. 12, ἐν παντὶ καὶ ἐν πᾶσιν μεμύημαι, καὶ χορτάζεσθαι καὶ πεινᾶν.

[4] 2 Cor. xi. 23 ff.; cf. also i. 8 ff.; iv. 7 ff.; vi. 4 ff.; xii. 10; 1 Cor. iv. 9–13; xv. 31 f.; Rom. viii. 35 f.

And now we see this man, feeble in health, brutally ill-treated, brought down by hunger and perhaps by fever, nevertheless completing a lifework that as a mere physical performance challenges our admiration. One should just measure the mileage of St. Paul's journeys by water and by land and compare it with the distances covered by modern archaeologists and geographers.

Or try the experiment of going over the routes of St. Paul at the present day. With special passport and diplomatic recommendations in your pocket you have taken your seat in the comfortable up-to-date carriage of the Anatolian Railway, and in the evening twilight you are running on a track that engineering skill and dynamite have forced to pierce the rocks and cross the streams, towards the destination where your coming has already been announced by telegraph. As the train carries you without exertion over the top of the pass the last gleam of daylight shows you far away below the ancient road, narrow and stony, climbing its way up the pass, and on this road a few people on foot or on donkeys, or at best on horseback, are hurrying towards the poor-looking dirty inn. It must be reached before night has fallen, for the night is no man's friend: the wild dogs kept by the rough shepherds bar the way furiously, robbers have designs on cloak and steed, and the daemons of fever threaten the tired and over-heated traveller in the cold night air that is already beginning to blow down the side valleys.

Or, leaving the modern Levant hotel with its lift and French menu, go into the miserable khan at the top of the pass known as the Syrian Gates on the road to Antioch, and sleep for a single night on the hard boards of its unsavoury plank-beds, tortured by bad air, cold, and vermin. Or sail towards Italy from the east on one of the big Mediterranean steamers of the North German Lloyd; the storm that tosses you up and down in the dark night, and perhaps makes you a little seasick, cannot turn the mighty vessel from her course, but the little sailing ship, with no stars and no compass to guide her, is the plaything of the waves, and is thrown by the storm on reef or sandbank, and the few survivors drift about for days on fragments of the wreck, enduring agonies of hunger and thirst.

On that darkening road we have seen St. Paul; on those hard boards Paul sought repose when weary; and it was Paul who drifted backwards and forwards on that ship's plank, a night and a day[1]—Paul, the man who suffered so much from sickness. On my two journeys in Anatolia in 1906 and 1909 I had the great happiness and privilege of going over almost all the routes traversed by St. Paul; one of the most lasting impressions derived from these journeys, which were mostly made with modern means of locomotion, is my unspeakable amazement at the purely physical accomplishment of St. Paul the traveller, who truly might say not without reason that he buffeted his body and brought it into subjection like a slave.[2] Strength is made perfect in weakness!

Another of the great contradictions in St. Paul is this. He is of great humility, and yet again

[1] 2 Cor. xi. 25, *νυχθήμερον ἐν τῳ βυθῷ πεποίηκα.*

[2] 1 Cor. ix. 27, *ὑπωπιάζω μου τὸ σῶμα καὶ δουλαγωγῶ.*

capable of uttering words of truly majestic self-confidence. Especially characteristic here is the confession in the first letter to the Corinthians [1]:—

> 'I am the least of the apostles. . . . But by the grace of God I am what I am. . . . I laboured more abundantly than they all: yet not I, but the grace of God which was with me.'

These are no mere phrases, but genuine confessions; with an almost Greek horror of arrogance [2] he combines manly consciousness of strength: before God a worm, before men an eagle!

A result of his bodily weakness, but also no doubt of the whole structure of his soul, is that periods of deep inward depression alternate with great moments in which he is completely emancipated and feels an intoxicated sense of victory in having overcome the world. He speaks from his very own experience of 'the earnest expectation of the creature,' [3] and no less so of being cast down, of being straitened and pressed, of distresses, anxieties, heavy cares.[4] His soul thrills with a longing for death,[5] and yet the dissolution of the earthly tent-house is a horrible thought to him.[6] Out of his own most personal experience he discovered the simplest and yet most powerful

[1] 1 Cor. xv. 9 f., *ἐγὼ γάρ εἰμι ὁ ἐλάχιστος τῶν ἀποστόλων . . . χάριτι δὲ θεοῦ εἰμὶ ὅ εἰμι . . . περισσότερον αὐτῶν πάντων ἐκοπίασα, οὐκ ἐγὼ δὲ ἀλλὰ ἡ χάρις τοῦ θεοῦ σὺν ἐμοί.*

[2] Cf. the frequent warnings in the letters of St. Paul against boasting.

[3] Rom. viii. 19 ff., *ἡ ἀποκαραδοκία τῆς κτίσεως.*

[4] 2 Cor. iv. 8 ff.; vi. 4 ff.; 1 Cor. iv. 9 ff. and other passages.

[5] Phil. i. 23.

[6] 2 Cor. v. 2 ff.

chord expressive of all human sorrow in the *De profundis* of the letter to the Romans [1]:—

'O wretched man that I am!'

And again the same man cries out for joy in complete exaltation above all the troubles and perplexities of this life.[2] It is bad psychology to refer the words significant of depression exclusively to Paul's pre-Christian period, and to make only Paul the Christian speak the words from on high. Even as a Christian Paul was swallowed up by the deep, just as no doubt when he was a pious Jew he saw the mountains from whence cometh our help.

This great contrast in St. Paul's experience is closely connected with another. His is a tender nature. He weeps, and speaks with the frankness of antiquity about his weeping.[3] He enters with hesitation, 'in fear, and in much trembling,' a new sphere of missionary work.[4] He is capable of the most affectionate feeling, calls the mother of a friend in popular hearty tone his own mother,[5] writes as a father,[6] nay, feels even as a mother.[7] Words of most touching affection flow from his lips. Standing proofs of this tenderness are found in the letters to the Philippians and to Philemon, both full of the truest delicacy of feeling. So too

[1] Rom. vii. 24, ταλαίπωρος ἐγὼ ἄνθρωπος.
[2] The most splendid passage is Rom. viii. 35 ff.
[3] 2 Cor. ii. 4; Phil. iii. 18; cf. Acts xx. 19, 31.
[4] 1 Cor. ii. 3, ἐν ἀσθενείᾳ καὶ ἐν φόβῳ καὶ ἐν τρόμῳ πολλῷ.
[5] Rom. xvi. 13.
[6] 1 Thess. ii. 11; 1 Cor. iv. 14 f., etc.
[7] Gal. iv. 19; cf. 1 Thess. ii. 7.

the great thirteenth chapter of 1 Corinthians, the song of songs with brotherly love for its subject, streamed forth from his brotherly soul, and in the mirror of this stream we see the tender heart of the man most clearly reflected.

At times, however, this tender Paul who coaxes so gently, who can be so very tolerant[1] towards others upon occasion, shows himself a hard man; he writes like a taskmaster, he gets angry, and his wrathful words dart like lightning upon the offenders.[2] The effect of such words upon those to whom they are applied is most crushing: his opponents object scornfully[3] that Paul, the weakling in bodily presence, should write such outspoken and severe letters when he is at a distance. Still more characteristic is the account received by St. Paul himself[4] of the effect of a letter (no longer extant) which he had written to the Corinthians[5] when in a state of great depression. The letter gave immediate and deep offence to the church, and possibly the Corinthians tore it up in their first anger, or did away with it on purpose afterwards, because it contained so much that was painful to them—that would be the easiest explanation of the disappearance of this no doubt magnificent letter.

To his opponents he is inexorably hard; not shrinking from even the bitterest tone, he coins polemical expressions of positively fanatical coarse-

[1] Cf. especially his attitude towards the 'weak' brethren, 1 Cor. viii., Rom. xiv. 1–xv. 13.

[2] Cf. the beginning of Galatians, and many other passages.

[3] 2 Cor. x. 10.

[4] 2 Cor. vii. 8 ff.

[5] 2 Cor. ii. 4; cf. p. 14 n. 1 above.

ness,[1] the mortal sting of which is hardly felt when excited aftercomers, who are not worthy to unloose the latchet of his shoes, have the hardihood to take his sword in their hands at the present day. St. Paul even doubted occasionally the *bona fides* of his opponents.[2]

One observation in especial is typical here: St. Paul is full of irony, inexorable, biting irony.[3] Many of his sayings are intelligible on no other explanation; they quiver like a sword-blade when they are once grasped as ironical words of the controversialist.

By this mixture of mildness with severity St. Paul reminds us, as he does in so much else, of Luther; compare, for instance, the reformer's delightful letter to his son Hänsichen and his deadly words in controversy with the Pope.

It is readily intelligible that a personality of such polar contrasts made a very different impression upon different people. Seldom probably has any one been at once so ardently hated and so passionately loved as St. Paul.

He quotes from time to time opinions of his opponents concerning himself which, though of course caricatures, are highly instructive. At close quarters, they said, he was meek, at a distance full of boldness;[4] his letters were outspoken and powerful, but in bodily presence he was weak and his speech of no account;[5] he tried to talk people

[1] Gal. v. 12; Phil. iii. 2, 18; 2 Cor. xi. 13 ff., 20; Rom. xvi. 18.

[2] Gal. i. 7; ii. 4; iv. 17; vi. 12.

[3] Cf. as an especially typical example 2 Cor. xi.

[4] 2 Cor. x. 1, 2.

[5] 2 Cor. x. 10.

into doing things;[1] he did not write what he thought;[2] he was beside himself.[3] They did not even shrink from accusing him behind his back of deceit, uncleanness, and guile,[4] nor from whispering of acts of dishonesty that he had committed in money matters.[5] We understand now the troublesome precautions with which St. Paul managed the whole business of the collections. The poor folk who made up his churches and who lived on obols and denarii, envious persons who even, as St. Paul once says,[6] 'bite and devour one another,' and who by trooping before pagan judges in their miserable disputes over some mere bagatelle exposed the brotherhood to mockery[7]—these people (it is the obverse of the medal as regards the social structure of infant Christianity) were not inaccessible to vulgar suspicion and unworthy gossip about a great man. On the apostle's own testimony there were not wanting in the Corinthian church at any rate persons who formerly had been none too scrupulous as to *meum* and *tuum*—'thieves' and 'extortioners,' says St. Paul in plain language.[8] Certain though it is that the whole of this gossip did bitter injustice to the apostle, there was perhaps in other reproaches a grain of truth, no doubt untruly turned to account. We can see this particularly well in one case: the impulsiveness with which on one occasion St. Paul

[1] Gal. i. 10. [2] 2 Cor. i. 13.
[3] 2 Cor. v. 13. [4] 1 Thess. ii. 3 f.
[5] 2 Cor. xii. 16.
[6] Gal. v. 15, ἀλλήλους δάκνετε καὶ κατεσθίετε.
[7] 1 Cor. vi. 1–11.
[8] κλέπται . . . ἅρπαγες, 1 Cor. vi. 10, compared with verse 11. Cf. also Eph. iv. 28.

changed his plans for a journey is seized hold of by his opponents to his disadvantage,[1] and they accuse him of frivolously saying 'yea, yea and nay, nay' in one breath.

But there is also no lack of evidence of quite enthusiastic devotion to him. St. Paul reminds his Galatians of the time of their first love, when they received him 'as an angel of God, even as Christ Jesus' Himself,[2] and would have 'counted themselves blessed' if they might have 'plucked out their eyes' for him. The Philippians, as his letter to them shows, loved him still deeper, because more steadily.

From all this we may draw conclusions as to the personality of St. Paul. Being himself both tender and severe, he made the men who came in contact with him either his friends or his foes. The ordinary man's comfortable tranquillity was unknown to him; he went his way through the fires and tempests of love and hate.

It of course goes without saying that the man Paul who has so far engaged our attention was an ancient, not a modern man. But as a warning against every attempt at modernisation it is as well to formulate the sentence expressly. At the same time it must not be forgotten that in the great emotions of the human soul the difference between the so-called modern man and the ancient man is not so very great. The historically trained eye recognises the differences that really exist.

The world of St. Paul is that ancient world which we have already tried to sketch in outline, and the ancient naïve cosmology with its distinction

[1] 2 Cor. i. 17. [2] Gal. iv. 13 ff.

between the upper and the lower region forms the background of his religious certainties. His belief in daemons, which underlies many passages in his letters, is genuinely ancient. Just as countless other men of antiquity, whose leaden tablets with verse and curse have survived to the present day, 'deliver' their opponents to the gods of the lower world,[1] so he 'delivers' the blasphemers Hymenaeus and Alexander to Satan,[2] and so he advises the Corinthians to 'deliver' a transgressor with due solemnity to Satan.[3] The counterpart of this would be the farewell scene at Miletus,[4] where St. Paul says to the elders of the assembly at Ephesus :-

> 'And now I commend you to God, and to the word of His grace.'

He has much to say of the wiles of Satan,[5] but he trusts also that ere long God will crush the Evil One under the feet of the saints.[6]

We see St. Paul as one of the ancients in every case where the social culture of the great cities of antiquity appears as the background of his missionary work. His figurative language, very unlike that of Jesus the Galilean, which is fresh as the dew and gay with colour, reflects the culture of the ancient great city—the athletics of the stadium,[7]

[1] Cf. *Light from the Ancient East*, pp. 303 ff.
[2] 1 Tim. i. 20. [3] 1 Cor. v. 3–5.
[4] Acts xx. 32.
[5] 1 Thess. ii. 18; 2 Thess. ii. 9; 1 Cor. vii. 5; 2 Cor. ii. 11; iv. 4; xi. 14; xii. 7; Eph. vi. 11 f.; 1 Tim. v. 15; 2 Tim. ii. 26.
[6] Rom. xvi. 20.
[7] 1 Cor. ix. 24; Phil. iii. 14; 2 Tim. iv. 7 f. (this passage is quite in the style of an inscription relating to an athletic champion, *Light from the Ancient East*, p. 312).

the military life,[1] slavery,[2] the legal institutions, particularly trial scenes,[3] the theatre,[4] the home and family life,[5] building,[6] handicraft,[7] trade,[8] and navigation.[9] The military and legal institutions probably interested him most. His figures drawn from country life are rare and generally still more conventional than the others.

From passages in the letters we are able, if we have learnt how to look at fragments, to reconstruct scenes of the life of the people in an ancient great city.[10] We can imagine the bustle in the *macellum* at Corinth, the bazaar of the butchers, where the different kinds of meat cause anxious Christians terrible scruples of conscience[11]; afterwards again, when the meat, which perhaps came from a pagan offering to idols, is served as a roast in the house of a pagan it may cause embarrassment to a Christian who may happen to be bidden to the

1 1 Thess. v. 8; Eph. vi. 10 ff.; Philemon 2; 1 Cor. ix. 7; xiv. 8; 2 Cor. x. 3 ff.; Phil. ii. 25; 2 Tim. ii. 3. Especially characteristic is the figure of a triumphal procession, 2 Cor. ii. 14; Col. ii. 15.

2 Numerous passages.

3 Numerous passages, especially those in which use is made of the concepts κατακρίνειν, 'to condemn,' and δικαιοῦν, 'to justify' (*i.e.*, 'acquit'). When St. Paul (Rom. iii. 24) lays stress on the fact that God acquits us *freely* (without our paying Him anything, δωρεάν), no doubt earthly judges who were bribable occupy the background of the figure (cf. Acts xxiv. 26).

4 1 Cor. iv. 9; Rom. i. 32 (συνευδοκοῦσι).

5 Many passages.

6 1 Cor. iii. 10 ff. Cf. especially the important metaphor of 'edification.'

7 Rom. ix. 21.

8 Eph. i. 14; 2 Cor. i. 22; v. 5; ii. 17.

9 1 Tim. i. 19.

10 The sayings of Jesus are in this respect far more abundant in their yield; they are classic documents of Palestinian folklore.

11 1 Cor. x. 25.

feast.[1] We see the Gnosis-Christian showing off his enlightenment and actually sharing the banquet in the pagan temple—a stumbling-block to the ascetically gloomy 'weak' brother[2] who watches him with venomous look, and who, though 'weak in faith,'[3] is strong in 'judging'[4] and 'speaking evil.'[5] Or we hear the clink of the money paid in as tribute and custom in the offices of the tax-gatherers,[6] among whom, as St. Paul hints with a smile, there are some rough worthies who require you not only to pay but to tremble as well.[7] Like summer lightning Paul's keen irony plays upon the learned class: the pagan sophists with their wisdom and their well-drilled rhetoric,[8] and the Jewish scribes with whom no business is to be done unless you offer them miracles.[9]

Of the quarrels of those who for the sake of a trifle run to the magistrate,[10] and of the dark pictures of moral corruption in the great city,[11] we have already spoken. Very telling pictures present themselves in the catalogues of domestic virtues contained in the letters to the Colossians[12] and the Laodiceans ('Ephesians'),[13] and also in the exhortations which display such a knowledge of life in the pastoral

[1] 1 Cor. viii. 10. [2] 1 Cor. x. 27 ff.
[3] Rom. xiv. 1. [4] 1 Cor. x. 29.
[5] 1 Cor. x. 30. [6] Rom. xiii. 7a.

[7] Rom. xiii. 7b. In the original there is a little pun on *φόρος*, 'tribute,' and *φόβος*, 'fear': *τῷ τὸν φόρον τὸν φόρον, . . . τῷ τὸν φόβον τὸν φόβον*. [By substituting 'money' for 'tribute,' and using the word 'gear' in its Scotch sense of 'money,' the pun can be imitated in English: 'gear to whom gear . . . fear to whom fear.' Tr.]

[8] 1 Cor. i. 19 ff.; ii. 4, 13. [9] 1 Cor. i. 20, 22.
[10] 1 Cor. vi. 1 ff.
[11] Rom. i. 24 ff.; Gal. v. 19 ff., etc.
[12] Col. iii. 12—iv. 1. [13] Eph. v. 15—vi. 9.

epistles—pictures that show us glimpses especially of family life. Their ethos is connected with the culture of the surrounding world by a broad basis of moral convictions common to the whole of antiquity.[1]

St. Paul as a man of the ancients stands out with wonderful clearness when we read his letters amid the ruins of places where he once laboured, which now in our day have risen again from the debris that covered them. We sit, for example, numbed by the oppressive solitude of the Ephesian landscape, in the theatre that witnessed the popular demonstration described in Acts xix., and we read in a letter that was written at Ephesus of the many Ephesian adversaries of the apostle.[2] Or again, on the height of the Acrocorinthus, with the sea bearing the sailing ships to Ephesus and Palestine on our right, and the Corinthian Gulf pointing Romewards on our left, we open the letter to the Romans, the letter in which, down yonder in Old Corinth, Paul swept his glance from Jerusalem to Rome and Spain.[3] Then Paul the ancient, the subject of the Emperor Nero, the contemporary of Seneca, becomes a living man.

The contemporary of Seneca! The later Christian writer who afterwards wrote a series of letters supposed to have been exchanged between St. Paul and Seneca places the apostle in direct relation with the literary man. As a matter of fact they do not stand

[1] Cf. in *Light from the Ancient East*, pp. 312–322, the hints concerning ancient popular ethics in the New Testament. The subject would repay fuller treatment.

[2] 1 Cor. xvi. 9.

[3] Rom. xv. 19, 23 f.

side by side. St. Paul stood once, an accused man, before the brother of Seneca—Gallio, the Proconsul of Achaia [1]—and the theme 'Paul and Seneca,' which would be more interesting to a later age, may have been suggested by this meeting at Corinth. But St. Paul does not rank with the philosophers. Seneca is one of the small upper class, St. Paul is one of the great crowd of the weary and heavy-laden. To the aristocratic men of letters in that age he would have been, if they had noticed him at all, absolutely a *homo novus*. But in reality—and here we must develop further a thought that we have already hinted at [2]—he was not particularly striking to his generation. Not a single contemporary historian mentions him. He was not a literary man to attract attention by his works, nor a man of learning to impress people by his theories of culture. The appearance of this one itinerant preacher of religion beside all the emissaries of other cults in the great cities of the Mediterranean coast was no more noticed then than the appearance of an American Adventist would be regarded in Berlin or Hamburg nowadays. The saying of his opponents, that he was 'unknown' [3]—which no doubt means that they did not recognise him as one of the genuine apostles of Jesus—contains a profound truth if we apply it to St. Paul's position in the world.

St. Paul is in this respect quite different from Luther. From 1517 onwards Luther was brought into publicity as a man of letters, as reformer, politician, and organiser. St. Paul remained in obscurity; not until long after his death did he attain to a place in the world's history.

[1] Acts xviii. 12 ff. Cf. Appendix I. below.

[2] Cf. pp. 58 f. above. [3] 2 Cor. vi. 9.

St. Paul has described in glowing words[1] the distance that separated the overwhelming majority of his Christian converts from the upper class possessors of culture, power, and noble birth. He feels the distinction in his own person and expresses it when he calls himself 'a layman in speech,'[2] when he speaks ironically of 'the wisdom of men'[3] and describes himself in comparison with the wise, the scribes, and the dialecticians as the herald of divine 'foolishness,'[4] or when he regards the wise no less than the unlearned as the subjects of his missionary work.[5] The same feeling of contrast with the great world speaks also in the bitterness of the passionate declaration that God had set forth the apostles as the 'last of all,' as the 'refuse' and 'offscourings' of humanity, fit to serve the world and angels and men as a spectacle[6] (like the wild beasts and criminals in the circus). Finally we may refer here once again to the non-literary Greek of the letters.

If it be objected that the letters of St. Paul, which now offer us so many puzzles in exegesis, were too 'high' for simple folk, and that St. Paul must have looked to find readers in an 'educated' public, the answer must be that the difficulty of interpretation proves nothing against our view. There are contemporary papyrus letters extant which certainly emanate from the lower classes and were certainly understood by their receivers, and which yet (or shall I say 'therefore'?) are extraordinarily difficult for us to understand. Moreover a great many of

[1] 1 Cor. i. 26 ff. [2] 2 Cor. xi. 6.
[3] 1 Cor. ii. 1 ff., 6–10; iii. 19 ff., etc.
[4] 1 Cor. i. 18–20. [5] Rom. i. 14.
[6] 1 Cor. iv. 9–13.

the 'difficulties' were introduced artificially into St. Paul's letters by the violence of dogmatists. 'Some things hard to be understood' remain, of course; the observation was rightly made by an early reader of the letters.[1] But nevertheless those six unknown persons,[2] Speratus, Nartzalus, Cittinus, Donata, Secunda, and Vestia, the martyrs of Scilli, who on 17 July, 180, were obliged to state in evidence before the Proconsul what was in their box, were certainly not speaking of unintelligible hieroglyphics but of their spiritual possession when they answered[3]:—

> 'The books in use among us, and besides these the letters of the holy man Paul.'

And at the present day plenty of unlearned Christians, who know their Bibles and have seen something of life, understand the letters of St. Paul quite well in the main particulars. That St. Paul himself was conscious of writing to simple folk, 'infants' and 'infirm,' is shown by occasional remarks of his.[4]

Does St. Paul lose anything by being thus contrasted as a *homo novus* with the dominant class of his time? Yes, he does lose something: the stilts that people had given him. Now he is put upon his own feet, upon the merits of his own personality. We measure him no longer by that which he received or is supposed to have received from without,

[1] 2 Pet. iii. 16, *δυσνόητά τινα.*

[2] 'Plainly all plebeian,' says Harnack, *The Mission and Expansion of Christianity in the First Three Centuries*, translated by James Moffatt, 2nd ed., London, 1908, ii., p. 278 n. 2.

[3] Acts of the Scillitanian Martyrs (Greek version, edited by Usener): *αἱ καθ' ἡμᾶς βίβλοι καὶ αἱ προσεπιτούτοις ἐπιστολαὶ* Παύλου *τοῦ ὁσίου ἀνδρός.*

[4] 1 Cor. iii. 1 ff.; Rom. vi. 19.

but by what he was originally. The virgin strength of the personality contained in this *homo novus* raises him above the masses surrounding him and makes him overtop his celebrated contemporaries of the upper class. There is no one belonging to the age of Nero who has left such permanent traces on the souls of men as Paul the *homo novus*.

The cosmopolitan touch which this unknown man shows clearly here and there is the one silent presage of his future in the world's history. Paul of Tarsus was not narrowed in by the walls of his workshop or by the narrow gloomy alleys of his ghetto. He is a citizen of the world, to the Jews a Jew, to the Hellenist a Hellenist.[1] His attitude is kindly towards the Roman state, of which he is a citizen,[2] and he even on one occasion throws out the colossal idea that there is something divine about the government of the state, and that power is part of the essence of that government.[3] What wonderful fruit these few lines of the tentmaker's letter afterwards bore in the theories of the state held by the canonists and civilians!

Moreover his large soul had without learned training absorbed much from the cosmopolitan civilisation of the east and west which was roaring around him, and not least from the common stock of ethics.[4] His secular education, as we might call it, is not drilled in, but breathed in. He has picked up several things from the rhetoricians, he knows pithy sayings from the poets and lines that lived in the mouth of the people;[5] he has had no dealings with the Asian prose-

[1] 1 Cor. ix. 20 f. [2] Acts xxii. 25 ff.
[3] Rom. xiii. 1–7. [4] Cf. p. 76 n. 1. above.
[5] 1 Cor. xv. 33; Acts xvii. 28; Tit. i. 12.

writers and their rhythm-beating,[1] which speaks for his good sense. He has his own opinion about paganism, based on his own observation. He adopts the usual polemics of Judaism against the Gentiles for their worship of images and their immorality,[2] but he does not like a narrow-minded zealot consider that paganism as such is altogether forsaken of God :—

> 'Is God the God of the Jews only? is He not the God of the Gentiles also? Yes, of the Gentiles also.'[3]

He finds among the pagans that unwritten Law, the Law of conscience;[4] he credits them with moral feeling;[5] and he reads on the altars of paganism a dedication which he explains as a cry of yearning for the One God.[6]

It goes without saying that he does not interpret an inscription like this as a modern epigraphist would. St. Paul looks at everything from a religious point of view.

And now we have come to the last clear characteristic of the man Paul, the characteristic which was destined to become, from the point of view of universal history, the real motive force in him. This great man was made what he was by his talent for religion.

[1] Cf. in the Theologische Literaturzeitung, 31 (1906) cols. 231 ff., my detailed criticism of the hypothesis entertained by Friedrich Blass.

[2] Rom. i. 18–32; Gal. ii. 15.

[3] Rom. iii. 29, ἢ Ἰουδαίων ὁ θεὸς μόνον; οὐχὶ καὶ ἐθνῶν; ναὶ καὶ ἐθνῶν.

[4] Rom. ii. 14 f. [5] 1 Cor. v. 1.

[6] Acts xvii. 23. A dedication probably resembling the one at Athens has recently been discovered at Pergamum; cf. Appendix II. below.

St. Paul is one of the few men to whom the much abused expression 'religious genius' may legitimately be applied. His is a mystical and prophetic nature, and in comparison with this characteristic the theological element vanishes almost entirely. He is mystical and prophetic also in the unusual sense that he is capable of ecstatic experiences. It is true he has a horror of the wild excesses of pagan [1] and Christian [2] ecstasy indulged in by unrestrained crowds, and at Corinth, where it once happened that a person in a state of ecstasy cursed Christ,[3] he opposed speaking with tongues, though he quite approved of it theoretically.[4] But he himself is gifted to speak with tongues,[5] and can tell of datable [6] ecstasies and special revelations of his own. Transported into the third heaven, into paradise, he has heard 'unspeakable words, which it is not lawful for a man to utter.'[7] In hours when he was unable to pray the Spirit has suddenly taken possession of his weakness and has prayed vicariously for him 'with groanings which cannot be uttered.'[8] Or it is vouchsafed him to hear the voices of the upper world in words that he can understand,[9] and dreams become to him divine inspirations.[10]

The enlightened Philistine smiles at the delusions of the enthusiast, the precise dogmatist passes over whatever is mystical by preference, or refers it to the philosophers or medical men. The historian of

[1] 1 Cor. xii. 2. [2] 1 Cor. xiv. 23.

[3] 1 Cor. xii. 3. [4] 1 Cor. xiv.

[5] 1 Cor. xiv. 18.

[6] 2 Cor. xii. 2; Gal. ii. 1. As to the dating of the ecstasy cf. Isaiah vi. 1, 'In the year that King Uzziah died. . . .'

[7] 2 Cor. xii. 2–4. [8] Rom. viii. 26 f.

[9] 2 Cor. xii. 9; Acts xxii. 17 ff.; ix. 4 ff., etc.; xx. 23; xvi. 6, 7.

[10] Acts xvi. 9; xxvii. 23 f.

religion knows that the experiences of the great 'enthusiast,' puzzling as they may be to himself, are the fountains of strength in the history of religion. Whoever takes away the mystical element from St. Paul, the man of antiquity, sins against the injunction of St. Paul[1] :—

'Quench not the Spirit.'

For our part we will let the sacred fire burn on, whose glow we trace in the letters: St. Paul is, in the deepest sense of the word, by the grace of God a *homo religiosus.*

And this soul predestined for the unspeakable mysteries of the most blessed communion with God was born into a human communion in which the mighty experiences of heroic saints of old, though relegated to text and letter, had not ceased to make themselves felt, a communion in which religion was everything. Paul the religious man was born and grew up a Jew.

[1] 1 Thess. v. 19, *τὸ πνεῦμα μὴ σβέννυτε.*

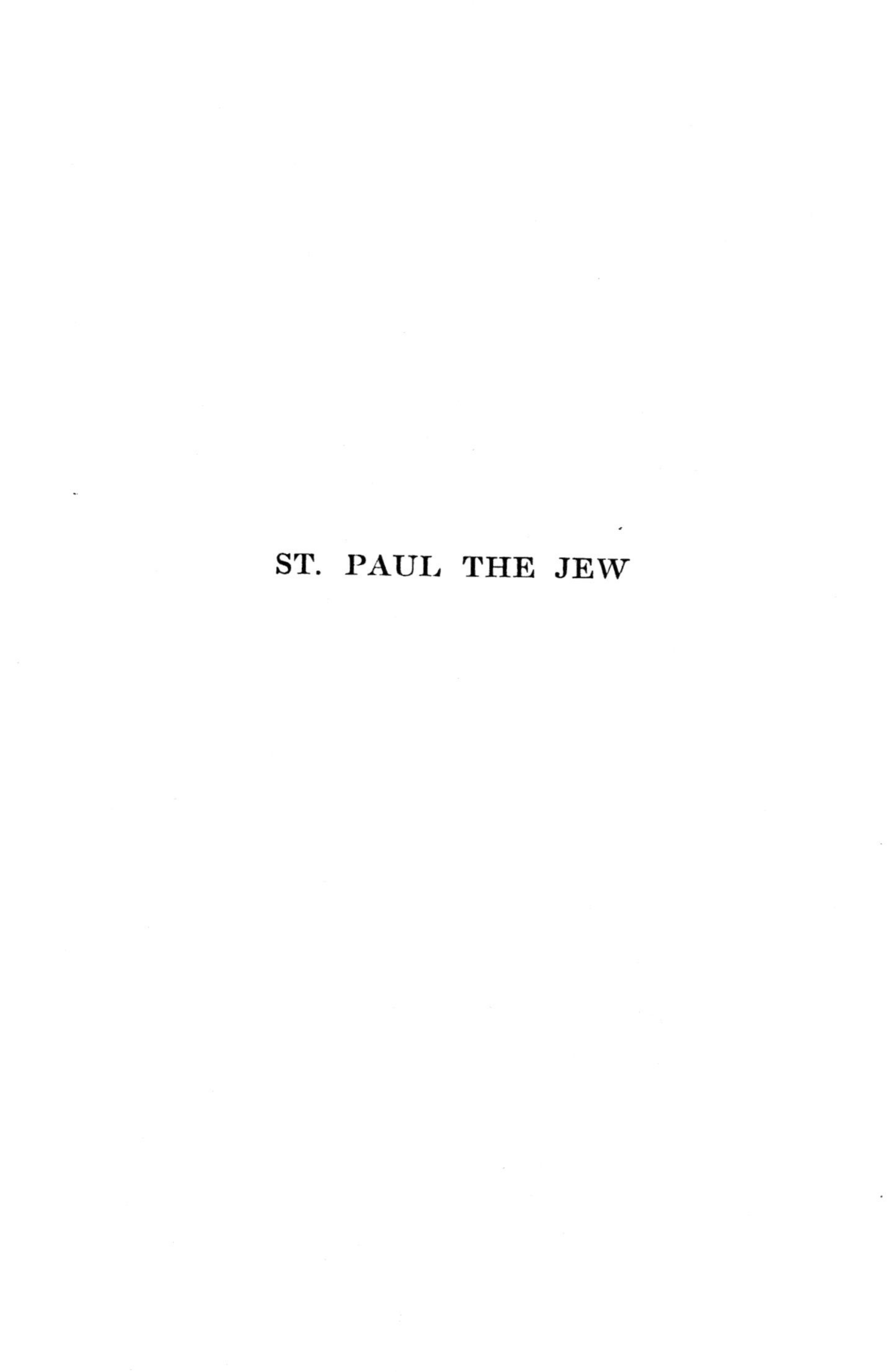

ST. PAUL THE JEW

CHAPTER IV

ST. PAUL THE JEW

In the time of the Emperors Augustus and Tiberius a traveller wandering through the lanes of a great Hellenistic city in the coastlands of the Mediterranean, after first admiring the glittering marble temples of the old gods and the shrines of deities more recently arrived from abroad, would probably notice in one of the more modest quarters a simpler religious edifice, without an altar. At best it was decorated with a frieze of vine-leaves or olive-branches, but apart from that there would be scarcely any external ornament, and in the interior bare walls and no image of a god. When the visitor entered, his eye fell only upon a chest of books written upon rolls, and when the attendant approached to unroll them for the stranger, they were seen to be in large Greek characters. A reading-desk and benches, candlestick and lamps completed the scanty inventory of the apartment.

In the cosmopolitan city of Alexandria, where the congregations that gathered round those rolls numbered thousands of members, including high officials, wealthy traders, and eminent men of letters, all this may have looked more costly and imposing. In other cities, however, that religious edifice was probably no better built and furnished than most of the synagogues now used by the Jewish population in the East, such as I have visited at Constantinople, Chalcis, and Tiberias. An inscribed stone discovered several years ago, which in the imperial period stood over the entrance to a Corinthian synagogue,[1] bears the now mutilated words 'Synagogue of the Hebrews,' in the same extremely poor-looking rude script that is known to us from other Jewish inscriptions of that age.

These modest Jewish synagogues up and down the Hellenistic world were a silent and, the history of religion tells us, extremely effective protest against the worship of images by the polytheistic pagans. More than a hundred and fifty Jewish congregations of the imperial period are already known to us within the olive zone of the Mediterranean basin;[2] their actual number was no doubt considerably greater.[3] They possessed in their Greek rolls, round

[1] Text and facsimile in *Light from the Ancient East*, p. 13, n. 7.

[2] The Jews of Mesopotamia, middle and upper Egypt, etc., are not included.

[3] My map shows about 143 places out of Palestine with Jewish settlements; but in several places there was more than one Jewish congregation, *e.g.*, we know the names of nine synagogues in Rome. The number given on the authority of Emil Schürer (*Gesch. d. jüd. Volkes*, III.,[4] Leipzig, 1909, pp. 1 ff.; *Hist. Jewish People*, 2nd Div., trs. Taylor and Christie, Edinburgh, 1885, ii., pp. 220–252 out of date for this point) and Johannes Oehler (Monatsschr. f. Gesch. u. Wiss. d. Judentums, N.S. 53 [1909], pp. 292 ff., 443 ff., 525 ff.) is being continually increased by new discoveries. While my map was being engraved I found Jews in a place called Syron Kome, near Babylon, in Egypt: three presumably poor Jews signed on 26 November, 59 A.D., an acknowledgment of a debt of 600 silver drachmae, the original of which is now extant at Hamburg (Hamburg Papyri, No. 2). Cf. *Griechische Papyrusurkunden der Hamburger Stadtbibliothek*,

which the congregation assembled Sabbath by Sabbath to pray and listen, a centre of religious power which even attracted numbers of pagans. By the sacred writings of the Old Testament, in the Greek translation of the Seventy Interpreters, the pious Jew of the Dispersion, who had become outwardly a Hellenist, and in general no longer understood the Semitic original, was brought into ever new contact with the traditions which told of the fortunes of his fathers and the providences by which they were guided. He was also constantly reminded of the religious experiences and hopes of the prophetic men whose giant figures loom so largely in the religious history of the Mediterranean world during the thousand years before Christ.

The religion of the saints of old, which remained a living thing in the Semitic Old Testament, had not been mummified in the Bible of the Seventy, nor had it been presented without some interposition of Hellenistic culture. The Septuagint translation represents not only in form but also (in several main points, indeed, very considerably) in substance a Hellenisation of Jewish monotheism. This Greek Bible, a book of the West and of the East in the light of universal history, is an adaptation of the eastern faith to the western world,[1] and rendered possible an extremely effective propaganda for the One God of the Jews among pagans who had become weary and doubtful under polytheism.

ed. by Paul M. Meyer, Leipzig, 1911, I., pp. 4 ff. These Jews in the neighbourhood of Babylon, in Egypt, and in the time of the apostles, are not without interest in connexion with 1 Pet. v. 13.

[1] Further details in my little work, *Die Hellenisierung des semitischen Monotheismus*, Leipzig, 1903 (reprinted from the Neue Jahrbücher für das klassische Altertum, etc., 1903).

Though apparently cut off from the Semitic home of his fathers by his Hellenistic Scriptures, the cosmopolitan Jew did not lose his close connexion with the centre of the Jewish religion, the Temple at Jerusalem. Everyone of full age contributed his tax of two drachmae yearly for Jerusalem, and everyone who could possibly afford it went on pilgrimage to the Holy City. Just as to-day in the weeks preceding the vernal full moon Jerusalem is the goal of many thousands of Jews, Christians, and Mohammedans—just as the whole world of Islam from Constantinople to the Sunda Islands, and from our African colonies to China and Japan, is vibrating with a constant movement towards Mecca—so in those days, to use the words of a contemporary writer,[1] many thousands from many 'thousands' of cities streamed at every feast towards the Temple. St. Luke's account[2] of what happened on the day of Pentecost gives an international list of pilgrims to Jerusalem who had remained behind in the Holy City.

And there, in the city of the Temple, the Jew, in spite of the foreign domination of the Romans, felt proud and privileged in the possession of great special rights. Warning inscriptions carved on stone in Greek and other languages, one of which has been preserved to the present day,[3] forbade everyone who was not a Jew to enter the sacred precinct of the Temple upon pain of death.[4] At this seat of grace, where the sacred fire of the altar of burnt offering never went out, the yearning of the pilgrims was

[1] Philo, *De monarchia*, ii. 1.
[2] Acts ii. 9 ff.
[3] Text and facsimile in *Light from the Ancient East*, pp. 74–76.
[4] Cf. also Acts xxi. 28, 31; xxii. 22.

fulfilled. Here they heard the choirs of singing-men and the rushing sound of the harps; here sat world-famed teachers of the law and gave of their best; here it was possible for one present in the sanctuary on the Great Day of Atonement to participate, however faintly, in the most solemn act of worship of the whole year. And here everyone breathed the glowing atmosphere of the most ardent national hopes of a Messiah.

Jews of strangely differing types met together in the court of the Temple, and to-day, as you stand on that same broad space before the rock-built fane at Jerusalem, you have only to close your eyes for a moment for those old shapes to reappear there once more: the rich Babylonian merchant, showing no signs of the hardships of his long caravan journey, fills the hand of the poor pilgrim from Rome, who is begging money to pay for his return voyage; the Cilician handicraftsman and the Alexandrian scholar speak shudderingly of the massacre wrought by Pilate among the pilgrims from Galilee.[1]

Not a few of the foreign pilgrims to the feast, as that Pentecostal list teaches us,[2] stayed on permanently or at least for a considerable time in the Holy City. Thus there arose in Jerusalem itself synagogues of foreign Jews who held together as fellow-countrymen, just as at the present day the Sephardim Jews and the Ashkenazim Jews always have their separate synagogues. In the Acts of the Apostles we have evidence of a congregation consisting of African Jews, and of a synagogue formed of Cilicians and others from Asia Minor.[3]

[1] Luke xiii. 1.

[2] Acts ii. 9 ff.

[3] Acts vi. 9, ἐκ τῆς συναγωγῆς . . . τῶν ἀπὸ Κιλικίας καὶ Ἀσίας.

It was probably in this synagogue of Cilicians and other Jews of Asia at Jerusalem that the Cilician Jew *Saul, who is also called Paul,*[1] found support and encouragement when in his younger years he spent some time at Jerusalem. Here no doubt he formed personal connexions for his future journeys in Asia Minor, of which, indeed, he can then have had no foreboding, and in daily conversation with travellers from afar he must have learnt the geography of the Dispersion and the main lines of travel. When we are told in the Acts of the Apostles that the man born in Tarsus[2] was 'brought up' at Jerusalem,[3] we are at first inclined to infer that Paul came when still a child to Jerusalem. We could connect this with the fact that he afterwards had relations in Jerusalem: after his arrest his sister's son did him a service.[4] Was St. Paul's sister then living at Jerusalem with her son? or was the nephew staying only for a short time in the Holy City as a pilgrim to the feast?

Judging, however, from the total impression made upon us by the St. Paul we know, it is nevertheless probable that the son of Tarsus spent his boyhood in the Hellenistic city of his birth. St. Paul appears so decidedly as a Jew of the Septuagint, and possesses

[1] Acts xiii. 9, Σαῦλος δὲ ὁ καὶ Παῦλος.

[2] Acts xxii. 3; ix. 11; xxi. 39. The statement found in St. Jerome (*In Philem.* 23 and *De viris inlustribus*, 5) referring to Giscala in Galilee as the home of St. Paul, may perhaps have originated in a tradition in his family that they had originally come from Giscala (cf. Theodor Mommsen, Zeitschrift für neutestamentliche Wissenschaft, 2 [1901], p. 83). Though St. Paul was certainly born at Tarsus, it is not altogether impossible that he had Galilean blood in his veins.

[3] Acts xxii. 3, ἀνατεθραμμένος δὲ ἐν τῇ πόλει ταύτῃ.

[4] Acts xxiii. 16 ff.

such sovereign command of the Hellenistic colloquial language, that we are bound to assume him to have been strongly influenced from his childhood by the Septuagint and the Hellenistic world surrounding him.

From his own statements we can discover with great probability something about the childhood of St. Paul. Belonging to the tribe of Benjamin,[1] but by birth also a Roman citizen,[2] the boy must early have been impressed by the fact that, like pious Jews at the present day,[3] he possessed two names of very different kind: one sacred—the famous old Jewish name of Saul, Graecised as *Saulos*—and one profane, the like-sounding Latin name also Graecised as *Paulos*.

Even in his old age there stood out clearly to his soul one experience of his childhood, concerning which he gives pathetic hints in his letter to the Romans.[4] We might speak of it as his fall:—

> 'For I was alive without the law once: but when the commandment came, sin revived, and I died. And the commandment, which was ordained to life, I found to be unto death. For sin, taking occasion by the commandment, deceived me, and by it slew me.'

---

[1] Rom. xi. 1; Phil. iii. 5. [2] Acts xxii. 28.

[3] According to information given to me by Salomon Frankfurter, and referred to in my little book, *Die Urgeschichte des Christentums im Lichte der Sprachforschung*, Tübingen, 1910, p. 16. On the problem of the double name cf. the discussion of Hermann Dessau's important essay "Der Name des Apostels Paulus" (Hermes 45 [1910], pp. 347 ff.) in the second edition of my *Bibelstudien*.

[4] Rom. vii. 9–11, *ἐγὼ δὲ ἔζων χωρὶς νόμου ποτέ· ἐλθούσης δὲ τῆς ἐντολῆς ἡ ἁμαρτία ἀνέζησεν, ἐγὼ δὲ ἀπέθανον. καὶ εὑρέθη μοι ἡ ἐντολὴ ἡ εἰς ζωὴν αὕτη εἰς θάνατον. ἡ γὰρ ἁμαρτία ἀφορμὴν λαβοῦσα διὰ τῆς ἐντολῆς ἐξηπάτησέν με καὶ δι' αὐτῆς ἀπέκτεινεν.*

St. Paul is probably thinking here in the first place of his earliest childhood, which he elsewhere[1] describes as the time of childish immaturity; the idea of 'sin' and the sense of guilt were both still unknown to him. But then came a sad day that he could never forget. In the synagogue the child had seen from afar with awe and curiosity the dumb rolls of the Law in their brilliant embroidered coverings,[2] but now for the first time the 'thou shalt' of the Law, conveyed to him no doubt by the mouth of a parent, entered commandingly into his consciousness. The Law's 'thou shalt' was, however, closely followed by the child's 'I will not' and transgression. St. Paul does not say what the occasion was. But he indicates that this first sin wrought terrible havoc in his sensitive young soul: he felt himself deceived, it was as if he had tasted death:—

'I died.'

We do not know when this tragedy took place in the soul of the youthful St. Paul; many of us know from personal experience what agony the sense of guilt can cause even in childish years. Jewish teachers, at least of a later period, seem to have assumed[3] that a child grew to the age of nine without knowing anything of sin; but that then, with the awakening of the 'evil instinct,' sin began. More important, however, than the explanation of this experience in detail is the fact which, I think, can be certainly concluded from it. The man who experienced this fall cannot have had a sunny, happy youth; the Law, sin, and death had already cast

[1] 1 Cor. xiii. 11. [2] 2 Cor. iii. 14.

[3] Tanchuma (late commentary on the Pentateuch) on Gen. iii. 22.

their gloomy shadows upon the soul of the gifted boy, and the prevailing tone of his mind as he matured more and more into the conscious Jew may be described according to his own indication as one of slavish anxiety [1]—that is, not merely the fear of God in the old Biblical sense,[2] but the deep distress of one 'born under the Law'[3] concerning his soul's salvation :—

> 'O wretched man that I am! Who shall deliver me out of this body of death?'

Even in his Christian period St. Paul is capable of such cries for help [4] when the old distress wakes in him again.

This distress drove the poor man in his anxiety to the strictest school of Judaism; Paul became a Pharisee.[5] Perhaps this took place while he was still at Tarsus;[6] we know that the propaganda of Pharisaism extended over land and sea.[7] At Jerusalem, however, where he settled for some time in order to receive a thorough training in the Law [8] at the feet of the celebrated Rabban Gamaliel,[9] he was not only an adherent of Pharisaic Pietism, but within that extraordinarily active and precise body he was one of the most fanatical enthusiasts. When he

[1] Rom. viii. 15. [2] 2 Cor. vii. 1; Rom. iii. 18.

[3] Gal. iv. 4.

[4] Rom. vii. 24, ταλαίπωρος ἐγὼ ἄνθρωπος· τίς με ῥύσεται ἐκ τοῦ σώματος τοῦ θανάτου τούτου;

[5] Phil. iii. 5; Acts xxvi. 5; xxiii. 6. [6] Acts xxiii. 6.

[7] Matt. xxiii. 15 is not merely hyperbolic.

[8] This is probably the best interpretation of the expression 'brought up,' in Acts xxii. 3; the great teachers are the 'fathers.'

[9] Acts xxii. 3.

compared himself with his contemporaries who sat crouching near him in the hall of instruction, committing their traditional wisdom to memory, he could say that he was 'exceedingly zealous of the traditions of the fathers.'[1] All the pride of a scribe learned in the Law communicated itself to him in those days :—

'A guide of the blind,
A light of them which are in darkness,
An instructor of the foolish,
A teacher of babes'—

these words in the letter to the Romans,[2] written many years afterwards, shine with the reflected splendour of that proud self-consciousness.

On the other hand, his searching, serious eye could not fail to notice the fearful contrast that continually presented itself between his own will and performance,[3] and that other contrast between external piety and inner corruption which existed in his surroundings just as everywhere else in the world. In one zealot he noticed thievery,[4] in another immorality,[5] and he seems once to have caught one of his co-religionists, probably a Jew of the Dispersion, a man who used to speak with scorn of the heathen idols, enriching himself through these idols by acting as a receiver of goods stolen from a temple[6]—just as a modern Christian Anatolian, who looks down with

[1] Gal. i. 14; cf. Acts xxii. 3.

[2] Rom. ii. 19 f., ὁδηγὸν τυφλῶν, φῶς τῶν ἐν σκότει, παιδευτὴν ἀφρόνων, διδάσκαλον νηπίων.

[3] Rom. vii. 15 ff. [4] Rom. ii. 21.

[5] Rom. ii. 22a.

[6] So I should attempt to explain the obscure passage in Rom. ii. 22b. The remarkable sentence, 'thou that abhorrest idols, dost thou rob temples?' must surely enshrine a definite recollection of St. Paul's.

contempt on Islam, might have no objection to offering for sale in a quiet corner of his little shop carpets stolen from a mosque.

Observations like this no doubt made Paul the Pharisee, even in his Jewish period, profoundly appreciative of the great conception of the old prophets [1] concerning 'circumcision of the heart' [2] as distinguished from the merely outward circumcision of which many a Jew openly boasted,[3] while others, probably from fear of pagan ridicule at the baths or in the stadium, tried to conceal the token of Judaism.[4]

His perception of the fact that beside the 'secret,' [5] that is, genuine Jews there were many merely 'outward,' [6] ordinary Jews, who were condemned as sinners by good pagans,[7] combined probably with the deeply humiliating experiences of his own often futile struggle for 'righteousness' by personal performance,[8] to make blaze forth occasionally in the glowing soul of Paul the Jew thoughts of extraordinary and pre-eminent acts of religious sacrifice. At times he was tempted to what seemed the highest degree of piety, the ideal of the Maccabean martyrs, 'to give his body to be burned' [9]

1 Deut. x. 16; xxx. 6; Jer. iv. 4.
2 Rom. ii. 29, περιτομὴ καρδίας.
3 Rom. ii. 28.
4 1 Cor. vii. 18.
5 Rom. ii. 29, ὁ ἐν τῷ κρυπτῷ Ἰουδαῖος.
6 Rom. ii. 28, ὁ ἐν τῷ φανερῷ Ἰουδαῖος.
7 Rom. ii. 26 ff.
8 Rom. vii. 14 ff.
9 1 Cor. xiii. 3, ἐὰν παραδῶ τὸ σῶμά μου ἵνα καυθήσομαι. In spite of Adolf Harnack's exhaustive defence of the reading καυχήσωμαι, 'that I may glory' (Sitzungsberichte der Kgl. Preuss. Akademie der Wissenschaften, 1911, pp. 139 ff.), I take καυθήσομαι (for καυθήσωμαι; the future subjunctive occurs also in the papyri) to be the original. I cannot admit that martyrdom by fire

for God's sake. He would have been capable of doing so too, just as afterwards, when a Christian, he would have gladly sacrificed himself for his people.[1]

The most genuine characteristics of the Jewish nature were preserved by Paul when he became a Christian. 'St. Paul the Jew' does not mean that Paul was a Jew only before his conversion and afterwards no longer. Paul remained a Jew even when he was a Christian, in spite of his passionate polemics against the Law. This is not meant merely ethnologically—he of course did not change his race at baptism—it applies also to his religion and temperament. In opposition to mechanical divisions of the Jewish and the Christian elements in him, we need not hesitate to call him the great Jew-Christian of the earliest age. His worship of God comes to him 'from his forefathers.'[2] We may well assume that

was not yet within the apostle's mental vision (p. 142). Daniel iii. 28 is an important passage, but the Second Book of Maccabees, which gives an exact description of a martyrdom by fire (2 Macc. vii. 3 ff.), is more important still, and so especially is the Fourth Book of Maccabees, which was quite recent in the time of St. Paul and fairly revels in details of the burning of martyrs (4 Macc. v. 32; vi. 24 ff.; vii. 4, 12; viii. 13; ix. 17, 19 ff.; x. 14; xi. 18 ff.; xii. 1, 10–20; xiii. 5, 9; xiv. 9 f.; xv. 14 f., 20, 22; xvii. 1; xviii. 20; cf. my remarks in Kautzsch's *Apokryphen und Pseudepigraphen*, ii. pp. 149–177). Victory in the martyrdom of fire is looked upon as the highest proof of faith, as shown by Heb. xi. 34 (cf. 4 Macc. xvi. 21 ff.; xviii. 12, 14). Even the age of St. Paul had witnessed the burning of Jews in the Jewish massacres at Alexandria under Caligula (Schürer, I.3, p. 498; Eng. trs. First Division, vol. ii. p. 93). These Alexandrian victims of the fire were martyrs in the religious sense, for their offence was refusal to worship the Emperor.—The change of the reading *καυθήσομαι* would be suggested afterwards by the reflection that St. Paul's martyrdom was not by fire.

[1] Rom. ix. 3.

[2] 2 Tim. i. 3.

in his own family there had been a continuity of serious piety for generations similar to that which he praises in Timothy's mother Eunice and grandmother Lois: their 'unfeigned faith' had been inherited by the son and grandson.[1]

St. Paul never withdrew from the national and religious union constituted by his people. He adopts with pride the name of 'Hebrew,'[2] and also the still weightier names of 'Israelite'[3] and 'seed of Abraham,'[3] just as he certainly reckons himself with 'the Israel of God,'[4] speaks of the Jews in the desert as 'our fathers,'[5] and of course boasts of 'our forefathers'[6] and 'father'[7] Abraham, and 'our father'[8] Isaac. He calls even the unbelieving Jews his 'kinsmen according to the flesh,' for whom he would gladly take the curse upon himself, if he could thereby save them.[9] Or he boasts of his membership of the tribe of Benjamin,[10] which he shares with King Saul,[11] and his circumcision on the eighth day.[12] So also in neutral things: for instance he reckons the dates of journeys by the Jewish calendar of festivals.[13] Though standing himself above the letter of the Law, he still as an apostle observed the hallowed customs of his people; I regard the notices to this effect in the Acts of the Apostles[14] not as later touches by some one

1 2 Tim. i. 5.
2 2 Cor. xi. 22; Phil. iii. 5.
3 2 Cor. xi. 22; Rom. xi. 1.
4 Gal. vi. 16.
5 1 Cor. x. 1.
6 Rom. iv. 1.
7 Rom. iv. 16.
8 Rom. ix. 10.
9 Rom. ix. 3.
10 Rom. xi. 1; Phil. iii. 5.
11 Acts xiii. 21.
12 Phil. iii. 5, περιτομῇ ὀκταήμερος.
13 1 Cor. xvi. 8; Acts xxvii. 9.
14 Acts xvi. 3; xviii., 18; xxi. 26.

who favoured the Jews, but as applications of the principle enunciated by St. Paul himself,[1] that he was 'to the Jews a Jew.'

The sensation of contrast which the Jew felt towards the 'sinful'[2] people who were not Jews is not unknown to St. Paul. Feeling as a Hellenist he sometimes separates the 'Greeks' from the 'Barbarians,'[3] and in the same way, feeling as a Jew, he often employs the old Jewish contemptuous expression, 'the heathen' ('the Gentiles'),[4] for those who were not Jews. The Romans applied the same word, also no doubt contemptuously, to the provincials.[5] Here too belongs the metaphor by which the Jews are the cultivated olive-tree, the 'Gentiles' only a 'wild olive.'[6]

How greatly St. Paul loved his ancestral people is shown by the flaming testimonies in the letter to the Romans.[7] He is tormented not by a merely

[1] 1 Cor. ix. 20, καὶ ἐγενόμην τοῖς Ἰουδαίοις ὡς Ἰουδαῖος.

[2] Gal. ii. 15.

[3] Col. iii. 11; Rom. i. 14.

[4] [According to one theory] our word *heathen* [which has cognates in all the Germanic languages] is a borrowing from the Greek. The earliest recorded form [the Gothic word *haiþnō*, 'a heathen woman'], occurring in the Gothic [translation of Mark vii. 26 (where the original has Ἑλληνίς)], is explained as an adaptation of ἔθνος, pronounced with the aspirate ἕθνος (W. Schulze, Sitzungsber. d. Berliner Akad. d. Wissenschaften, 1905, pp. 747 ff.). [I have ventured to modify this note by the addition of the words in square brackets, because Schulze's etymology has not commended itself to specialists in Germanic philology. See F. Kaufmann, Zeitschrift für deutsche Philologie 38 (1906), pp. 433–436; F. Kluge, Zeitschrift für deutsche Wortforschung 11 (1909), pp. 21–27; R. Much, ibid. pp. 211–218. TR.]

[5] For ἔθνη in the sense of provincials cf. for instance A. von Domaszewski in *Strena Helbigiana*, Lipsiae, 1899, p. 53; and David Magie, *De Romanorum iuris publici sacrique vocabulis* . . ., Lipsiae, 1905, p. 59.

[6] Rom. xi. 17 ff.

[7] Rom. ix.–xi.

theoretical question but by grief for his people, who had turned away from the Messiah Jesus. The question whether God might have rejected His people pierces his soul.[1] Little as St. Paul was able to find a logical solution of the problem, he doubtless at last, in the enthusiasm of his faith and in his love for his people, succeeded in putting the torturing question from him.

The observation that St. Paul after his conversion shows nothing of the renegade's hatred, certainly adds a sympathetic touch to the whole impression of the man. The occasional hard sayings against the Law are counterbalanced by other statements in which he is at pains to do justice to the Law; and, indeed, he not infrequently continued to use the Law as an authority, just in the manner of his fathers.[2]

This brings us to the most characteristic feature of Paul the Jew. Paul was to the last a pious Bible Jew, a Septuagint Jew. What distinguished him in this respect from other pious Jews of the Dispersion was the perception that in Christ the Law had lost its binding force and the promises had found their fulfilment. But the total religious and ethical content of the Septuagint is for him the obvious condition precedent to his Christian piety.

St. Paul the Christian never withdrew from the divine world of the Hellenistic Old Testament. To understand the whole of St. Paul, and not merely a part of him, from the point of view of religious history, we must know the spirit of the Septuagint. Not the Hebrew Old Testament, not necessarily that

[1] Rom. xi. 1.

[2] Cf. for instance 1 Cor. ix. 9; Gal. iii. 13, etc.

which we now call 'Old Testament theology, supplies the historic premises of St. Paul's piety, but the faith contained in the Greek Old Testament. The task of reconstructing from the Septuagint, conceived as a compact and uniform Bible, the Jewish premises for St. Paul's Christianity, has scarcely been recognised as such by scholars, let alone solved. It resolves itself into a number of separate problems, of which only a few need here be pointed out: the certainties about God in the Septuagint; the Spirit and Christ in the Septuagint; faith and righteousness in the Septuagint, etc.

In many points, of course, the result of these separate investigations will come into touch with the results of 'Old Testament theology' established from the Hebrew Old Testament, but in many points it will not. 'Old Testament theology' regards the Old Testament as the historical document of a complex of facts in religious history which extended over several thousand years and gradually developed in a number of separate phases. The student of the Septuagint, on the other hand, regards the Greek Old Testament essentially in the same way as St. Paul regarded it, and as a pious layman to-day regards the Old Testament—as something in itself relatively uniform. The Greek translation has in fact almost entirely obliterated the numerous lines by which in the Hebrew text the stages in the gradual stratification and development are marked for the historian. In the Septuagint Bible statements in the prophets, in Genesis, and in quite late Psalms, which in the Hebrew original perhaps cannot possibly be combined, unite together without difficulty, because the religious reader of the Septuagint hears much more clearly the same unalterable spirit of the same revelation speaking from all the rolls of his Holy Scriptures.[1]

How large an admixture of Septuagint piety there was in the religious psyche of St. Paul is apparent from the great number of Greek Biblical quotations which we find in his letters. It is not improbable that St. Paul made use of a text of the Septuagint which had in places undergone a Jewish revision.[2]

St. Paul's connexion with the Septuagint is shown still more strikingly by the whole of his religious and ethical vocabulary. It becomes clearest of all to us when, possessing already an accurate acquaintance with St. Paul's letters, we read the Septuagint itself—not merely single lines quoted by St. Paul, but the book as a whole, regarded as the Hellenistic Bible. Unfortunately there is still too little methodical reading of the Septuagint done amongst us; but for the student of St. Paul there can hardly be anything more interesting and instructive.

The exegesis that St. Paul bestowed upon the Greek Bible shows us very vividly St. Paul the Jew. It is the exegesis of a completely authoritative document. Although St. Paul regards a part of this document, the Law, as repealed in Christ, he does occasionally, as already mentioned, quote passages of the Law with the weighty and significant words, 'It is written.' In the Hellenistic world the phrase 'It is written' was then the formula with

[1] Cf. the work mentioned at p. 89 n. 1 above.

[2] Further details in my work, *Die Septuaginta-Papyri und andere altchristliche Texte der Heidelberger Papyrus-Sammlung*, Heidelberg, 1905, p. 69 f.

which people referred to the terms of an unalterable agreement;[1] St. Paul uses it in exactly the same way. What is written cannot be called in question; every quotation from Scripture is a proof from Scripture. God Himself speaks in the Scripture, the Scripture itself is actually personified,[2] and it is laid down as a principle[3]:—

'Not to go beyond the things which are written.'

With such an attitude towards the letter of the Bible, St. Paul as an exegete might seem to have been slavishly fettered from the very first. But we know that means had long ago been found, in spite of the tyranny of the letter, to get beyond the letter. This means, which St. Paul is fond of using, is allegorical exegesis. It was not invented by the Jews; they probably adopted it from Hellenism, which interpreted the poets allegorically, in order to explain away their religious coarseness to a cultured generation that had become prudish.

The Jews, however, adopted it gladly, for it was what they wanted. It would be an injustice to the allegorical exegesis of the Bible by Jews and early Christians to regard it as the monstrous product of a completely irrational theosophical craze. The mere observation that no less a person than Philo Judaeus makes extensive use of it ought to make us more cautious. As a matter of fact, in an age of insistence on mechanical and literal inspiration, allegorical exegesis was the only means available for all prophetic, creative minds to escape from

[1] Instances of the legal use of γέγραπται in my *Bibelstudien*, p. 109 f., *Neue Bibelstudien*, p. 77 f. (both in English as *Bible Studies*, Edinburgh, 1901, second edition 1903, pp. 112 f., 249 f.).

[2] *E.g.*, Gal. iii. 8, 22.

[3] 1 Cor. iv. 6, μὴ ὑπερ ἃ γέγραπται.

being stifled by the letter.[1] In Philo as well as in St. Paul, paradoxical as it may seem to say so, allegorical exegesis is rather a proof of freedom than of constraint, though it has led both men to great violence of interpretation.

An instance of such violence in St. Paul is his explanation to the Galatians[2] of the word 'seed'[3] as if it were to be understood in the singular, although the idea was really meant to be plural and is elsewhere so explained by St. Paul.[4] Or we might point to the subtle interpretation of the story of the Fall in favour of the man.[5] Another example would be his explanation of the saying about the ox that was not to be muzzled when treading out the corn,[6] as referring to the apostles.[7] In the course of this explanation, moreover, St. Paul hints casually that God does not trouble Himself about oxen. This feeble, unpractical remark of the town-dweller, who cannot take a natural view of animals because he has not lived in close touch with them, shows how far he is from the strong, splendid realism of the faith held by Jesus, who had grown up with animals and plants about Him. Jesus will not suffer a sparrow to fall to the ground without God's will,[8] and makes the flowers of the Galilean spring to be clothed by God Himself in their array of more than kingly gorgeousness.[9]

[1] G. Klein gives a similar verdict with regard to allegorical exegesis (*Der älteste christliche Katechismus und die jüdische Propaganda-Literatur*, Berlin, 1909, p. 42 f.).

[2] Gal. iii. 16.
[3] In Gen. xiii. 15.
[4] Rom. iv. 18; ix. 8.
[5] 1 Tim. ii. 13 f.
[6] Deut. xxv. 4.
[7] 1 Cor. ix. 9 f.; cf. 1 Tim. v. 18.
[8] Matt. x. 29; Luke xii. 6; cf. Matt. vi. 26; Luke xii. 24.
[9] Matt. vi. 28 ff.; Luke xii. 27 f.

On the other hand St. Paul, the allegorical expounder of Scripture, does, by the aid of his method, succeed in producing magnificent religious meditations. The parallel contrasting of Sarah and Hagar as the two testaments,[1] the identification of the rock which gave water in the wilderness with the Spiritual Christ[2]—these, viewed in their ancient setting, are revelations of a great genius, and no modern objections can diminish them. The Jewish habit of allegorising, which has so often lent crutches to the small masters of theology, here gives a religious genius wings to soar aloft like an eagle.

In various other details of his handling of Scripture St. Paul the Jew is dependent on his rabbinical traditions, especially those peculiar to the body of edifying legend known as the Haggadah. This is the source of the theory in the letter to the Galatians,[3] which is found also elsewhere,[4] that the Law was given not by God Himself but by the angels; this too is the source of the number 430, also in the letter to the Galatians,[5] and of that touch,[6] so popular in its appeal, about the rock which gave water in the wilderness having followed the Israelites on their wanderings.

In St. Paul's dialectic, as it is generally called, we again see the influence of his Jewish teachers, and especially the influence of the methods of teaching and demonstrating associated with oral disputation in the house of instruction. The letters of St. Paul being mostly dictated orally, the methods of oral demonstration are quite appropriate. Apart from

[1] Gal. iv. 22 ff. [2] 1 Cor. x. 4.
[3] Gal. iii. 19 (cf. also Col. ii. 16, combined with ii, 18).
[4] Acts vii. 53; Heb. ii. 2.
[5] Gal. iii. 17. [6] 1 Cor. x. 4.

the proof of all proofs—proof by Scripture—St. Paul is very fond of proof by analogy. For instance, analogies from nature are used to illustrate the relation of the earthly to the heavenly body,[1] analogies from agricultural and military life to illustrate the right of the apostles to the means of subsistence.[2] Analogies from legal life, in which St. Paul as a city-resident was strongly interested, are special favourites with him, *e.g.*, an outsider cannot add a clause to a testament;[3] the heir who is not yet of age is under the authority of the guardian and the steward for as long as the father has appointed.[4] We find farther the analogical conclusion from the less to the greater[5] ('simple and complex' the Rabbis called it), and also the conclusion from the greater to the less.[6] The magnificent parallel contrasts drawn between Adam and Christ in 1 Corinthians and Romans[7] are also typically rabbinical.

On the whole, however, St. Paul's rabbinical dialectic, and indeed his dialectic altogether, has been in my opinion much too highly rated. Demonstration in the strict sense is not St. Paul's strong point. Hoping to arrive with him at the end of a straight road, you sometimes find yourself brought back to the starting-point of a circle. In controversy, for instance, St. Paul is of much too impulsive a nature to be a great dialectician. Rather than refute his opponents at length he disposes of them with an angry look; and in the treatment of religious problems he generally succeeds better with

[1] 1 Cor. xv. 35 ff.
[2] 1 Cor. ix. 7.
[3] Gal. iii. 15.
[4] Gal. iv. 1.
[5] *E.g.*, Rom. xi. 12, 24.
[6] *E.g.*, 1 Cor. vi. 1 ff.; Rom. xi. 21.
[7] 1 Cor. xv. 22 ff., 45 ff.; Rom. v. 12 ff.

the intuitive and contemplative than with the speculative.

How far St. Paul's talent for intuition and contemplation is a Jewish feature I do not venture to say. In the mystical literature of later times there are analogies not a few, especially no doubt among the classics of mysticism in the Middle Ages. In any case the idea of contemplation seems to me to characterise what is distinctive in the religious production of St. Paul (and afterwards of the evangelist St. John) better than the idea of theological speculation.

By contemplation I understand a submersion or steeping of oneself in the great certainties of faith, a wrestling with practical problems which are not interesting from the point of view of scientific theology, but torturing problems of religion. Contemplation speaks in sentences that are not hard and rigid, but soft, living, working like leaven; they do not fly like hissing arrows straight to their mark, they circle round their prey like an eagle in noiseless flight. But often there is something hesitating and brooding about contemplation; it shows less forward than downward progress of thought. It cannot attain to a uniform system, because it is the surging to and fro of a soul stirred to its depths.

A typical example of this tossing to and fro of the perturbed soul is the celebrated contemplation in Romans on God's ways with Israel.[1] To some extent it is a logical problem, but to a much greater extent it is religious agony that here moves St. Paul the Jew. As already pointed out,[2] a logical solution is not found; in spite of many attempts to free himself

[1] Rom. ix.–xi.

[2] Cf. p. 101 above.

St. Paul gets entangled again and again in the net of the problem, and in the answers that he gives he does not free himself by speculation, he tears the net by the irresistible force of his religious intuition.

The stream of St. Paul's contemplative production flows most purely in the letter to the Colossians and in the closely related letter to the Laodiceans (the so-called Epistle to the Ephesians). In these two letters there were no special problems of church life to discuss, and so St. Paul could here give vent to solemn utterances, which even in point of style are striking for their grave and as it were priestly earnestness.

I repeat, however, that I am not certain whether this strongly contemplative strain in St. Paul constitutes a specifically Jewish side of his character. We might say that his contemplation is Jewish in its want of system and in its inequalities on the side of theory, Jewish in its constructive aids, especially its proof by Scripture. The essential thing, however, is perhaps not derivable from anywhere, but to be regarded as the outcome of St. Paul's own specific genius.

Be that as it may, for the rest St. Paul the Jew stands clearly before us, with all the power contained in Judaism, and also with some of the limitations that surrounded it.

The characteristic features of St. Paul the Jew come out still more clearly when we place him beside another of his race, who, known the world over as "the Jew" *par excellence* of the Hellenistic age, has become almost one of the Fathers of the Church—Philo of Alexandria.

The two men, Philo Judaeus and St. Paul the Jew,

are contemporaries. Both are Jews of the Dispersion, city-dwellers, with marked cosmopolitan traits. Both live and move in the Septuagint Bible. Both are capable of ecstatic and mystical experiences, and have many points of contact in details.

And yet they stand in very strong contrast to one another, a contrast which reminds us of the opposition between Seneca and St. Paul,[1] and which recurs again in some main lines in the case of Erasmus and Luther. Philo writes, St. Paul speaks (even his letters are spoken); Philo's name has probably made its way to St. Paul, but not St. Paul's to Philo; Philo is an author, St. Paul is not; Philo leaves literary works behind him, St. Paul non-literary letters. Philo is a philosopher, St. Paul the fool pours out the vials of his irony upon the wisdom of the world. Philo belongs to the upper class, St. Paul to the middle and lower classes; Philo represents high literary culture, St. Paul the strength that wells up from the people. Philo is a pharos, St. Paul a volcano. Philo is a student, a theologian, St. Paul a prophet and herald. Philo works at his desk for the great literary public, St. Paul hurries from the loom to the market and the synagogue, to meet his audience face to face. Philo's nephew, Tiberius Julius Alexander, was Procurator of Palestine and Praefect of Egypt; not only is his name immortalised by Josephus, Tacitus, and Suetonius, he has also a monument in stone on the wall of the propylon of a temple in the Great Oasis—one of the most famous inscriptions of the early imperial period.[2]

[1] Cf. p. 77 above.

[2] Dittenberger, *Orientis Graeci Inscriptiones Selectae*, No. 669. Reproduced from a photograph in *Light from the Ancient East*, p. 362.

St. Paul's nephew, trembling for his uncle's safety and interrogated by Roman officers,[1] is an unknown person from the nameless masses, appearing for a moment and then vanishing. Philo goes to Rome as an ambassador and is received by the Emperor, St. Paul only has relations with imperial slaves,[2] and is transported to Rome as a prisoner.

The whole mass of contrasts between the man of Alexandria and the man of Tarsus may be summed up thus: Philo is a Platonist, St. Paul will be what he will be in Another; Philo the Jew stands at the end of ancient culture, St. Paul the Jew stands at the beginning of the new world-religion.

It is true that, before St. Paul the Jew has taken his place on the threshold of the new era, we see him as a fanatical keeper of the Pharisaic tradition with his face turned backward to the past: St. Paul the Jew became at first the persecutor of the infant Church of Christ. In the passionate zeal which he here displayed he is a thorough Jew. The picture drawn of the persecutor in the Acts of the Apostles[3] is no doubt correct in the main; its principal features are confirmed by painful self-tormenting confessions in St. Paul's letters.[4] Historically the attitude of the young man is easy enough to explain. The conflict to which Jesus had fallen a victim was a conflict with the leading party of the Pharisees; Paul the persecutor is Paul the Pharisee, continuing the warfare waged by his party against Jesus by warfare waged against the church of the Crucified.

[1] Acts xxiii. 16 ff. [2] Phil. iv. 22.

[3] Acts vi. 9; vii. 58; viii. 1 ff.; ix. 1 ff.; xxii. 3 ff.; xxvi. 4 ff.

[4] Gal. i. 13 f., 23; 1 Cor. xv. 9; Phil. iii. 6; 1 Tim. i. 13.

ST. PAUL THE CHRISTIAN

CHAPTER V

ST. PAUL THE CHRISTIAN

The primitive apostolic cult of Jesus—The conversion of St. Paul —St. Paul's spiritual experience of Christ

THE death of Jesus on the cross had the immediate effect of scattering his little band of adherents from Galilee and Jerusalem. In the great religious conflict with the powerful Pharisees, Jesus seemed to have been finally defeated, although He had foretold in prophetic words of foreboding to His followers both His martyrdom and His coming again after His martyrdom.

Very soon, however, after their terrible experience caused by the execution of Jesus, we find these fearful and despairing individuals again assembled in the Holy City, and whereas formerly they had scarcely been united into an organised church, they are now closely bound together in the fellowship of the breaking of bread and of prayer, longingly waiting for the last great revelation of their Messiah.

It was Easter experiences of St. Peter and the others[1] that had brought about this great change.

Those experiences can never be completely analysed

[1] The most important authority for this statement is 1 Cor. xv. 1 ff.

by historical means, but the substance of them is described by men and women in like manner: Jesus appeared to them in divine glory as the One whom God had raised from the dead, with words of encouragement and promise upon His lips.

These experiences of the apostles are the psychological starting-point of the earliest cult of Jesus in Palestine, the *sine qua non* for the growth and organisation of Christian churches. Owing to them the prophet of the Kingdom of God became the object of the apostles' piety, for they set the seal to His Messianic revelations about Himself. They invested the form of the Messiah with the resplendence of Deity itself, turned the torturing problem of the Cross into a miracle of grace, opened the sacred writings of the old prophetic period and roused up new confessors and prophets in a great revival.

In order to understand Primitive Christianity in the light of religious history it is of the greatest importance to learn to regard these beginnings of the organised church of Christ as the beginnings of a new cult, the cult of Jesus Christ.

Jesus Himself had founded no new cult; he had brought the new age. But even during His earthly life His person had been the centre of attraction to His faithful followers: His great consciousness of His own personality had exerted a selective and combining influence upon men. The real *cult* of Christ, however, arose out of the mysteries of the apostles' Easter experiences. Though the torches of exact scholarship are powerless to penetrate the sacred twilight of those mysteries, and to analyse all that is ancient and mysterious into crystal-clear phenomena self-evident to the modern mind, we have displayed to us in the beginnings of the cult of Jesus an example, probably unique in ancient religious history, of the rise of a new cult. Apart from the real intrinsic worth of the apostles' piety, the new cult was distinguished from all others by the circumstance that the central figure of the cult did not remain veiled in the mist of mythology, but had been personally known to most of the earliest sharers of the cult [1] as a man of flesh and blood, and was daily present to them in a living stream of tradition conveying His imperishable and incomparable sayings.

The outward characteristics of the primitive apostolic cult of Jesus are recognisable clearly enough from the Acts of the Apostles. That book, of course, being a pious record for popular reading, does not speak of the first church in the dry tone that might be adopted by an ecclesiastical bureaucracy publishing its tables of statistics, but with the pious earnestness which we are accustomed to associate with missionary gatherings. The writer of the first missionary history becomes enthusiastic, and makes his readers enthusiastic, over the church of the saints, which is viewed of course only in a transfigured light. But the historic lines are unmistakable. The adherents of the cult of the living Jesus Christ had already adopted the rudiments of an organisation based on brotherhood; they possessed in baptism and the Lord's Supper two institutions which may be called, in the ancient technical sense of the word, the two Primitive Christian mysteries; and they had early begun

[1] Several hundred eyewitnesses were still alive between 50 and 60 A.D. (1 Cor. xv. 6).

within the neighbourhood of Palestine, as far as to Phoenicia, Syria, and Cyprus, to carry on a propaganda[1] so as to gather together a church that should be worthy of the coming Kingdom of God.

Historically the most remarkable trace left by the earliest Palestinian cult of Jesus Christ is an Aramaic hieroglyph which we afterwards find in the mouth of St. Paul,[2] but which, because it is an Aramaic word, must come from the primitive Aramaic-speaking church. It is the cry of prayer which was probably sent up yearningly to Christ by the faithful at the end of the communion festival[3] :—

'Marana tha' (Our Lord, come!)

Thus the infant church prays to her Lord for His advent in divine glory in order to the final epiphany of the Kingdom of God.

The self-sacrificing enthusiasm of the infant church soon came in conflict with the same powerful authorities to which Jesus had succumbed. The blood of the first martyr is shed, and at the death of Stephen, who bore witness with his blood, we find present as one of those morally responsible[4] the Pharisee and zealot Saul who is also called Paul.

[1] See on the map at the end of the volume the sites of the primitive apostolic cult of Christ, marked by a red double cross, the names being doubly underlined.

[2] 1 Cor. xvi. 22, Μαρανα θα. Cf. Rev. xxii. 20.

[3] Cf. the occurrence of the cry in the oldest Christian communion prayer, Didache, x. 6, εἴ τις ἅγιός ἐστιν, ἐρχέσθω. εἴ τις οὐκ ἔστι, μετανοείτω. Μαρανα θα. ἀμήν. 'If any is holy, let him come. If any is not, let him repent. Our Lord, come! Amen.'

[4] Acts vii. 58; viii. 1.

The young man from the burning Cilician plain must have been inspired with fanatical hatred against the adherents of Jesus of Nazareth, whose denunciations of woe against the piety of the Pharisees were not forgotten. The gospel propaganda was quickly followed by the counter-propaganda of force; it was organised by Saul *alias* Paul. In the service of the same disciplinary authority whose scourgings were afterwards to lacerate his own back, he hastened—an apostle already in this—northward to Damascus [1] to smother the flames of the new cult which were already faintly burning there.

On this journey, close to the city of Damascus itself,[2] came the experience that meant total transformation to St. Paul, namely his conversion.

Concerning this event, which no pagan historian took notice of, though in its effects it was of world-wide importance, we possess two sources of information: the hints of the apostle himself, and three sketches in the Acts of the Apostles,[3] which are not completely reconcilable with one another, but which must, from the nature of the case, be somehow derived from accounts given by St. Paul himself.

Here too, as with the appearances of Christ to St. Peter and the others who saw Him at the first Easter, we shall never succeed in unravelling the experience psychologically and analysing it without any residue, not even if we call to our aid the

[1] Gal. i. 13 ff.; Acts ix., xxii., xxvi.

[2] This is stated explicitly in Acts ix. 3, xxii. 6, xxvi. 12, but could also be inferred by combining Gal. i. 13 with i. 17.

[3] Acts ix. 1 ff.; xxii. 3 ff.; xxvi. 10 ff.

numerous analogies to the incident of conversion which the history of religion affords. But we can state with great certainty how St. Paul himself conceived of the incident.

He describes it once [1] with the word which occurs in the Septuagint as a technical expression for appearances of the Divinity, and which he also uses with reference to the appearances of Christ to the other apostles [2] :—

'He appeared to me also.'

It was the living Christ who appeared, and St. Paul hints that the manifestation of Christ to him was the last in the series.

Another time [3] he says, with still more of ancient vividness :—

'I have seen Jesus our Lord,'

or he confesses [4] :—

'I was apprehended by Christ Jesus.'

A fourth time,[5] however, he speaks of his experience almost as a modern psychologist would, as a revelation of the Son of God brought about by God 'in' him. A fifth time [6] he says in still more general terms that the mystery of Christ was made known

[1] 1 Cor. xv. 8, ὤφθη κἀμοί.

[2] 1 Cor. xv. 5, 6, 7, ὤφθη.

[3] 1 Cor. ix. 1, in the form of a rhetorical question, οὐχὶ Ἰησοῦν τὸν κύριον ἡμῶν ἑόρακα ;

[4] Phil. iii. 12, κατελήμφθην ὑπὸ Χριστοῦ Ἰησοῦ.

[5] Gal. i. 16, ἀποκαλύψαι τὸν υἱὸν αὐτοῦ ἐν ἐμοί.

[6] Eph. iii. 3, κατὰ ἀποκάλυψιν ἐγνωρίσθη μοι τὸ μυστήριον.

to him by revelation. In his memory of what happened near Damascus there was always, I think—we see it hinted in the second letter to Corinth[1]—the impression of a great blaze of light, comparable to God's first shining day that broke forth out of the darkness at the creation. So too, in the Acts of the Apostles,[2] the whole thing is painted, with the universal colours of antiquity, in the magnificent flood of light always employed to represent manifestations of the divine.

An experience which St. Paul looks upon as caused by God, which betokens with absolute certainty that the living Christ has been revealed to him, or that he himself has been taken possession of by Christ, and which includes also the inward transformation and at the same time apostolic commission[3] of the man who hitherto had been a persecutor—all this the event near Damascus was to St. Paul himself. And this description of the incident of his conversion is amply sufficient for the historian. We can, however, taking this one experience in connexion with the whole of St. Paul's later mystical experience of Christ, gain one more important result by combining two statements in the letter to the Galatians. To the man who describes his position as a Christian by saying,[4]

'Christ liveth *in me*,'

---

[1] 2 Cor. iv. 6, *ὁ θεὸς ὁ εἰπών· ἐκ σκότους φῶς λάμψει, ὃς ἔλαμψεν ἐν ταῖς καρδίαις ἡμῶν πρὸς φωτισμὸν τῆς γνώσεως τῆς δόξης τοῦ θεοῦ ἐν προσώπῳ Χριστοῦ.*

[2] Acts ix. 3; xxii. 6, 9; xxvi. 13.

[3] Gal. i. 16, *ἵνα εὐαγγελίζωμαι αὐτὸν ἐν τοῖς ἔθνεσιν.*

[4] Gal. ii. 20, *ζῇ δὲ ἐν ἐμοὶ Χριστός.*

Damascus was the beginning of this indwelling of Christ:—

> 'It was the good pleasure of God . . . to reveal His Son *in me*.' [1]

The incident near Damascus must therefore not be isolated, but must be regarded as the foundational experience in mysticism of a religious genius to whom also in later life extraordinary ecstatic experiences were vouchsafed.

The conversion of the persecutor to the follower, and of the apostle of the Pharisees to the apostle of Christ, was a sudden one. But it was no magical transformation; it was psychologically prepared for, both negatively and positively.

Negatively, by the experiences which the soul of the young Pharisee, in its passionate hunger for righteousness, had had under the yoke of the Law. We hear the echo of his groanings even twenty or thirty years afterwards in the letters of the convert: like a curse there had come upon him the awful discovery [2] that even for the most earnest conscience, in fact especially for the most earnest conscience, it is impossible really to keep the whole Law.

Positively the conversion was no doubt prepared for on the one hand by the prophetic inwardness of the old revelation acting on Paul the Jew, and on the other hand by a relatively close familiarity with genuine tradition about Jesus and the effects that Jesus was able to produce in the persons of the confessors of Jesus whom Paul persecuted. I do not consider it probable that the young zealot

[1] Gal. i. 16. See note 5, p. 120.

[2] Gal. iii. 10, and many sad regrets in Romans (*e.g.* vii. 14 ff.).

was ever personally acquainted with the earthly Jesus, although weighty voices have again declared recently in favour of this hypothesis.[1] But it is most certainly probable that the Pharisee was acquainted with his opponent as far as He remained an influence in His words and in His disciples.

Thus the lightning of Damascus strikes no empty void, but finds plenty of inflammable material in the soul of the young persecutor. We see the flames shoot up, and we feel that the glow then kindled has lost none of its force a generation later in the man grown aged: Christ is in Paul, Paul in Christ.

With these words we have not only grasped the secret of all St. Paul's religion—we have also described it in terms made sacred by St. Paul:—

Christ in Paul,[2] Paul in Christ.[3]

It is no doubt generally admitted that St. Paul's religion centred in Christ, but how differently people conceive of the Christ-centred Christianity of St. Paul! Often it has been represented as identical with Christological Christianity. But the religion of St. Paul is Christ-centred in a far deeper and far more realistic sense: it is not first of all a doctrine concerning Christ, it is 'fellowship' with Christ.[4] St. Paul lives 'in' Christ, 'in'

[1] 2 Cor. v. 16 must be otherwise understood. If the words 'we have known Christ after the flesh (κατὰ σάρκα)' referred to personal acquaintance with the earthly Jesus, the conclusion, 'now we know Him no more,' would be trivial.

[2] Gal. ii. 20, etc.

[3] Numerous passages.

[4] 1 Cor. i. 9; x. 16; Phil. iii. 10. The word used is κοινωνία, an inimitably vivid expression.

the living and present spiritual Christ, who is about him on all sides, dwells in him,[1] speaks to him,[2] speaks in and through him.[3] To St. Paul Christ is not a person of the past, with whom he can have intercourse only by meditating on his words that have been handed down, not a great 'historic' figure, but a reality and power of the present, an 'energy'[4] whose life-giving power is daily made perfect in him.[5]

We must first of all try to understand this Christ of the apostle. The attempt is usually made under the heading, 'the Christology' of St. Paul. But it would be more accurate, because more historical, to inquire concerning the apostle's 'knowledge of Christ,' or 'experience of Christ,' or 'Christ as revealed to St. Paul.' Anything that tends to petrify the fellowship with Christ, which was felt at the beginning and felt so vividly, into a doctrine about Christ, is mischievous. We ask, What Christ did Paul know and experience? The answer can only be: it is the spiritual, living Christ, of whom Paul is certain.

This certainty of Christ, however, is of varying quality. Always, it is true, the living, risen Christ is the centre, but we can distinguish two opposite extremes of feeling.

At one time Christ is to the apostle the Son of God who has been 'highly exalted'[6] to the Father, who now dwells in heaven above in glory with the

[1] Gal. ii. 20. [2] 2 Cor. xii. 9.
[3] 2 Cor. xiii. 3.
[4] Phil. iii. 21; Col. i. 29; Eph. i. 19.
[5] 2 Cor. xii. 9; Phil. iii. 10; 1 Cor. i. 24; v. 4.
[6] Phil. ii. 9, ὁ θεὸς αὐτὸν ὑπερύψωσεν.

Father, 'at the right hand of God,'[1] and shall soon 'come' as a judge upon earth.[2]

This assurance about Christ, which is strongly Jewish in tone, and especially influenced by Psalm cx., might be called by doctrinaire theologians an assurance of the transcendence of Christ. It would be more in the spirit of St. Paul and therefore historically more correct to describe it as an assurance of Christ the 'highly exalted.' This word 'highly exalted' is characteristically Pauline,[3] and although it afterwards gave a very strong stimulus to the development of dogma, it was originally not a dogmatic expression at all, but a religious formulation of a conviction about Christ in plain, popular style.

Still more characteristic of St. Paul is the second, more Hellenistic and mystical phase of his experience of Christ: the living Christ is the Spirit. As Spirit (*pneuma*) the Living One is not far away beyond clouds and stars, but present on this poor earth, where He lives and rules among His own. Here, too, there are inspirations to be found in the Septuagint, and St. Paul himself is responsible for some significant formulations :—

'The Lord is the Spirit,'[4]

'The last Adam became a life-giving Spirit,'[5]

'He that is joined unto the Lord is one Spirit,'[6]

---

[1] Rom. viii. 34; Col. iii. 1; Eph. i. 20; following LXX Psa. cx. 1.

[2] Cf. the numerous παρουσία passages in St. Paul's letters.

[3] ὑπερυψόω, Phil. ii. 9 (cf. ὑψόω, John iii. 14; viii. 28; xii. 34). Isa. xxxiii. 10 in the LXX sounds like a preliminary announce-

[For notes 4 to 6 see next page.

and so on. Still more important perhaps than lines of such symbolical character as these is the fact that in numerous passages St. Paul makes statements about Christ and about the Spirit in precisely equivalent terms. This is specially observable in the parallelism of the mystical formulae 'in Christ' and 'in the (Holy) Spirit.' The formula 'in the Spirit,' which occurs only nineteen times in St. Paul, is connected in nearly all these passages with the same specifically Pauline fundamental notions as the formula 'in Christ.' Faith,[1] righteousness,[2] justification,[3] being,[4] standing,[5] rejoicing and joy,[6] free gift (by grace),[7] love,[8] peace,[9] sanctification,[10] sealing,[11] circumcision,[12] bearing witness,[13] speaking,[14] being filled,[15] one

1 Gal. iii. 26, etc.: 1 Cor. xii. 9.
2 2 Cor. v. 21, etc.: Rom. xiv. 17.
3 Gal. ii. 17: 1 Cor. vi. 11.
4 1 Cor. i. 30, etc.: Rom. viii. 9.
5 Phil. iv. 1, etc.: Phil. i. 27.
6 Phil. iii. 1, etc.: Rom. xiv. 17.
7 Rom. vi. 23: 1 Cor. xii. 9.
8 Rom. viii. 39, etc.: Col. i. 8.
9 Phil. iv. 7: Rom. xiv. 17.
10 1 Cor. i. 2: Rom. xv. 16 [the Greek has ἐν], etc.
11 Eph. i. 13, etc.: Eph. iv. 30.
12 Col. ii. 11: Rom. ii. 29
13 Eph. iv. 17: Rom. ix. 1.
14 2 Cor. ii. 17, etc.: 1 Cor. xii. 3.
15 Col. i. 10: Eph. v. 18.

Continuation of notes to p. 125.]
ment of the Pauline and Johannine 'Christology': νῦν ἀναστήσομαι, λέγει κύριος, νῦν δοξασθήσομαι, νῦν ὑψωθήσομαι, 'Now will I rise, saith the Lord, now will I be glorified, now will I be exalted.'

4 2 Cor. iii. 17, ὁ δὲ κύριος τὸ πνεῦμά ἐστιν.

5 1 Cor. xv. 45, ἐγένετο . . . ὁ ἔσχατος Ἀδὰμ εἰς πνεῦμα ζωοποιοῦν.

6 1 Cor. vi. 17, ὁ δὲ κολλώμενος τῷ κυρίῳ ἓν πνεῦμά ἐστιν.

body,[1] a temple of God[2]—all these things the Christian sees and experiences and is 'in Christ,' and also 'in the Spirit'; that means in fact 'in Christ who is the Spirit.' Therefore also the technical expressions 'fellowship of the Son of God' and 'fellowship of the Holy Spirit' are parallel in St. Paul;[3] for the same experience is meant, whether St. Paul says that Christ lives in him[4] or that the Spirit dwells in us,[5] whether he speaks of Christ's making intercession for us with the Father[6] or of the assistance of the Spirit in prayer.[7]

Doctrinaire theologians might call this experience of Christ by the apostle an experience of the immanence of Christ. It would be more in the manner of St. Paul, and therefore historically more correct, to speak of the experience of the Spirit-Christ.

This assurance of the nearness of Christ is much more frequent with St. Paul than the upward look to the distant Christ 'highly exalted' to heaven.

'Christ in me'

—that is indeed a confession poured forth from the

1 Rom. xii. 5 : 1 Cor. xii. 13.

2 Eph. ii. 21 : Eph. ii. 22.

3 1 Cor. i. 9 : 2 Cor. xiii. 13 [14] ; Phil. ii. 1.

4 Gal. ii. 20; cf. 2 Cor. xiii. 5; Rom. viii. 10.

5 Rom. viii. 9; 1 Cor. iii. 16; vi. 19.

6 Rom. viii. 34 f.

7 Rom. viii. 26 ff. In St. John, who calls the Spirit (John xiv. 16, 26; xv. 26; xvi. 7) and Jesus Christ (1 John ii. 1) 'advocate' (παράκλητος), this great Pauline conviction is still more realistically worked out than in Romans.

very depths of the soul, the confession of an assurance, a certitude, which brings light to the lowest recesses of the ego and takes commanding possession. Corresponding with this is the other assurance: 'In Christ.' Christ is Spirit; therefore He can live in Paul and Paul in Him. Just as the air of life which we breathe is 'in' us and fills us, and yet we at the same time live and breathe 'in' this air, so it is with St. Paul's fellowship of Christ: Christ in him, he in Christ. This thoroughly Pauline watchword, 'in Christ,' is meant vividly and mystically, and so is the analogous 'Christ in me.' The formula 'in Christ' (or 'in the Lord,' etc.) occurs 164 times in St. Paul: it is really the characteristic expression of his Christianity. Greatly misunderstood by the commentators, rationalised, often applied to the 'historic' Jesus and so weakened in effect, often ignored, this formula—so closely connected in meaning with the other: 'in the Spirit'—must be conceived as the peculiarly Pauline expression of the most intimate fellowship imaginable of the Christian with the living, spiritual Christ.[1]

Related, if not identical, is the formula 'through Christ,' which has also been often misunderstood, but which in by far the greatest number of cases is also to be referred to the spiritual Christ.[2]

We may now ask, What was St. Paul's conception of this spiritual Christ? The answer will depend on how we define 'spirit' (*pneuma*) as used

[1] On this, and on the whole chapter, cf. my book, *Die neutestamentliche Formel 'in Christo Jesu,'* Marburg, 1892.

[2] Cf. Adolph Schettler, *Die paulinische Formel 'Durch Christus,'* Tübingen, 1907.

by St. Paul. It is best to start from the sharp contrast in which the *pneuma* always stands to *sarx*, 'the flesh.' The 'spirit' is certainly something not fleshly,[1] not earthly,[2] not material. The spiritual Christ has indeed a *soma*, a 'body,' but it is a spiritual,[3] that is heavenly[4] body,[5] consisting of divine effulgence. Sharp, philosophically pointed definition of the concept 'spiritual' there is happily none in St. Paul. The apostle remains popular and, in true ancient style, vivid in his formulation. He probably thought of some light, ethereal form of existence, such as he doubtless attributed also to God. But there is no binding definition; we have the greatest possible latitude if we should wish to transplant the apostle's ideas concerning Christ into our own religious thought. To Paul the Spirit, God, the living Christ is a reality, the reality of all realities; therefore there was no need for him to puzzle over definitions. The Spirit that is living in Paul searches all things, even the deep things of God,[6] but it excogitates no definitions of God. Religious definitions are always attempts to save something.

If Paul had given a definition, he would have defined as a man of the ancients, in a manner more realistic, more massive, and more concrete than a speculative thinker of our own time, but certainly not materialistically. There is nothing fleshly, nothing earthly about the Spirit; it is divine, heavenly, eternal, holy, living, and life-giving—these are all predicates that St. Paul gives

[1] The *locus classicus* is 1 Cor. xv. 35 ff.
[2] 1 Cor. xv. 47 ff.
[3] 1 Cor. xv. 45 f.
[4] 1 Cor. xv. 47 ff.
[5] Phil. iii. 21.
[6] 1 Cor. ii. 10.

or could give to it, and they may all be applied to the spiritual Christ.

What St. Paul formally new created or rather introduced into the mysticism of Christ was not definitions, but an abundant store of technical phrases expressing, often in popular figurative language, the spiritual fellowship between Christ and His own. The not unimportant problem of reproducing this technical language of St. Paul, some details of which we have touched, has not yet been solved connectedly, and it can only be mentioned as a problem here. He that will solve it must be at home in the atmosphere and language of Eastern and Western mysticism.

The question, 'What, according to St. Paul, brings about the fellowship of Christ?' is answered from the hints which we have given concerning St. Paul's conversion. It is God who brings about fellowship with Christ.[1] Not that every Christian has an experience equal to that of St. Paul on the road to Damascus, but every one who possesses the living Christ or the Spirit has received the gift from God Himself, or is 'apprehended' by Christ Himself.[2] There are numerous passages[3] in which God is celebrated as the giver of the Spirit.

The assertion that in St. Paul baptism is the means of access to Christ, I take to be incorrect. There are passages which, if isolated, might be held

[1] 1 Cor. i. 9, 30; 2 Cor. i. 21 f.; iv. 6. Here too belong all the passages in which St. Paul speaks of our being chosen and called by God. They must not be isolated as a special piece of doctrine.

[2] Phil. iii. 12.

[3] Gal. iv. 6; Rom. v. 5; viii. 15; 1 Cor. vi. 19; ii. 12.

to prove it,[1] but I think it is nevertheless more correct to say that baptism does not bring about but only sets the seal to the fellowship of Christ. In St. Paul's own case at any rate it was not baptism that was decisive, but the appearance of Christ to him before Damascus; nor did he consider himself commissioned to baptize, but to evangelise.[2] The Lord's Supper, again, was to him not the real cause of fellowship with Christ, but an expression of this fellowship; it was an especially intimate contact with the Lord.[3] The Lord's Supper does not bring about the fellowship, it only brings it into prominence. Neither baptism nor the Lord's Supper is regarded as of magical effect.[4] In every case it is God's grace that is decisive. St. Paul's Christians can say with him [5]:—

'By the grace of God I am what I am.'

Powerful and original as St. Paul's spiritual experience of Christ is, there are not wanting influences that acted upon him as stimuli, chiefly coming from the piety of the Septuagint. In the Greek Old Testament there are a considerable number of prominent passages—and here, I think, an important Hellenisation of the original is revealed—in which the formulae 'in God' and 'in the Lord' are used in a mystical sense. The words of the prophet,[6]

'Yet I will exult in the Lord,'

[1] *E.g.*, Gal. iii. 27.
[2] 1 Cor. i. 17.
[3] 1 Cor. x. 16.
[4] 1 Cor. x. 1–13.
[5] 1 Cor. xv. 10, *χάριτι δὲ θεοῦ εἰμὶ ὅ εἰμι.*
[6] LXX Hab. iii. 18, *ἐγὼ δὲ ἐν τῷ κυρίῳ ἀγαλλιάσομαι.*

sound like the prelude of St. Paul's Jubilate,[1]

'Rejoice in the Lord!'

The formula 'in God,' which is especially frequent in the Septuagint Psalms, is a great favourite with St. Paul[2] and occurs also united with the formula 'in Christ.'[3] The confession in the speech on Mars' Hill,[4]

'In Him (God) we live and move and have our being,'

is part of Paul's pre-Christian mysticism, inspired by the Septuagint; Paul the Christian's rallying-cry, 'in Christ,' is the more vivid substitute for the old sacred formula.

It is justifiable, I think, to speak of Hellenistic influence here, when we remember the importance in Greek mysticism of inspired persons who are filled with their god, and gifted with power in their god.[5] Placed in the great coherent body of mysticism in general, the piety of St. Paul acquires the stamp which really distinguishes it in the history of religion: it is mysticism centred in Christ.

A quarter of a century ago, in my undergraduate days, a heavy hand had stretched out from the side of the dogmatists and had banished mysticism from German lecture-rooms. The study of St. Paul, like other things, suffered under this hand. The few scholars who then emphasised to us the mystic element in St. Paul might have appealed to the

[1] Phil. iii. 1; iv. 4, *χαίρετε ἐν τῷ κυρίῳ.*

[2] 1 Thess. ii. 2; Rom. ii. 17; v. 11; Col. iii. 3; Eph. iii. 9.

[3] 1 Thess. i. 1; 2 Thess. i. 1.

[4] Acts xvii. 28, *ἐν αὐτῷ γὰρ ζῶμεν καὶ κινούμεθα καὶ ἐσμέν.*

[5] Valuable material is now offered by R. Reitzenstein, *Die hellenistischen Mysterienreligionen*, Leipzig and Berlin, 1910.

authority of greater teachers than Albrecht Ritschl.[1] Luther and Calvin brought a congenial sympathy to the understanding of the apostle's mysticism about Christ, and if we go farther back we find the real St. Paul alive in the ancient Church, especially in the Greek Fathers. The greatest monument of most genuine appreciation of St. Paul's mysticism, however, is the Gospel and the Epistles of St. John; their Logos Christ is the Spirit Christ, made once more incarnate for the congregation of saints in a time of bitter conflict by an evangelist who is equally inspired by the earthly Jesus and by St. Paul.

There can be no doubt that St. Paul became influential in the world's history precisely by reason of his mysticism about Christ. The spiritual Christ was able to do what a dogmatic Messiah never could have done. The dogmatic Messiah of the Jews is fettered to his native country. The spiritual Christ could move from place to place; coming from the East, He could become at home in the West, could bid defiance to the changing centuries and spread His arms over every generation:—

> 'The Spirit bloweth where it listeth.'[2]

St. Paul of course could not have exerted this

[1] [The Göttingen theologian (1822–1889), author of *The Christian Doctrine of Justification and Reconciliation* (translated by J. S. Black, Edinburgh, 1872, and by H. R. Mackintosh and A. B. Macaulay, Edinburgh, 1900) and other influential works. Cf. A. E. Garvie, *Ritschlian Theology*, Edinburgh, 1899; J. K. Mozley, *Ritschlianism*, London, 1909; E. A. Edghill, *Faith and Fact: a Study of Ritschlianism*, London, 1910. Tr.]

[2] John iii. 8.

great influence if the fires of mysticism had consumed away the ethical element in him. But the ethos in his case stood the ordeal of fire. The Pauline fellowship of Christ is no magic transformation, nor is it an orgy of enthusiasts who are left mere yawning sluggards when the transport is over. St. Paul himself subordinated ecstasy to ethos.[1] The mysticism of Christ in him is rather a glowing than a flaming fire. The man whom Christ has 'apprehended' says with all humility[2] :—

> 'Not that I have already seized [Him] . . . . !'

But he also makes the heroic confession[3] :—

> 'I can do all things in Him that strengtheneth me.'

Similarly, too, the gift of the Spirit set the saints of St. Paul's churches mighty tasks. Having 'put on Christ'[4] they are to put Him on anew daily,[5] and 'in' this Christ only that faith is of value which proves its energy by love.[6]

Let us look back for a moment. Christ the Living, highly exalted with the Father, but also as Spirit living in Paul, and Paul in Him by God's grace—that is the Apostle Paul's assurance of Christ and experience of Christ. According to the doctrinaire view 'Paulinism' establishes at this point an 'antinomy' through the 'dualism' of the transcendence and immanence of Christ. But in

1 1 Cor. xiii. 1–3.
2 Phil. iii. 12 ff., οὐχ ὅτι ἤδη ἔλαβον . . .
3 Phil. iv. 13, πάντα ἰσχύω ἐν τῷ ἐνδυναμοῦντί με.
4 Gal. iii. 27. 5 Rom. xiii. 14.
6 Gal. v. 6, πίστις δι' ἀγάπης ἐνεργουμένη.

fact we see two moods of St. Paul's piety, both of which could exist side by side in his capacious soul. They no more represent an internal contradiction than the experiences of the transcendent and immanent God which every believer knows. The polar contradiction of these two moods gives rather to the inner life of the apostle its prophetic tension.

This tension relieves itself in an abundance of great detailed assurances, particular experiences, and confessions.

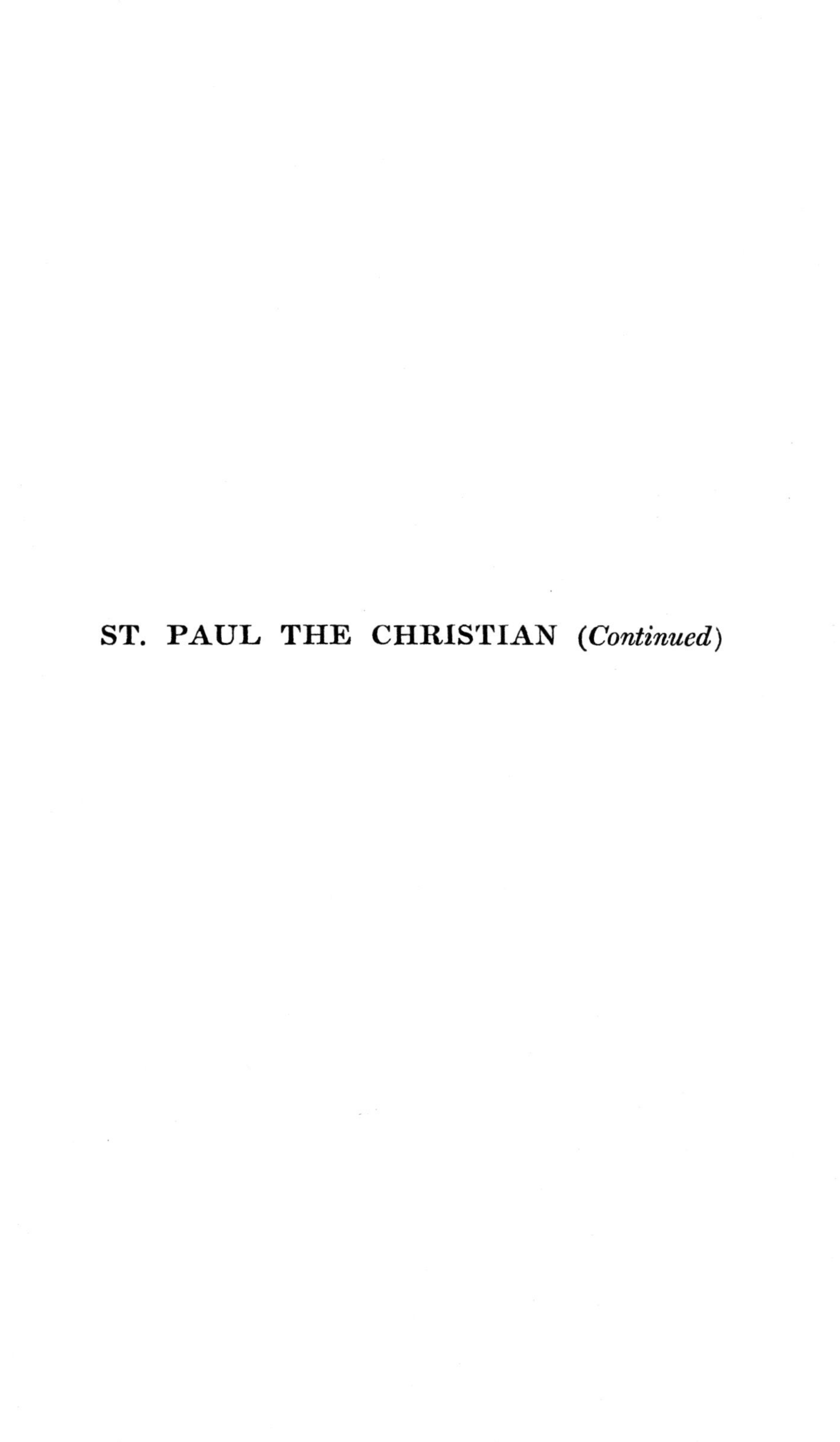

ST. PAUL THE CHRISTIAN (*Continued*)

CHAPTER VI

ST. PAUL THE CHRISTIAN (*Continued*)

Faith in God 'in Christ' the experience of salvation—The unity of the faith and the variety of its forms of expression

WITH the assurance of Damascus, 'Christ in me,' and that other assurance of equal content, 'I in Christ,' there is concentrated in the deep and to religious impulses extremely sensitive soul of the convert an inexhaustible religious energy. In all directions St. Paul now radiates 'the power of Christ'[1] that possesses him, and dispenses 'the riches of Christ,'[2] 'the blessing of Christ,'[3] and 'the fulness of Christ'[4] which have accrued to him.

To designate this abundant 'power of Christ,' which streamed through him and took effect from him, St. Paul employed a well-known technical religious term, the Greek word *pistis*, which we are accustomed to translate as 'faith.'

Though it is one of the most frequently discussed of Pauline 'conceptions,' the apostle's faith can, I think, be still more precisely formulated than it usually is. The term 'faith' as used by St. Paul is generally defined as 'faith in Christ,' with no

[1] 2 Cor. xii. 9, *ἡ δύναμις τοῦ Χριστοῦ*. Cf. 1 Cor. v. 4.

[2] Eph. iii. 8, *τὸ πλοῦτος τοῦ Χριστοῦ*. Cf. ii. 7.

[3] Rom. xv. 29, *εὐλογία Χριστοῦ*.

[4] Eph. iv. 13, *τὸ πλήρωμα τοῦ Χριστοῦ*.

special stress on the preposition, so that the phrase is equivalent to 'believing in' or, in the archaic language of the English Bible, 'believing on Christ.' We might therefore conceivably employ, as Carlyle would have done, a hyphen between 'in' and the preceding word. Again, the not infrequent genitival combination 'faith of Christ Jesus,'[1] and the prepositional phrases 'faith in Christ Jesus'[2] and 'to believe in Christ Jesus'[3] are identified with 'believing-in' or 'believing-on' Christ.

I consider that this procedure obliterates a characteristic feature of St. Paul in a most important particular. Faith with St. Paul is faith 'in Christ' with accent on the 'in,' and hyphen between 'in' and 'Christ.' That is to say, faith is something which is effected in the vital union with the spiritual Christ. That is the meaning of the passages in which St. Paul combines the preposition 'in'[4] with the words 'faith,' 'faithful,' and 'believe,' and also of the passages in which the genitival combination occurs.

It has not yet been generally recognised[5] that St. Paul's use of the genitive, 'of Jesus Christ,' is altogether very peculiar. There are a number of passages in St. Paul in which the ordinary gram-

[1] πίστις Χριστοῦ Ἰησοῦ, Gal. ii. 16, 20; iii. 22; Eph. iii. 12; Phil. iii. 9; Rom. iii. 22, 26 (R.V. marg.).

[2] πίστις ἐν Χριστῷ Ἰησοῦ, Gal. iii. 26; v. 6; Col. i. 4; ii. 5 (εἰς, cf. n. 4 below); Eph. i. 15; 1 Tim. i. 14; iii. 13; 2 Tim. i. 13; iii. 15.

[3] πιστεύειν εἰς Χριστὸν Ἰησοῦν, Gal. ii. 16; Phil. i. 29; (Eph. i. 13, ἐν); cf. also 'the faithful in Christ,' πιστοὶ ἐν Χριστῷ Ἰησοῦ, Eph. i. 1; Col. i. 2.

[4] ἐν or εἰς. The difference between the two is not great in popular Greek.

[5] A forthcoming work by Otto Schmitz will submit the whole subject to discussion.

matical scheme of 'subjective genitive' and 'objective genitive' proves insufficient. Later Greek (and Latin) possesses in addition to these a genitival use, sometimes rather remarkable, which to some extent is the result of the survival of a very ancient type. So too in St. Paul it would be possible to establish a peculiar type of genitive, which we might call the 'mystic genitive,' because it expresses the mystic fellowship. 'Of Jesus Christ' is here in the main identical with 'in Christ.'

'The faith of Christ Jesus' is the faith 'in-Christ,'[1] and many other religious root ideas are also combined with the mystic genitive.[2] Side by side with 'the faith of Christ' we find in St. Paul 'the love of Christ,'[3] 'the hope of Christ,'[4] 'the peace of Christ,'[5] 'the meekness and gentleness of Christ,'[6] 'the tender mercies of Christ,'[7] 'the patience of Christ,'[8] 'the obedience of Christ,'[9] 'the truth of Christ,'[10] 'the fear of Christ,'[11] 'the

[1] For references see p. 140 n. 1, 2, 3.

[2] [In German the mystic genitive can be best imitated by a compound substantive, says the author at this place. Accordingly in the next sentence he writes 'Christ-faith,' 'Christ-love,' 'Christ-hope,' 'Christ-gentleness,' 'Christ-mercy,' etc. Such forms are conspicuous and might cause a false impression in English. In German, which is more tolerant of compounds, they are accepted just as readily as the time-honoured genitival forms. Tr.]

[3] 2 Cor. v. 14; Eph. iii. 19; Rom. viii. 35, ἡ ἀγάπη τοῦ Χριστοῦ.

[4] 1 Thess. i. 3, ἡ ἐλπὶς τοῦ κυρίου ἡμῶν Ἰησοῦ Χριστοῦ.

[5] Col. iii. 15, ἡ εἰρήνη τοῦ Χριστοῦ.

[6] 2 Cor. x. i, ἡ πραΰτης καὶ ἐπιείκεια τοῦ Χριστοῦ.

[7] Phil. i. 8, σπλάγχνα Χριστοῦ Ἰησοῦ.

[8] 2 Thess. iii. 5, ἡ ὑπομονὴ τοῦ Χριστοῦ.

[9] 2 Cor. x. 5, ἡ ὑπακοὴ τοῦ Χριστοῦ.

[10] 2 Cor. xi. 10, ἀλήθεια Χριστοῦ.

[11] Eph. v. 21, φόβος Χριστοῦ. Cf. 2 Cor. v. 11.

circumcision of Christ,'[1] 'the sufferings of Christ,'[2] 'the afflictions of Christ,'[3] and other similar technical expressions.[4] In each case it is presumed that the particular experience or assurance of soul in the Christian takes place in the mystical and spiritual fellowship with Christ.

So too 'the faith of Christ'[5] is the faith which is alive in the fellowship with the spiritual Christ, and it is 'faith-in God' (='believing-on God'[6]), identical in content with the faith which Abraham in the sacred past had held, that is to say, unconditional trust in the living God in spite of all temptations to doubt. This 'faith of Abraham,'[7] heroic by its 'Nevertheless,'[8] was afterwards made impossible by the Law,[9] but is now again possible to us and effectual in Christ. Separated from Christ, St. Paul says once, we are in the cosmos without God;[10] in union with Christ we have boldness to approach God.[11]

1 Col. ii. 11, ἡ περιτομὴ τοῦ Χριστοῦ.

2 2 Cor. i. 5; Phil. iii. 10, τὰ παθήματα τοῦ Χριστοῦ.

3 Col. i. 24, αἱ θλίψεις τοῦ Χριστοῦ. On these last two expressions cf. Arnold Steubing, *Der paulinische Begriff 'Christusleiden'* (a Heidelberg dissertation), Darmstadt, 1905.

4 Cf., for example, the conceptions noted on p. 139 above, 'the power of Christ,' 'the riches of Christ,' 'the blessing of Christ,' 'the fulness of Christ.'

5 ['Christ-faith.' See p. 141, n. 2. Tr.]

6 This 'on' or 'in' (ἐπί) in St. Paul is nearly always connected with 'God' (Rom. iv. 5, 24; [ix. 33; x. 11]); with 'Christ' only in 1 Tim. i. 16.

7 Rom. iv. 12, 16, πίστις Ἀβραάμ.

8 [The Psalmist says, 'I was as a beast before Thee. *Nevertheless* I am continually with Thee; Thou hast holden me by my right hand . . .,' Ps. lxxiii. 23. Cf. Rom. viii. 35–39. Tr.]

9 Gal. iii. 12, 23.

10 Eph. ii. 12, ἦτε . . . χωρὶς Χριστοῦ . . . ἄθεοι ἐν τῷ κόσμῳ.

11 Eph. iii. 12, ἐν ᾧ ἔχομεν τὴν παρρησίαν καὶ προσαγωγὴν ἐν πεποιθήσει διὰ τῆς πίστεως αὐτοῦ.

St. Paul's faith, therefore, is the union with God which is brought about in the fellowship with Christ, and which is an unshakable confidence, like that of Abraham, in the grace of God.

And now we must try to recognise the apostle's 'faith of Christ' as the centre of energy from which radiate all his confessions concerning salvation in Christ. To use another metaphor, we must try to realise the rich variety of Pauline experience and testimony about salvation which is contained in the confessions in St. Paul's letters as refractions of one single ray—'the faith of Christ.'[1]

Here, in my opinion, lies the most important problem for the student of St. Paul, so far as St. Paul's inmost self is concerned. The solution of the problem lies in perceiving that the Pauline testimonies about salvation are psychically synonymous.

In the older days of Pauline study it was the general rule first of all to isolate the so-called 'concepts' of justification, redemption, reconciliation, forgiveness, etc., and then from these isolated and thereby theologised 'concepts' to reconstruct the 'system' of 'Paulinism.' In the writings of some, Paulinism appeared like a triangle; in the writings of others, like a square or a hexagon—but in any case it looked very geometrical and regularly conventionalised.

With our theory we also see straight lines, but they do not unite to form figures. They run like rays in all directions, unlimited and immeasurable, from the one point of light constituted by the experience of Christ.

[1] [See p. 142 n. 5.]

It was the result of the isolative and dogmatising method that 'Paulinism' looked so hard and cold, so calculated and scholastic, so angular and complicated, and so difficult of assimilation, and that on account of Paulinism St. Paul seemed to many people the evil genius of Christianity.

If, however, we may draw conclusions as to character from historical effects, then we may say: the message of Christ which the tentmaker of Tarsus preached to simple folk in the great Hellenistic cities in the age of the Caesars must have been simple, or at least intelligible to the simple, transporting and inspiring to the multitude. And there is one way to realise the popular simplicity of the Pauline gospel even to-day. We must take seriously the observation that the countless statements about Christ made by the letter-writer in unsystematic sequence do not represent a diversity of many objects but a diversity in the psychological reflection of the *one* object of piety to which St. Paul bears testimony in figurative expressions with constantly new variation of kindred meanings, and often with the parallelism of prophetic emphasis. It is our business to grasp the figurativeness, the ancient and popular figurativeness, of these testimonies.

Here we will only select those of St. Paul's metaphors for salvation in Christ to which most violence has been done by the exponents of 'Paulinism.' There are many other synonyms besides, but the five following are the most important: justification, reconciliation, forgiveness, redemption, and adoption.

These now classical expressions exerted an enormous influence on later dogma, and in consequence they have themselves in the course of centuries become overlaid with a patina so strongly dogmatic that at the present day many people find it difficult to recognise their original meaning. But to the plain man of antiquity in the days before dogma the original meaning was clear.

In all five of these figurative expressions man stands before God, each time in a different guise before the same God: first as an accused person, secondly as an enemy, thirdly as a debtor, fourthly and fifthly as a slave.

As an accused person[1] man stands before God's judgment seat as part of the mighty complex of religious imagery which surrounds the fundamental word 'justification,' and which has its psychological starting-point in the old Jewish and old apostolic expectation of the last judgment. In Christ the accused becomes 'unaccused';[2] he is awarded not condemnation[3] but liberty.[4] 'Acquittal'—that is the meaning of St. Paul's 'justification';[5] and the acquittal experienced 'in Christ' coincides with justification 'out of faith'[6] or 'through faith,'[7] because faith is union with Christ.[8]

St. Paul's justification 'out of' faith or 'through' faith has often been misunderstood, and is often

[1] Rom. viii. 33, *τίς ἐγκαλέσει κατὰ ἐκλεκτῶν θεοῦ;*

[2] 1 Cor. i. 8; Col. i. 22, *ἀνεγκλήτους*.

[3] Rom. viii. 1, *οὐδὲν ἄρα νῦν κατάκριμα τοῖς ἐν Χριστῷ Ἰησοῦ.*

[4] Rom. viii. 2, *ὁ γὰρ νόμος τοῦ πνεύματος τῆς ζωῆς ἐν Χριστῷ Ἰησοῦ ἠλευθέρωσέν σε ἀπὸ τοῦ νόμου τῆς ἁμαρτίας καὶ τοῦ θανάτου.*

[5] Gal. ii. 17; 2 Cor. v. 21; Rom. iii. 24; viii. 33; Phil. iii. 9.

[6] Greek *ἐκ* generally translated 'by' (except in R.V. marg.) or 'of,' Gal. ii. 16; iii. 8, 24; v. 5; Rom. iii. 26, 30; v. 1; ix. 30; x. 6.

[7] Gal. ii. 16; Rom. iii. 22, 25, 28 (variant), 30.

[8] Cf. p. 143 above.

misunderstood by uneducated Protestantism at the present day, in something like this form: justification is reckoned as the reward given by God to man for his performance of faith. St. Paul himself perhaps gave occasion to this misunderstanding by the emphatic use which he made of a text from the Septuagint[1] concerning the faith of Abraham, especially in the fourth chapter of Romans.[2] The phrasing of this quotation,

'His faith was reckoned,'[3]

lends support to the mechanical interpretation just mentioned.

But we must not isolate this passage, and on no account may we look upon 'reckon' as the characteristic word to use in connexion with justification. St. Paul employs the word 'reckon' under compulsion of the terms of his quotation. When due regard is paid to the whole of St. Paul's utterances concerning faith and righteousness, then it must be said: faith according to St. Paul is not a human performance before God, but a divine influence upon man in Christ, and justification 'out of' faith or 'through' faith is in fact justification 'in' faith,[4] justification 'in Christ,'[5] justification 'in the name

[1] LXX Gen. xv. 6 (in the form quoted by St. Paul), *ἐπίστευσεν δὲ Ἀβραὰμ τῷ θεῷ, καὶ ἐλογίσθη αὐτῷ εἰς δικαιοσύνην.*

[2] Rom. iv. 3 f., 9 f., 22 ff.; cf. also Gal. iii. 6.

[3] *ἐλογίσθη.*

[4] The formula 'in (the) faith' (*ἐν [τῇ] πίστει*) is often used in St. Paul: Gal. ii. 20; 1 Cor. xvi. 13; 2 Cor. xiii. 5; Col. ii. 7; and still more frequently in the Pastoral Epistles. It does not occur in combination with 'justify' anywhere in the letters, as far as I can see, but that is an accident. The contrasted formula 'in the law' (*ἐν νόμῳ*) is so combined in Gal. iii. 11; v. 4.

[5] Gal. ii. 17.

of the Lord Jesus Christ,'[1] justification 'in His blood.'[2] Faith is not the condition precedent to justification, it is the experience of justification.

Being justified in Christ, the believer possesses a 'righteousness of God' in Christ.[3] This frequent technical expression,[4] once replaced by the phrase 'righteousness from God,'[5] is used by St. Paul to describe the normal condition vouchsafed to us of grace by God in Christ. That it is nothing of the nature of a magical transformation is shown by a passage in Galatians[6] which speaks of 'waiting for' the desired righteousness: before all men lies the last judgment, which will at length bring definitive justification. The justified man is therefore not a completely righteous man: he has still a goal of righteousness before him. In the apostle's thoughts on justification as elsewhere we see the peculiar dynamic tension between the consciousness of present possession and the expectation of future full possession.

As an enemy[7] man stands before God in the second group of metaphors which clusters round the idea of 'reconciliation'; and in the marriage problem as treated by St. Paul, which contemplates the separation and reconciliation of a husband and wife,[8] we have a human example to help us to understand the figure. As an enemy man is alienated from God

[1] 1 Cor. vi. 11.
[2] Rom. v. 9 (cf. below, p. 174).
[3] 2 Cor. v. 21, *δικαιοσύνη θεοῦ ἐν αὐτῷ.*
[4] 2 Cor. v. 21; Rom. i. 17 (not iii. 5); iii. 21, 22, 25, 26; x. 3.
[5] Phil. iii. 9, *τὴν ἐκ θεοῦ δικαιοσύνην.*
[6] Gal. v. 5, *ἡμεῖς γὰρ πνεύματι ἐκ πίστεως ἐλπίδα δικαιοσύνης ἀπεκδεχόμεθα.*
[7] Rom. v. 10; Col. i. 21, *ἐχθροί*; cf. Rom. viii. 7, *ἔχθρα εἰς θεόν.*
[8] 1 Cor. vii. 11.

and far off from God;[1] through Christ we become reconciled again with God.[2] We must not suppose that God is conciliated: it is God[3] who changes us in Christ from enemies to persons reconciled. Therefore we have 'peace with God through our Lord Jesus Christ,'[4] or 'the peace of God in Christ,'[5] or, to sum up everything[6]:—

'Christ is our peace.'

It is perfectly clear that the 'conception,' often so highly dogmatised, of reconciliation in St. Paul coincides completely in meaning with the undogmatic idea of 'peace.'[7]

As a debtor[8] man stands before God in the third cycle of metaphors, in which the apostle is clearly following up the old Gospel[9] estimate of sin as a debt. In Christ the debtor experiences the remission of his debt;[10] for of His grace God presents us in Christ with the amount of the debt which has grown up through our trespasses.[11] 'Remission,' that is the meaning of the word 'forgiveness,' and I do

[1] Col. i. 21, ἀπηλλοτριωμένους; Eph. ii. 13, οἵ ποτε ὄντες μακράν.
[2] 2 Cor. v. 18 ff.; Rom. v. 10.
[3] 2 Cor. v. 18 ff.; Col. i. 20.
[4] Rom. v. 1, εἰρήνην ἔχομεν πρὸς τὸν θεὸν διὰ τοῦ κυρίου ἡμῶν Ἰησοῦ Χριστοῦ.
[5] Phil. iv. 7, ἡ εἰρήνη τοῦ θεοῦ . . . ἐν Χριστῷ; cf. John xvi. 33, 'that in Me ye might have peace.'
[6] Eph. ii. 14, αὐτὸς γάρ ἐστιν ἡ εἰρήνη ἡμῶν.
[7] Cf. especially Rom. v. 1 compared with v. 11.
[8] Cf. Col. ii. 14, τὸ καθ' ἡμῶν χειρόγραφον.
[9] Matt. vi. 12; Luke xi. 4.
[10] Col. i. 14, ἐν ᾧ ἔχομεν . . . τὴν ἄφεσιν τῶν ἁμαρτιῶν; Eph. i. 7, ἐν ᾧ ἔχομεν . . . τὴν ἄφεσιν τῶν παραπτωμάτων.
[11] Col. ii. 13, χαρισάμενος ἡμῖν πάντα τὰ παραπτώματα.

not believe that there is any great difference between the two Greek words which St. Paul here uses.[1] Any one who has seen one of the many acknowledgments of debt that have come down to us on papyrus from ancient times, will realise that the metaphor which St. Paul carries out so remarkably of the bond nailed to the Cross, after being first blotted out and so cancelled,[2] was especially popular in its appeal.

And now comes the important series of metaphors, obviously valued and loved above others by the apostle, which centres in the word 'redemption.' It is probably the most often misunderstood; but, viewed in connexion with the civilisation of the ancient world in which St. Paul lived, there is no mistaking its simplicity and force. Though not immediately intelligible to us, this cycle of metaphors offered no difficulty at all to the ancient Christians, because it is connected with slavery, a social institution common to the whole of antiquity. As a slave man stands here before God, and there are various powers which St. Paul regards as the 'masters' of the unfree man—sin,[3] the Law,[4] idols,[5] men,[6] death (corruption).[7] In Christ the slave obtains freedom.[8] This liberation of the slave in Christ[9] is hinted also by the word 'redemption':[10] as justification is the acquittal of the accused, so redemption is the eman-

[1] ἄφεσις, Col. i. 14; Eph. i. 7; and πάρεσις, Rom. iii. 25.

[2] Col. ii. 14.

[3] Rom. vi. 6, 17, 19, 20; Tit. iii. 3.

[4] Gal. iv. 1–7; v. i.

[5] Gal. iv. 8, 9.

[6] 1 Cor. vii. 23.

[7] Rom. viii. 20 f.

[8] Gal. ii. 4, τὴν ἐλευθερίαν ἡμῶν ἣν ἔχομεν ἐν Χριστῷ Ἰησοῦ. Cf. Gal. v. 1; John viii. 36.

[9] Rom. iii. 24; Col. i. 14; Eph. i. 7.

[10] ἀπολύτρωσις, 1 Cor. i. 30; Rom. iii. 24; viii. 23; Col. i. 14; Eph. i. 7, 14; iv. 30.

cipation of the slave by purchase. It is not improbable that St. Paul was following up a saying of Jesus,[1] to which he no doubt also alludes elsewhere.[2]

> "The Son of man came not to be ministered unto, but to minister [as a slave], and to give His life a ransom for many [slaves]."

The greatest impetus to the elaboration of metaphors of emancipation by purchase came, however, from the custom of sacral manumission, which was widely spread in the ancient world—and continued to be of effect among Hellenistic Jews and afterwards even among Christians—and which we have once more become acquainted with, thanks chiefly to inscriptions.[3] Among the various legal forms by which in the time of St. Paul the manumission of a slave could take place we find the solemn rite of purchase of the slave by a deity. The owner comes with the slave to the temple, sells him there to the god, and receives from the temple treasury the purchase money, which the slave has previously deposited there out of his savings. The slave thus becomes the property of the god, but as against all the world he is a free man.

From this point of view the words which twice occur in 1 Corinthians,[4]

> 'ye were bought with a price,'

---

[1] Mark x. 45 = Matt. xx. 28, *καὶ γὰρ ὁ υἱὸς τοῦ ἀνθρώπου οὐκ ἦλθεν διακονηθῆναι, ἀλλὰ διακονῆσαι καὶ δοῦναι τὴν ψυχὴν αὐτοῦ λύτρον ἀντὶ πολλῶν.*

[2] Phil. ii. 7, *μορφὴν δούλου λαβών*, 'taking the form of a slave.'

[3] Detailed evidence in *Light from the Ancient East*, pp. 323–334.

[4] 1 Cor. vi. 20; vii. 23, *τιμῆς ἠγοράσθητε.*

like the sentence in Galatians[1] about Christ redeeming them that were under the Law, become vividly intelligible, especially when we see that St. Paul uses formulae that recur regularly in inscriptions relating to manumissions, and when we remember that among the people to whom St. Paul wrote there were slaves who of course must have known all about that particular form of law. Having been freed through Christ (or 'in'[2] Christ, as 'in' the temple of the god), those who have hitherto been the slaves of sin, slaves of the Law, etc., are now slaves of Christ,[3] the property of Christ,[4] bondmen incorporate with Christ,[5] but otherwise free men,[6] who must not be made slaves again.[7]

The same contrast between the present possession and the future full possession which we found in the apostle's assurance of justification,[8] can be also observed in his idea of redemption: those who have already been redeemed are still 'waiting for' 'the redemption of the body';[9] 'the day of redemption' is still before them.[10]

Instead of slaves we become free men in Christ.

1 Gal. iv. 5, ἵνα τοὺς ὑπὸ νόμον ἐξαγοράσῃ. Cf. iii. 13.

2 Gal. ii. 4.

3 Gal. i. 10; Eph. vi. 6; and other passages.

4 Gal. iii. 29; v. 24; 1 Cor. i. 12 [—where Deissmann puts a stop after "Cephas," taking the next words to be Paul's rejoinder, "But I am Christ's"—TR.]; iii. 23; xv. 23; 2 Cor. x. 7.

5 1 Cor. xii. 27, etc.

6 Gal. v. 1, 13.

7 Gal. ii. 4; v. 1; 1 Cor. vii. 23.

8 Page 147 above.

9 Rom. viii. 23, ἡμεῖς καὶ αὐτοὶ ἐν ἑαυτοῖς στενάζομεν υἱοθεσίαν ἀπεκδεχόμενοι, τὴν ἀπολύτρωσιν τοῦ σώματος ἡμῶν.

10 Eph. iv. 30, εἰς ἡμέραν ἀπολυτρώσεως.

How little St. Paul binds himself dogmatically with this metaphor is shown by the fact that he occasionally employs the figure of a slave for the sake of a different contrast: instead of slaves we become in Christ 'sons of God.'[1] In drawing this contrast, St. Paul is employing the ancient legal conception of adoption. Numerous inscriptions have not only enabled us to illustrate by quotations the word[2] which St. Paul here uses, but have taught us how common adoption was in the Hellenistic world at that time, and how readily understood by the people the apostle's metaphor must have been. This is especially true of a thought which is entitled to a place in this cycle of metaphors, and which St. Paul found in the Septuagint[3] and in the sayings of Jesus,[4] that God has drawn up a 'testament'[5] in our favour, and that we therefore may expect an 'inheritance'[6]:—

> 'And if children,
> Then heirs;
> Heirs of God,
> And joint-heirs of Christ.'[7]

---

[1] *υἱοὶ θεοῦ*, Gal. iv. 5 f.; iii. 26; Rom. viii. 14.

[2] *υἱοθεσία*, 'adoption,' Gal. iv. 5; Rom. viii. 15, 23; Eph. i. 5. Quotations from ancient sources in *Neue Bibelstudien*, p. 66 f., (= *Bible Studies*, p. 239).

[3] Where it is very frequent.

[4] Cf. especially His words at the Last Supper, in the light of Luke xxii. 29.

[5] *διαθήκη*, Gal. iii. 15 ff.; iv. 24; 1 Cor. xi. 25; 2 Cor. iii. 6.

[6] *κληρονομία*, Gal. iii. 18; iv. 1 ff.; Col. iii. 24; Eph. i. 14, 18; v. 5, etc.

[7] Rom. viii. 17, *εἰ δὲ τέκνα, καὶ κληρονόμοι· κληρονόμοι μὲν θεοῦ, συγκληρονόμοι δὲ Χριστοῦ.*

How clear and comforting must these words, and others like them [1]—

> 'Thou art no longer a slave but a son;
> And if a son, then an heir through God'—

have rung in the heart of a man of antiquity who from the legal practice of the world he lived in was familiar with the testament in which the testator adopts some one as his son and makes him the heir! [2]

But this series of ideas also is not made dogmatically rigid: the adoption by God which we have experienced in Christ [3] is also still the object of our 'expectation'; [4] and of our 'inheritance' we possess through the Holy Spirit at present only 'earnest money.' [5]

That all these 'concepts' of justification, reconciliation, forgiveness, redemption, adoption, are not distinguishable from one another like the acts of a drama, but are synonymous forms of expression for one single thing, is proved by a peculiarity which occurs again and again in St. Paul's letters—a mark of the holy warmth of their enthusiasm. The apostle is fond of adding one conception to another, so as to explain the one by the other: adop-

[1] Gal. iv. 7, *ὥστε οὐκέτι εἶ δοῦλος, ἀλλὰ υἱός· εἰ δὲ υἱός, καὶ κληρονόμος διὰ θεοῦ.*

[2] On this ancient form of testament (adoption by testament, with simultaneous appointment as heir), cf. F. Schulin, *Das griechische Testament verglichen mit dem römischen*, a 'programm,' Basel, 1882, especially pp. 15 ff. and 52.

[3] Rom. viii. 15 ff., *ἐλάβετε πνεῦμα υἱοθεσίας, ἐν ᾧ κράζομεν· Ἀββᾶ ὁ πατήρ.*

[4] Rom. viii. 23, *υἱοθεσίαν ἀπεκδεχόμενοι.*

[5] Eph. i. 14, *ὅς ἐστιν ἀρραβὼν τῆς κληρονομίας.*

tion stands side by side with redemption;[1] justification[2] and forgiveness[3] are explained by redemption; or justification by forgiveness.[4] Illegitimate catachreses from the rhetorical point of view, these pilings up of mixed metaphors were no doubt, for the purposes of the popular preacher, exceedingly effective. Utterances like this sentence in 1 Corinthians[5]:—

> 'But of Him are ye in Christ Jesus,
> Who was made unto us wisdom from God,
> And righteousness and sanctification, and redemption'—

were no doubt not dogmatically vivisected by St. Paul's churches, but appreciatively shared like the exultation of a psalmist.

It is furthermore remarkable that all five of the groups of metaphors just mentioned are taken from the practice of the law. This is not the only proof of St. Paul's fondness for legal imagery, which would present itself especially easily to the city-resident.

We shall not comprehend St. Paul until we have heard all these various testimonies concerning salvation sounding together in harmony like the notes of a single full chord. Once accused before God, an enemy of God, a debtor, and slave—now in Christ acquitted and redeemed, free from debt, the friend of God, and son of God—the man who makes this confession testifies that in Christ he has ceased to be 'far off' from God and has come 'near' God.[6] To

[1] Gal. iv. 5; Rom. viii. 23.
[2] Rom. iii. 24.
[3] Col. i. 14; Eph. i. 7.
[4] Rom. iv. 6–8.
[5] 1 Cor. i. 30, *ἐξ αὐτοῦ δὲ ὑμεῖς ἐστὲ ἐν Χριστῷ Ἰησοῦ, ὃς ἐγενήθη σοφία ἡμῖν ἀπὸ θεοῦ δικαιοσύνη τε καὶ ἁγιασμὸς καὶ ἀπολύτρωσις.*
[6] Eph. ii. 13, *νυνὶ δὲ ἐν Χριστῷ Ἰησοῦ ὑμεῖς οἵ ποτε ὄντες μακρὰν ἐγενήθητε ἐγγὺς ἐν τῷ αἵματι τοῦ Χριστοῦ* (on this last formula, cf. p. 175 below).

raise scholastically pointed questions, which the controversial theology of exegesis finds indispensable, such as, 'What is the relation of justification to reconciliation in St. Paul? or of forgiveness to redemption?' is simply to break the strings of the harp and twist them into a tangle that it is hopeless to unravel. Surely it has no more value than to ask what is the relation of an accused person to an enemy or of a debtor to a slave. Such questions may furnish matter for pamphlets and make examination candidates uneasy, but they do not further our understanding of St. Paul.

It is more profitable to search in St. Paul himself for utterances in which the harmony of that chord is completed, and surely there is not a finer line to be found than the shout of triumph in the second letter to the Corinthians [1]:—

> 'If any man is in Christ, he is a new creature.'

That is the second chapter of the Pauline Genesis, on the first page of which was written the sudden blaze of light near Damascus.[2] Living in Christ, St. Paul divides his life into two great periods,[3] that of the old Paul, and that of the Paul newly created. The 'old man'[4] had lived in other spheres: 'in' the flesh,[5] 'in' sins,[6] 'in' Adam,[7] with his death-appointed destiny, 'in' the Law,[8] 'in' the world,[9]

1 2 Cor. v. 17, εἴ τις ἐν Χριστῷ, καινὴ κτίσις. Cf. Gal. vi. 15.

2 2 Cor. iv. 6; cf. p. 121 above.

3 2 Cor. v. 17.

4 Rom. vi. 6; Eph. iv. 22, ὁ παλαιὸς (ἡμῶν) ἄνθρωπος.

5 Rom. vii. 5; viii. 8, 9.

6 1 Cor. xv. 17.

7 1 Cor. xv. 22.

8 Gal. v. 4; Rom. iii. 19; ii. 12, ἐν (τῷ) νόμῳ.

9 Eph. ii. 12.

'in' sufferings.[1] The 'new man'[2] in Christ stands within the sacred precinct, into which all those gloomy things of the past cannot penetrate:—

> 'The old things are passed away;
> Behold, they are become new.'[3]

The flesh has no power over the new man, because as a follower of Christ he has 'crucified' the flesh.[4]

As a new creature Paul the Christian is also free from sin.[5] He has been loosed from sin, but is he also sinless, incapable of sinning? In theory certainly St. Paul might subscribe to the statement that the Christian does not sin.[6] But the awful experiences of practice would give him cause to doubt. Paul the shepherd of souls retained a sober judgment; freedom from sin is not conceived of as something mechanical and magical. Side by side with all his moral exhortations to Christians to battle against sin there are confessions of Paul the Christian himself, especially in his letter to the Romans,[7] witnessing that even the new-created feels at times the old deep sense of sin. But in Christ the grace of God is daily vouchsafed to him anew, and daily he experiences anew the renovating creative power of that grace.

The new Paul is also quit of that fellowship with Adam which is a fellowship of death.[8] He is no longer 'in Adam' but 'in Christ,' and in Christ

[1] 2 Cor. vi. 4.
[2] Col. iii. 10, τὸν νέον (ἄνθρωπον).
[3] 2 Cor. v. 17, τὰ ἀρχαῖα παρῆλθεν· ἰδοὺ γέγονεν καινά.
[4] Gal. v. 24, οἱ δὲ τοῦ Χριστοῦ τὴν σάρκα ἐσταύρωσαν.
[5] Rom. vi. 1–14. [6] Cf. Rom. vi. 2, 6, 11.
[7] Particularly Rom. vii.
[8] 1 Cor. xv. 22; Rom. v. 12 ff.

he has the guarantee that death has been overcome.[1]

Paul the Christian is also a new creature because in Christ he is free from the Law:—

'Christ is the end of the Law.'[2]

The 'letter' is overcome by the 'spirit.'[3] The problem of the Law was especially torturing to the former Pharisee, and it occupies a large amount of space in the letters owing to St. Paul's polemical position with regard to the Judaisers. But it was not solved by one single statement in round terms; Paul the antinomist remained a pious Bible Christian and could still upon occasion quote the words of the Law as an authority.[4] His polemic against the Law, though often harsh,[5] seeks to preserve for the Law at least a portion of its dignity.[6] Freedom from the slavery of the Law is conceived in no sense favourable to libertinism;[7] like Jesus,[8] St. Paul proclaims that the quintessence of the Law is contained in the commandment to love one's neighbour.[9]

How high the new Paul felt himself to be elevated above the 'world' and its satanic and daemonic

[1] 1 Cor. xv. 22, *ὥσπερ γὰρ ἐν τῷ Ἀδὰμ πάντες ἀποθνήσκουσιν, οὕτως καὶ ἐν τῷ Χριστῷ πάντες ζωοποιηθήσονται.*

[2] Rom. x. 4, *τέλος γὰρ νόμου Χριστός.*

[3] Rom. vii. 6; 2 Cor. iii. 6.

[4] Cf. pp. 103 f. above.

[5] The worst is probably the polemic against Moses in 2 Cor. iii. 13 f.

[6] Cf. especially Gal. iii. 21 ff.

[7] Gal. v. 13, *μόνον μὴ τὴν ἐλευθερίαν εἰς ἀφορμὴν τῇ σαρκί.*

[8] Matt. xxii. 39 and parallels.

[9] Gal. v. 14; Rom. xiii. 8.

powers, is shown by many powerful sayings which derive their force from being combined with Christ. The mightiest song of triumph is surely that in his letter to the Romans[1] :—

'Who shall separate us from the love of Christ?
Shall tribulation, or anguish, or persecution?
Or famine, or nakedness?
Or peril, or sword?
As it is written:
"For Thy sake we are killed all the day long;
We are accounted as sheep for the slaughter."
Nay, in all these things we are more than conquerors
Through Him that loved us.
For I am persuaded,
That neither death, nor life,
Nor angels, nor principalities,
Nor things present, nor things to come,
Nor powers, nor height, nor depth,
Nor any other creature,
Shall be able to separate us from the love of God,
Which is in Christ Jesus
Our Lord.'

Finally there is one characteristically Pauline conviction, little regarded by doctrinaire students who are more interested in the theories of Primitive Christianity than its psychic forces, namely, the conviction of being in Christ elevated especially above suffering. St. Paul has here given form[2] to

[1] Rom. viii. 35–39, *τίς ἡμᾶς χωρίσει ἀπὸ τῆς ἀγάπης τοῦ Χριστοῦ; θλῖψις ἢ στενοχωρία ἢ διωγμός; ἢ λιμὸς ἢ γυμνότης; ἢ κίνδυνος ἢ μάχαιρα; (καθὼς γέγραπται, ὅτι ἕνεκεν σοῦ θανατούμεθα ὅλην τὴν ἡμέραν, ἐλογίσθημεν ὡς πρόβατα σφαγῆς.) ἀλλ' ἐν τούτοις πᾶσιν ὑπερνικῶμεν διὰ τοῦ ἀγαπήσαντος ἡμᾶς. πέπεισμαι γὰρ ὅτι οὔτε θάνατος οὔτε ζωὴ οὔτε ἄγγελοι οὔτε ἀρχαὶ οὔτε ἐνεστῶτα οὔτε μέλλοντα οὔτε δυνάμεις οὔτε ὕψωμα οὔτε βάθος οὔτε τις κτίσις ἑτέρα δυνήσεται ἡμᾶς χωρίσαι ἀπὸ τῆς ἀγάπης τοῦ θεοῦ τῆς ἐν Χριστῷ Ἰησοῦ τῷ κυρίῳ ἡμῶν.*

[2] Cf. p. 142 above.

one of the deepest, most pregnant conceptions that we owe to him: since he suffers in Christ, his sufferings are to him 'sufferings of Christ'[1] or 'afflictions of Christ.'[2] The sufferer is not the old Paul but the new Paul, who is a member of the Body of Christ, and who therefore shares mystically in all that that Body experienced and now experiences: he 'suffers with Christ,'[3] is 'crucified with Christ,'[4] 'dies,'[5] is 'buried,'[6] is 'raised'[7] and 'lives'[8] with Christ. Thus suffering is not an anomaly in Paul's life, but, being the suffering of Christ, it is a normal part of his state as a Christian, and a certain fixed measure of 'afflictions of Christ' must according to God's plan be 'filled up' by Paul.[9]

In this Pauline mysticism of suffering it is easy to recognise what I have called the undogmatic element in St. Paul. Dogmatic exegesis is puzzled by such passages; it tortures itself to find a meaning in them, and yet cannot express the inwardness of the mystic contemplation of suffering in theological formulae. But under the cross of Jesus a suffering man will be able even to-day to experience for himself the depth of meaning and the comfort implied by Paul's 'sufferings of Christ.' Similarly the ancient Christians were easily able to comprehend the mystic application of the several stages of baptism[10] to death, burial, and

[1] 'Christ-sufferings,' 2 Cor. i. 5; Phil. iii. 10.

[2] 'Christ-afflictions,' Col. i. 24.

[3] Rom. viii. 17, *συμπάσχομεν*.

[4] Gal. ii. 20, *Χριστῷ συνεσταύρωμαι*.

[5] Rom. vi. 8, *ἀπεθάνομεν σὺν Χριστῷ*. Cf. Col. ii. 20; iii. 3; 2 Tim. ii. 11.

[6] Rom. vi. 4, *συνετάφημεν αὐτῷ*. Cf. Col. ii. 12.

[7] Col. ii. 12, *συνηγέρθητε*. Cf. iii. 3; Rom. vi. 4 f.

[8] Rom. vi. 8, *συνζήσομεν αὐτῷ*; cf. 2 Tim. ii. 11.

[9] Col. i. 24, *ἀνταναπληρῶ τὰ ὑστερήματα τῶν θλίψεων τοῦ Χριστοῦ*.

[10] Rom. vi. 3 ff.; Col. ii. 12.

resurrection with Christ, because, having been baptized as adults, they had an indelibly vivid recollection of the ceremony as performed on them by immersion.

Paul in Christ, Christ in Paul! Paul is full of Christ, and no matter which of his confessions we choose to contemplate, we have found that it ultimately points to the same assurance of salvation, to his normal position with regard to God attained in Christ.

This then would be the place in which, to speak in doctrinaire terms, St. Paul's 'theology' in the narrower sense, that is to say, his doctrine of God, should be treated. It is more correct to speak of St. Paul's convictions concerning God. They are mirrored in many occasional utterances, and not least in the words of prayer contained in Paul's letters.

Absolutely 'new' features there are none in the content of these convictions.

The presumptions on which they are founded are the piety inculcated by the Septuagint, such other Jewish religion as showed any sign of life, and the revelations of God given by Jesus. St. Paul's experience of God is specially closely related to that of Jesus as reflected in the oldest traditions of His sayings. The fact that there is no contrast between Jesus and St. Paul receives outward illustration from the old Jewish word *abba* for beginning a prayer to the Father, which Jesus used, and which St. Paul took with him in its Aramaic form into the Hellenistic world.[1]

[1] Gal. iv. 6; Rom. viii. 15. Cf. the similar remark about *Marana tha*, p. 118 above.

There are two certainties pervading in equal measure the Gospel words of Jesus and the letters of St. Paul: God the majestic Lord of heaven and of earth, the Holy One, whose demands upon us are infinite, and God the loving Father, who enfolds us with His mercy, helps us, and gladly gives His grace even to sinners. In one saying of St. Paul's [1] :—

'The goodness of God leadeth thee to repentance'—

the two certainties unite in the form of the one old Gospel truth: God is holy love.

Here, however, at the centre of all piety there is a difference between Jesus and Paul, a difference not in the doctrinal formulation of the idea of God, but in the independent energy of the experience of God.

Jesus, in His experience of God, is self-supported; He needs no intermediate agency; the Son knoweth the Father.[2]

Paul, in his experience of God, is not self-supported. He needs an intermediate agency. As a pious Pharisee he had stood on the bridge of the Law, hoping to reach God by dint of his own righteousness, by hard walking as it were. But, apart perhaps from rare moments of grace, he had remained far from God. The moment near Damascus brought him near to God; into his weak humanity there streamed the divine power of the living Christ, and through that Christ and in that Christ he obtained 'access.' [3] Now he could really say 'Abba.' [4]

[1] Rom. ii. 4, *τὸ χρηστὸν τοῦ θεοῦ εἰς μετάνοιάν σε ἄγει.*

[2] Matt. xi. 27.

[3] Rom. v. 2; Eph. iii. 12.

[4] Gal. iv. 6; Rom. viii. 15.

Henceforth he can do all things in that Christ.[1] His whole judgment of the Person of Christ, and more than that, the energy of his love and the enthusiasm of his hope are rooted in his union with Christ.

[1] Phil. iv. 13, *πάντα ἰσχύω ἐν τῷ ἐνδυναμοῦντί με.* Cf. 1 Tim. i. 12.

ST. PAUL THE CHRISTIAN (*Continued*)

CHAPTER VII

ST. PAUL THE CHRISTIAN (*Continued*)

Contemplation of Christ—The love of Christ—The hope of Christ

As a product of the fellowship of Christ there grew up St. Paul's fruitful contemplation of Christ, or, to speak in doctrinaire terms, his Christology. *Tantum Christus cognoscitur, quantum diligitur.*[1]

It is true that even before the episode at Damascus most of the elements were present which afterwards became constitutive of the Pauline 'Christology.' Strong stimuli came particularly from the Septuagint Bible, the Jewish tradition of a Messiah, the witness of Jesus to Himself as current in unwritten records of the Gospel, the language of the primitive apostolic cult, and also from the storehouse of sacred concepts and imagery belonging to the non-Jewish world in the East and in the West.

Nevertheless it must not be imagined that St. Paul pieced together a Christology like mosaic work out of the older titles of honour and names that had been used in worship—such as 'Son of God,' 'Spirit of God,' 'Image of God,' 'the Anointed,' 'Judge,' 'Man,' 'Root of Jesse,' 'Son

[1] 'We know Christ in the same measure as we love Him.' [The author has modified the words of St. Bernard of Clairvaux by substituting 'Christ' for 'God.' Tr.]

of David,' 'Slave,' 'One that became poor,'[1] 'Brother,' 'Crucified,' 'Lord,' 'Saviour,' etc.—and that then on the basis of this Christology the doctrines of justification, reconciliation, redemption, etc., arose and were elaborated by him. On the contrary, being full of Christ, and growing daily more incorporate with Christ, Paul knows himself to be justified, reconciled, and redeemed in Christ, and out of this conviction of salvation in Christ there grows up in his contemplative soul the understanding of the mysteries which are hidden in the Person of Christ. In his attempt to explain the mysteries this man whom Christ has taken possession of can but adopt the magnificently glowing language of ancient worship.

Nor will it be otherwise at the present day. We must first be taken possession of by Christ in some way or another, and then the Christology will come of its own accord. Every merely intellectual Christology that does not arise out of a religious union with Christ is of no value. But every religious Christology will be, even to-day, in some form or another Pauline.

Pauline Christology, as it is called, is by no means mainly intellectual,[2] it is much rather contemplative, and inspired most strongly by the mystic experience of Christ and by the worship of Christ. Hence it is, therefore, that St. Paul's confessions of Christ, regarded as a whole, do not strike us as a system patched up out of motley rags of tradition. Though they are mostly couched in the terms of older worship they generally have the look of being St. Paul's own creation.

[1] [2 Cor. viii. 9; cf. p. 170 n. 1 below. Tr

[2] 1 Cor. ii. 9 f.

At the same time we may notice that in the form of expression in which these confessions of Christ are conveyed, anything specifically Jewish is generally rejected by St. Paul. The apostle of the world gives us a picture of Christ which is world-wide, instinct with humanity throughout. The fact, so infinitely important to the Jewish Christian, that Jesus was the son of David, is to St. Paul merely something external, affecting the flesh.[1] The Jewish and apocalyptic expression, 'Son of Man,' does not occur in his letters, the brilliance of that star being eclipsed by the morning splendour of the 'Son of God.'[2] The Jewish title 'Messiah' also retires into the background: in many passages the word 'Christ' is already a proper name in St. Paul.[3] And the honorific designation of 'Lord,' which St. Paul particularly loved to apply to Christ, is also, in spite of its use by the primitive apostles before St. Paul, world-wide[4]: it even carries with it the prediction of a conflict between the cult of Christ and the cult of the Caesars that stands out in the world's history.[5] It might be urged that 'Lord' as a title of dignity was world-wide, but only in the ancient sense of that term; St. Paul's fundamental certitude, however, that Christ is 'the Spirit,' is formulated not only for all nations but for all times.[6]

[1] Rom. i. 3 f.

[2] Rom. i. 4, and many other passages.

[3] On these facts relating to the history of ideas see pp. 31 ff. of the little work mentioned at p. 93 n. 3 above.

[4] Phil. ii. 9 f.

[5] Cf. generally the section on 'Christ and the Caesars' in *Light from the Ancient East*, pp. 342–384.

[6] Cf. p. 133 above.

Only in one single point of importance has the cosmopolitan apostle's spiritual picture of Christ preserved its native Jewish characteristics. Jesus Christ as He that should come, He that should come to judgment, He that should come to fulfil the Kingdom of God, He to whom the prayer *Marana tha*[1] was addressed—this Christ St. Paul could not give up. So too the inseverable connexion of the spiritually present Christ with the historic Jesus, and particularly the identity of the Living with the Crucified, saved St. Paul's religious contemplation from dissipating itself in mythological infinitudes.

This Jewish, this historical backbone to the figure of the spiritual Christ was of great importance to the popular effect of St. Paul's gospel. The religion of the people is not nourished by stuffed specimens contained in dogmatic compendiums, it draws its inspiration from the many-hued world of wonders revealed to observation.

The outlines of the Pauline Christ are perhaps most clearly visible in the second chapter of Philippians.[2] Paul the prisoner seeks to impress upon the souls of his simple converts the image of his adored object, drawn with vigorous lines but without any display of mythological imaginings. He who

[1] 1 Cor. xvi. 22; cf. p. 118 above.

[2] Phil. ii. 6–11, ὃς ἐν μορφῇ θεοῦ ὑπάρχων οὐχ ἁρπαγμὸν ἡγήσατο τὸ εἶναι ἴσα θεῷ, ἀλλὰ ἑαυτὸν ἐκένωσεν μορφὴν δούλου λαβών, ἐν ὁμοιώματι ἀνθρώπων γενόμενος καὶ σχήματι εὑρεθεὶς ὡς ἄνθρωπος. ἐταπείνωσεν ἑαυτὸν γενόμενος ὑπήκοος μέχρι θανάτου, θανάτου δὲ σταυροῦ. διὸ καὶ ὁ θεὸς αὐτὸν ὑπερύψωσεν καὶ ἐχαρίσατο αὐτῷ τὸ ὄνομα τὸ ὑπὲρ πᾶν ὄνομα, ἵνα ἐν τῷ ὀνόματι Ἰησοῦ πᾶν γόνυ κάμψῃ ἐπουρανίων καὶ ἐπιγείων καὶ καταχθονίων καὶ πᾶσα γλῶσσα ἐξομολογήσεται ὅτι κύριος Ἰησοῦς Χριστὸς εἰς δόξαν θεοῦ πατρός.

had lived eternally with the Father in divine spiritual glory did not strive to become equal to God; instead of ascending a stage higher He descended a stage lower, came down to earth, became man and slave, humbled Himself, was obedient to the Father unto death, even unto the death of the cross, and therefore was highly exalted again by God to heavenly glory, where He lives as Lord of all things created and rules to the honour of God:—

' . . . who, being in the form of God,
Made no grasping claim to be on an equality with God,
But emptied Himself,
Taking the form of a slave,
Being made in the likeness of men, and being found in fashion as a man;
He humbled Himself, becoming obedient even unto death,
Yea, the death of the cross.

Wherefore also God highly exalted Him,
And gave unto Him the name which is above every name:
That in the name of Jesus every knee should bow,
Of things in heaven and things on earth and things under the earth,
And that every tongue should confess
That Jesus Christ is Lord,
To the glory of God the Father.'

These lines are not written in the hard tone of a theological thesis, they are not calculated for discussion by modern western Kenoticists, nor for fanatics lusting for formulae to promote disunion. The words we have just heard have a soul of their own, and that a very different one. They are a confession of the primitive apostolic cult, made by Paul the prisoner in order to rally his fellow-worshippers of Jesus Christ round the object of their cult, round a form at once divine, human, and again divine. The confession can be understood only by the pious simplicity of silent devotion. Let us leave all our commentaries at home and ask an Anatolian Christian to read us the original text of this confession in the soft tones and psalm-like rhythm with which the Christian East is accustomed to hear portions of the Greek Bible read in the twilight gloom of the churches—then a part of the undertones of the old psalm becomes lifelike again, we are freed from our pitiful dependence on history, and we come into at least distant contact with the poor saints of Macedonia, who were the first possessors of the treasure.

In the second letter to Corinth[1] the confession is simpler, but marked by the same essential lines :—

> 'Though He was rich, yet for your sakes He became poor,
> That ye through His poverty might become rich."

The eternity of Christ in the past—in doctrinaire terminology the 'pre-existence' of Christ—is therefore absolutely beyond question to the apostle. This certainty, however, is only the result of a simple contemplative inference backwards from the fact of the spiritual glory of the present Christ: the Spirit (*pneuma*) must be and must always have been eternal. The inference is rendered easier by old Bible sayings about the Spirit,[2] and by ancestral beliefs of the Jews concerning the eternity of the most important messengers of revelation. It is quite in the Pauline manner of speaking when afterwards

[1] 2 Cor. viii. 9, . . . *ἐπτώχευσεν πλούσιος ὢν, ἵνα ὑμεῖς τῷ ἐκείνου πτωχείᾳ πλουτήσητε.*

[2] *E.g.* LXX Gen. i. 2, Job xxxiii. 4.

the second Epistle of Clement[1] tells us that Christ the Lord, who saved us, was first Spirit and then became flesh; and the celebrated lines in St. John's prologue[2] concerning the eternity and incarnation of the Word are also, though somewhat differently formulated, as regards their contents altogether on the same level with St. Paul.

All further testimonies to the pre-existent Christ spring from this certainty, especially the statements that He took part in the creation of the world,[3] and that He was present with the fathers in the wilderness in the form of the spiritual Rock.[4]

The earthly life of Jesus, therefore, was appreciated by St. Paul, at least in the letters that have come down to us, more for its character as a whole than for its details. But even in his letters a considerable number of details are referred to, *e.g.*, the descent of Jesus from David,[5] and the fact that, being a Jew, He was born under the Law.[6] Paul was himself acquainted with James the brother of Jesus,[7] and the apostle's celebrated prayer thrice repeated to Christ for removal of the 'thorn in the flesh'[8] presupposes a knowledge of the abundant Gospel tradition concerning the powers of healing possessed by Jesus. St. Paul, moreover, mentions the night of the betrayal[9] and the Last Supper,[10] and quotes precisely the words spoken by Jesus on that

[1] 2 Clem. ix, Χριστὸς ὁ κύριος ὁ σώσας ἡμᾶς ὢν μὲν τὸ πρῶτον πνεῦμα ἐγένετο σάρξ.

[2] John i. 1, 14. On the incarnation cf. Rom. viii. 3.

[3] 1 Cor. viii. 6; Col. i. 15 ff.

[4] 1 Cor. x. 4.

[5] Rom. i. 3; 2 Tim. ii. 8.

[6] Gal. iv. 4.

[7] Gal. i. 19; ii. 9.

[8] 2 Cor. xii. 8 f.

[9] 1 Cor. xi. 23.

[10] 1 Cor. xi. 23 ff.

occasion.[1] Other sayings of Jesus are also quoted as an unimpeachable authority.[2] The good confession witnessed 'before Pontius Pilate,'[3] the sufferings of Jesus,[4] His death on the cross,[5] and burial,[6] are of course familiar. One thing is particularly noticeable: St. Paul not only knows that the death of Jesus was brought about by a conflict with the authorities,[7] but he also, no doubt as a consequence of reports of what occurred at Gethsemane, regards it as a proof of the obedience of Jesus to the Father.[8] That St. Paul is influenced generally by the current tradition of our Lord's words, even where he does not expressly cite them, is shown by the moral exhortations in his letters[9] and other silent adaptations of sayings by Jesus.[10] In his oral mission work[11] the

[1] 1 Cor. xi. 24 f.

[2] 1 Thess. iv. 15; 1 Cor. vii. 10; ix. 14; Acts xx. 35; 1 Tim v. 18.

[3] 1 Tim. vi. 13.

[4] Cf. the passages already quoted at pp. 142 and 159 above concerning the 'sufferings of Christ,' which refer to sufferings endured by St. Paul, but are only intelligible if Christ had Himself suffered.

[5] Numerous passages.

[6] 1 Cor. xv. 4; Rom. vi. 4.

[7] 1 Cor. ii. 8.

[8] Phil. ii. 8, *γενόμενος ὑπήκοος μέχρι θανάτου, θανάτου δὲ σταυροῦ* (cf. pp. 168 f. above).

[9] Gal. v. 14; 1 Cor. vi. 7; Rom. xii. 14; xiii. 8 f.; xvi. 19.

[10] 1 Thess. v. 2 f.; 1 Cor. xiii. 2; 2 Cor. i. 17 ff.; Gal. iv. 6; Rom. viii. 15.

[11] The fact is generally overlooked, often under the indirect influence of the theory of mechanical inspiration, that the letters of St. Paul, considered as historical sources, are merely fragments, so that their *testimonium e silentio* is only to be used with caution. We ought to be very sparing with the phrase 'unknown to St. Paul.' The proof from silence appears most open to objection in the books of noisy writers who have nothing to say themselves. Neither the professed theologians (even of the critical school) nor the amateurs who lose their bearings and found new religions

apostle no doubt made still more ample use of the Lord's words than was necessary in writing to Christians; he is able to assume on the part of his churches a certain acquaintance with the sayings of Jesus.[1] And even the total impression that St. Paul had of the life of Jesus as one of humiliation, poverty, and slavery, is itself dominated by the Gospel tradition.[2] How greatly this 'poor' man Jesus was able to move the souls of the insignificant many, is shown by the success of St. Paul's missionary labours.

At the commanding centre, however, of St. Paul's contemplation of Christ there stands the Living One who is also the Crucified, or the Crucified who is also alive. The death on the cross and the resurrection of Christ cannot in St. Paul be isolated as two distinct facts; as contemplated by him they are inseparably connected. This is shown even linguistically; the Greek perfect participle for 'crucified,' which might be rendered

'He who is the Crucified,'[3]

goes a great way farther than the aorist, which would be equivalent to

'He who was Crucified,'[4]

---

without having understood the old have yet really freed themselves inwardly as well as outwardly from the theory of mechanical inspiration. It is still an obstacle to right thinking in methodology.

[1] 1 Thess. v. 1 f.

[2] Matt. viii. 20; (Luke ix. 58); Mark x. 45; (Matt. xx. 28); Luke xxii. 27.

[3] ἐσταυρωμένος, Gal. iii. 1; 1 Cor. i. 23; ii. 2. The language of the cult is found already in Mark xvi. 6 (Matt. xxviii. 5).

[4] σταυρωθείς.

and which St. Paul has never applied to Christ in his letters.[1] The perfect tense no doubt indicates that the cross is not a bare fact in the historic past, but something whose influence is continued into the present; 'the Crucified' is a reality which can be experienced every day, and the Johannine picture[2] of the Living One who bears the wounds of the Crucified is as much Pauline as the double meaning of the Johannine word 'lift up,'[3] which indicates at one and the same time the death on the lofty cross and the 'exaltation' to spiritual glory in the sense of the passage in Philippians.[4]

Another observation akin to this may be added. St. Paul's use of the phrase 'the blood of Christ' as a term characteristic of the cult corresponds to his conviction of the identity of the Living One with the Crucified.[5] The term 'blood of Christ," in many passages at least, does not refer to the physical blood once shed at the historic martyrdom; it is a vivid way of realising the Living One who is also the Crucified, and with whom we live in mystic spiritual 'fellowship of blood.'[6] We need only recall the apostle's conviction that he stands in a fellowship of suffering, a fellowship of the cross, and a fellowship

[1] Once only he employs the aorist indicative, ἐσταυρώθη (2 Cor. xiii. 4), but here he is not speaking of the present beneficent efficacy of the crucifixion: Christ, he says, was crucified (at that time in the past) through weakness. The rude materialism of after generations is shown in the watchword of the Theopaschite controversy, 'God who was crucified' (θεὸς ὁ σταυρωθείς).

[2] John xx. 27.

[3] John xii. 32, 33; iii. 14; viii. 28.

[4] Phil. ii. 9.

[5] On what follows I refer to Otto Schmitz, *Die Opferanschauung des späteren Judentums und die Opferaussagen des Neuen Testamentes*, Tübingen, 1910, pp. 214 ff.

[6] 1 Cor. x. 16, κοινωνία τοῦ αἵματος τοῦ Χριστοῦ.

of life with the spiritual Christ.[1] In many passages in particular the formula 'in the blood of Christ' borders upon the formula 'in Christ' and might be translated appropriately to the sense:—

'in the fellowship of blood with Christ.'[2]

Were it possible in St. Paul's case to consider the death on the cross and the resurrection as two separable events, then we should certainly have to say that the central fact to the apostle is the resurrection of Christ, or, to express the matter more psychologically, the certainty revealed to him at Damascus that Christ was alive. Then and not till then the cross became transfigured to him. Without the living Christ the cross would be a stumbling-block; the living Christ makes the cross stand out in brightest morning splendour of transfiguration glory.

It is possible to collect quite a number of passages from St. Paul in which the raising of Jesus from the dead is described as of central significance among God's acts.[3] After our strong insistence on the mystical character of St. Paul's religion this stands in no need of explanation, for the condition indispensable to all mysticism devoted to Christ is the certainty that Christ is alive.

The following are St. Paul's convictions concerning the resurrection of Jesus, and we see how old Biblical and Pharisaic beliefs have amalgamated with old apostolic traditions[4] under the influence of his

[1] Cf. pp. 158 ff. above.

[2] Rom. iii. 25 (cf. Eph. i. 9, προέθετο ἐν αὐτῷ); Rom. v. 9 (cf. v. 10, ἐν τῇ ζωῇ αὐτοῦ); Eph. ii. 13.

[3] 1 Cor. xv. 14, 17; 2 Cor. xiii. 4; Rom. i. 4; iv. 25; v. 10; vi. 10; viii. 34.

[4] 1 Cor. xv. 3.

own personal experience on the road to Damascus. The resurrection is the miraculous work of God and took place on 'the third day according to the Scriptures.'[1] It is identical with the 'exaltation' and the recommencement of the spiritual life of Jesus in glory with the Father.[2] It is not fleshly,[3] but it gives to the now living Christ, probably by the process spoken of as 'changing'[4] or 'transformation'[5] a spiritual heavenly body.[6] It is victory over death,[7] and it does away with the puzzle of the cross.[8]

Thus we have reached the point of vantage from which we may understand the apostle's great utterances concerning the cross. The noble fervour with which he hymns the solemn praises of the Crucified, with ever new variation and modulation, stirring most profoundly the souls of the people by the popular force of his words, is psychologically intelligible as the reaction from his former blasphemies[9] against the Crucified. There is a reminiscence of his old polemic as a Pharisee against the cross in the statement in 1 Corinthians, that the Crucified was to the Jews a stumbling-block.[10] Since Christ

[1] 1 Cor. xv. 4, ἐγήγερται τῇ ἡμέρᾳ τῇ τρίτῃ κατὰ τὰς γραφάς. No doubt LXX Hos. vi. 2 was in the writer's mind: ἐν τῇ ἡμέρᾳ τῇ τρίτῃ ἐξαναστησόμεθα καὶ ζησόμεθα ἐνώπιον αὐτοῦ, 'on the third day we shall arise and live before Him.'

[2] Phil. ii. 9 suggests this.

[3] 1 Cor. xv. 50.

[4] 1 Cor. xv. 51, 52, ἀλλαγησόμεθα.

[5] Phil. iii. 21, ὃς μετασχηματίσει τὸ σῶμα τῆς ταπεινώσεως ἡμῶν.

[6] 1 Cor. xv. 35–51; Phil. iii. 21.

[7] 1 Cor. xv. 54 ff.

[8] 1 Cor. xv. 14, 17; 2 Cor. xiii. 4.

[9] 1 Tim. i. 13.

[10] 1 Cor. i. 23, Χριστὸν ἐσταυρωμένον, Ἰουδαίοις μὲν σκάνδαλον. Cf. Gal. v. 11.

has now become alive to him, he can annul his old imputations by confessing that the Crucified is 'the miracle of God, and the wisdom of God.'[1]

St. Paul did not attempt, and could not have attempted, to relegate this miracle of God to one poor doctrinal formula. We make it impossible for ourselves ever to understand his position at the foot of the cross if we begin by endeavouring to reconstruct 'the' doctrine of Paul concerning the death of Christ, in such a form, for instance, as to assert that 'the' Pauline doctrine of the death of Christ is the idea of sacrifice.

The idea of sacrifice in St. Paul has not even remotely the importance which is usually attached to it on the basis of a materialistic explanation of the passages where blood is mentioned and certain other statements.[2] The metaphor of sacrifice is clearly present in his letter to the Ephesians,[3] and possibly also in 1 Corinthians,[4] if the passover lamb is here regarded by St. Paul as a sacrificial animal. But even if we could add to the number of clear references to sacrifice, we should still have to say that the thought of sacrifice is but one of the many and various lines of light radiating from the Pauline contemplation of the cross, nor can those rays be brought together into a single geometrical figure.

We find in the first place simple historical allusions to the death of Jesus: it is an act committed in

[1] 1 Cor. i. 24, Χριστὸν θεοῦ δύναμιν καὶ θεοῦ σοφίαν.

[2] Especially those relating to justification, reconciliation, redemption, etc., which refer to the spiritually living Christ, and most particularly the passage in Rom. iii. 24 ff. For the rest cf. the book by Otto Schmitz mentioned at p. 174 n. 5 above.

[3] Eph. v. 2, παρέδωκεν ἑαυτὸν ὑπὲρ ἡμῶν προσφορὰν καὶ θυσίαν τῷ θεῷ εἰς ὀσμὴν εὐωδίας.

[4] 1 Cor. v. 7, καὶ γὰρ τὸ πάσχα ἡμῶν ἐτύθη Χριστός.

blindness by the rulers of this world,[1] a shameful death,[2] a defeat 'through weakness.'[3]

But it is also a work of God; it is according to Scripture,[4] and cannot have happened in vain;[5] it is a proof of divine love,[6] and came at the right time.[7] On the part of Christ it is a confirmation of His obedience towards God,[8] and of His love towards us.[9] It was a blow to sin[10] and a boon to sinners,[11] even to individuals.[12] And the cycles of Pauline metaphor which illustrate salvation 'in' Christ[13] extend also to the contemplation of the cross. By His death on the accursed tree Christ has redeemed us from the curse of the Law.[14] He has publicly nailed to the cross the bond of debt which He blotted out.[15] The enmity between Jews and Gentiles and between them both and God is done away by the cross;[16] reconciliation and peace are established.[17]

From the use he makes of these cycles of metaphor we clearly see, moreover, that in his contemplation of the cross as in other things St. Paul is undogmatic and unfettered. The cross presents itself to the soul of the redeemed not as a thing of the past, wooden, hard, and bare, but as a power in the present, revealed to him in the Living One.

This becomes particularly clear in the expressions, already mentioned more than once, in which St. Paul

1 1 Cor. ii. 8.
2 Phil. ii. 8.
3 2 Cor. xiii. 4.
4 1 Cor. xv. 3.
5 Gal. ii. 21.
6 Rom. v. 8 ff.
7 Rom. v. 6.
8 Phil. ii. 8; Rom. v. 19.
9 Gal. ii. 20; Eph. v. 2.
10 Rom. vi. 10.
11 Rom. v. 6; 1 Cor. xv. 3; 2 Cor. v. 14, etc.
12 Gal. ii. 20; 1 Cor. viii. 11; Rom. xiv. 15.
13 Cf. pp. 144 ff. above.
14 Gal. iii. 13.
15 Col. ii. 14.
16 Eph. ii. 16.
17 Rom. v. 10; Col. i. 20 ff.

treats the sufferings, crucifixion, death, burial, and resurrection of Christ as processes of salvation which he, Paul, and the other Christians share in ethically and mystically,[1] not only in baptism, but in continuous fellowship of suffering, of the cross, of blood, and of life with the transfigured Master. Of all the religious appreciations of the cross in St. Paul these are probably the deepest and most original: through the certainty of fellowship as a member of Christ the cross has become, instead of an historical conception, altogether a spiritual, mystically realised, and living reality. My late father[2] understood St. Paul when he got Schmitz, the glass-painter of Cologne, to put a window in the Evangelical Church at Erbach, in the wine-growing country of the upper Rheingau, representing the crucified Saviour in conjunction with St. John's allegory of the Vine.[3] The cross has struck root in the earth, the dead rood-tree has become the living Vine, and beneath the extended arms of the Saviour the mystic branches stretch down their bright green leaves and heavy clusters of grapes towards the communicants:

> 'I am the Vine,
> Ye are the branches.'

St. Paul's religious contemplation is not the only thing to be explained by the fellowship with Christ. The store of ethical convictions which he brought with him from Judaism and the Hellenistic world, and which was very greatly increased by Gospel traditions, acquires its real brilliance through the

[1] Cf. pp. 158 ff. and 174 f. above.

[2] [Adolf Deissmann, 1832–1900, pastor of Erbach and local historian. Tr.]

[3] John xv. 1 ff.

experience of Christ. Even the ethical element in St. Paul is made fast to Christ; 'the love of Christ'[1] means the power for good which the individual possesses, and the power of goodness which permeates the whole organisation of Christendom.

This latter, the element of social ethics in St. Paul, is unmistakably religious in tone. St. Paul is most fond of regarding the community of believers under three aspects—as a family, as a body, and as a temple. Each of these metaphors is given a religious setting.

Christians are a family because God is their Father,[2] and Christ as the 'firstborn' Son of God is their Brother,[3] whose rights to the inheritance they share.[4] Differences of nation, rank, and sex are of no more account 'in Christ':[5]

'Therein is neither Jew nor Greek,
Therein is neither slave nor freeman,
Therein is no male and female:
For ye are all one man in Christ Jesus.'

Of course the religious gulf between Jews and non-Jews is bridged over[6]:—

'Wherein there is no Greek and Jew,
Circumcision and uncircumcision,
Barbarian, Scythian, slave, freeman,
But Christ is all and in all.'

---

[1] 2 Cor. v. 14; Eph. iii. 19; (Rom. viii. 35).

[2] Numerous passages. [3] Rom. viii. 29.

[4] Rom. viii. 17.

[5] Gal. iii. 28, οὐκ ἔνι Ἰουδαῖος οὐδὲ Ἕλλην, οὐκ ἔνι δοῦλος οὐδὲ ἐλεύθερος, οὐκ ἔνι ἄρσεν καὶ θῆλυ· ἅπαντες γὰρ ὑμεῖς εἷς ἐστὲ ἐν Χριστῷ Ἰησοῦ.

[6] Col. iii. 11, ὅπου οὐκ ἔνι Ἕλλην καὶ Ἰουδαῖος, περιτομὴ καὶ ἀκροβυστία, βάρβαρος, Σκύθης, δοῦλος, ἐλεύθερος, ἀλλὰ πάντα καὶ ἐν πᾶσιν Χριστός.

St. Paul took the name of 'brother' very seriously:

> 'The brother for whose sake Christ died,'[1]
> 'Him for whom Christ died.'[2]

With such irresistible words as these he stamps even the most insignificant comrade with a value for eternity, and impresses upon the enlightened indifference of Corinth and Rome the duty of tender brotherly consideration, making all Christians together collectively responsible for the mutual care of souls[3]:—

> 'Brethren, even if a man be overtaken in any trespass, ye which are spiritual, restore such a one in a spirit of meekness; looking to thyself, lest thou also be tempted. Bear ye one another's burdens, and so fulfil the law of Christ.'

But of course the most striking memorial of St. Paul's sense of brotherhood is the 'way'[4] which he showed unto the Corinthians, the Song of Songs about brotherly love[5]:—

> 'If I speak with the tongues of men and of angels,
> But have not love,
> I am become sounding brass
> Or a clanging cymbal.

---

[1] 1 Cor. viii. 11, ὁ . . . ἀδελφὸς . . . δι' ὃν Χριστὸς ἀπέθανεν.

[2] Rom. xiv. 15, ἐκεῖνον . . . ὑπὲρ οὗ Χριστὸς ἀπέθανεν.

[3] Gal. vi. 1, 2, ἀδελφοί, ἐὰν καὶ προλημφθῇ ἄνθρωπος ἔν τινι παραπτώματι, ὑμεῖς οἱ πνευματικοὶ καταρτίζετε τὸν τοιοῦτον ἐν πνεύματι πραΰτητος, σκοπῶν σεαυτὸν μὴ καὶ σὺ πειρασθῇς. ἀλλήλων τὰ βάρη βαστάζετε, καὶ οὕτως ἀναπληρώσετε τὸν νόμον τοῦ Χριστοῦ.

[4] 1 Cor. xii. 31.

[5] 1 Cor. xiii, ἐὰν ταῖς γλώσσαις τῶν ἀνθρώπων λαλῶ καὶ τῶν ἀγγέλων, ἀγάπην δὲ μὴ ἔχω, γέγονα χαλκὸς ἠχῶν ἢ κύμβαλον

And if I have the gift of prophecy,
And know all mysteries and all knowledge
And if I have all faith,
So as to remove mountains,
But have not love,
I am nothing.

And if I share out all my goods, morsel by morsel,
And if I give my body to be burned,
But have not love,
It profiteth me nothing.

Love suffereth long,
Kind is love,
Not envious is love.
It boasteth not,
Is not puffed up,
Is not unseemly.

It seeketh not its own,
Is not provoked,
Taketh no account of evil.

ἀλαλάζον. καὶ ἐὰν ἔχω προφητείαν καὶ εἰδῶ τὰ μυστήρια πάντα καὶ πᾶσαν τὴν γνῶσιν, καὶ ἐὰν ἔχω πᾶσαν τὴν πίστιν ὥστε ὄρη μεθιστάναι, ἀγάπην δὲ μὴ ἔχω, οὐθέν εἰμι. καὶ ἐὰν ψωμίσω πάντα τὰ ὑπάρχοντά μου, καὶ ἐὰν παραδῶ τὸ σῶμά μου ἵνα καυθήσομαι, ἀγάπην δὲ μὴ ἔχω, οὐθὲν ὠφελοῦμαι. ἡ ἀγάπη μακροθυμεῖ, χρηστεύεται ἡ ἀγάπη, οὐ ζηλοῖ ἡ ἀγάπη, οὐ περπερεύεται, οὐ φυσιοῦται, οὐκ ἀσχημονεῖ, οὐ ζητεῖ τὰ ἑαυτῆς, οὐ παροξύνεται, οὐ λογίζεται τὸ κακόν, οὐ χαίρει ἐπὶ τῇ ἀδικίᾳ, συγχαίρει δὲ τῇ ἀληθείᾳ. πάντα στέγει, πάντα πιστεύει, πάντα ἐλπίζει, πάντα ὑπομένει. ἡ ἀγάπη οὐδέποτε πίπτει. εἴτε δὲ προφητεῖαι, καταργηθήσονται· εἴτε γλῶσσαι, παύσονται· εἴτε γνῶσις, καταργηθήσεται. ἐκ μέρους γὰρ γινώσκομεν καὶ ἐκ μέρους προφητεύομεν. ὅταν δὲ ἔλθῃ τὸ τέλειον, τὸ ἐκ μέρους καταργηθήσεται. ὅτε ἤμην νήπιος, ἐλάλουν ὡς νήπιος, ἐφρόνουν ὡς νήπιος, ἐλογιζόμην ὡς νήπιος· ὅτε γέγονα ἀνήρ, κατήργηκα τὰ τοῦ νηπίου. βλέπομεν γὰρ ἄρτι δι᾽ ἐσόπτρου ἐν αἰνίγματι, τότε δὲ πρόσωπον πρὸς πρόσωπον· ἄρτι γινώσκω ἐκ μέρους, τότε δὲ ἐπιγνώσομαι καθὼς καὶ ἐπεγνώσθην. νυνὶ δὲ μένει πίστις, ἐλπίς, ἀγάπη, τὰ τρία ταῦτα, μείζων δὲ τούτων ἡ ἀγάπη.

It rejoiceth not in unrighteousness,
But rejoiceth with the truth.
It covereth all things,
Believeth all things,
Hopeth all things,
Endureth all things.

Love never faileth.
But whether there be prophecies, they shall be done away;
Whether there be tongues, they shall cease;
Whether there be knowledge, it shall be done away.
For we know in part,
And we prophesy in part:
But when that which is perfect is come,
That which is in part shall be done away.

When I was a child,
I spake as a child,
I felt as a child,
I thought as a child:
Now that I am become a man
I have put away childish things.

For now we see in a mirror,
In a riddle;
But then face to face:
Now I know in part;
But then shall I fully know
Even as also I have been fully known.

But now abideth
Faith, hope, love,
These three;
But the greatest of these is love.'

Christians are a 'body,' and the Head is Christ or Christ is the Body, and Christians are the members.[1] St. Paul has here Christianised a well-known metaphor that the ancients were very fond of. His corporative idea, profound in its simplicity, was passed on by him to assist the progress of the future church.

The figure is no less popular when both the individual Christian[2] and the church[3] are spoken of as a 'temple' which is still building, and which, though already inhabited by God, requires to be more and more 'edified.' St. Paul had seen such unfinished temples on his journeys, in Jerusalem and in Asia Minor. The temple of Herod was not quite finished until the sixties of the first century, a short time before it was destroyed. In Asia Minor on the site of excavations among the ruins of ancient temples we saw again and again unfinished materials of ancient date which had never received the last stroke of the mason's mallet; and one delightful spring morning,[4] as we were rowing out to the Turkish steamer in the little bay of Panormus (Kovella), near Miletus and Didyma, we saw in the shallow water near the coast gigantic sections of marble columns which have now been waiting two thousand years for the teams to drag them, after their journey here by sea, up the hill to their destination in the Didymaeon. Like the medieval cathedrals, these Anatolian temples required 'edification' by the work of generations: hence the explanation of St. Paul's favourite idea of 'edification,' which has

[1] Col. i. 18, 24; ii. 19; Eph. iv. 15 f.; v. 23; 1 Cor. xii. 12; Rom. xii. 4 ff.

[2] 1 Cor. vi. 19.

[3] 1 Cor. iii. 16 ff.; 2 Cor. vi. 16; Eph. ii. 20 ff.

[4] 18 April, 1906.

acquired special importance in 1 and 2 Corinthians. We see the work going forward once more on the site where the new Christian community is being built up[1]:—

> 'According to the grace of God which was given unto me, as a wise master builder I laid a foundation; and another buildeth thereon. But let each man take heed how he buildeth thereon. For other foundation can no man lay than that which is laid, which is Jesus Christ. But if any man buildeth on the foundation gold, silver, costly stones, wood, hay, reed; each man's work shall be made manifest: for the day[2] shall declare it, because it is revealed in fire; and the fire itself shall prove each man's work of what sort it is.'

There are incapable persons who, instead of a temple that defies the fire, built of fine stone, and decorated with gold and silver, can only manage to erect light wooden sheds or even miserable huts of straw or reed, such as Herodotus mentions among the inhabitants of Sardis,[3] such as are still found to-day among the Yuruks in the plain of Ephesus,[4] and such as the one my companions and I visited in the evening twilight on the bank of the Maeander near the ruins of Magnesia.[5] Paul, the

[1] 1 Cor. iii. 10–13, *κατὰ τὴν χάριν τοῦ θεοῦ τὴν δοθεῖσάν μοι ὡς σοφὸς ἀρχιτέκτων θεμέλιον ἔθηκα, ἄλλος δὲ ἐποικοδομεῖ. ἕκαστος δὲ βλεπέτω πῶς ἐποικοδομεῖ· θεμέλιον γὰρ ἄλλον οὐδεὶς δύναται θεῖναι παρὰ τὸν κείμενον, ὅς ἐστιν Ἰησοῦς Χριστός. εἰ δέ τις ἐποικοδομεῖ ἐπὶ τὸν θεμέλιον χρυσίον, ἀργύριον, λίθους τιμίους, ξύλα, χόρτον, καλάμην, ἑκάστου τὸ ἔργον φανερὸν γενήσεται· ἡ γὰρ ἡμέρα δηλώσει, ὅτι ἐν πυρὶ ἀποκαλύπτεται, καὶ ἑκάστου τὸ ἔργον ὁποῖόν ἐστιν τὸ πῦρ δοκιμάσει.*

[2] The Day of Judgment.

[3] Hdt. v. 101.

[4] *Forschungen in Ephesos* veröffentlicht vom Österreichischen Archäologischen Institute, Wien, 1906, vol. i. pp. 12 f.

[5] 15 April, 1906.

city-resident, who no doubt on his journeys had often seen wretched habitations of this kind reduced to ashes in a moment, did not want the church of Christ to resemble them. The solid foundation, the like of which had never been seen, deserved to be crowned with a massive, noble edifice.

Nevertheless, St. Paul was far from formulating a fixed 'conception of the church' that would satisfy a lawyer. The apostle cannot be called the father of the constitutional church. His churches were 'assemblies'[1] summoned by God—God's levy. All of them together are spoken of as 'the assembly,'[2] and the single assemblies sometimes possessed also 'house-assemblies,'[3] that is, smaller fellowships meeting for edification at certain houses. In all these brotherhoods, smaller or greater, breathes the Spirit, perceptible in the wondrous effects produced, and bestowing on every brother the special grace (*charisma*) that the assembly needs. The first letter to the Corinthians is classical evidence of this 'charismatic' age before the days of the church.[4]

The modest beginnings of an external organisation were fairly obviously suggested by the needs themselves, but could also be adopted from the various models of associations that existed in antiquity, especially from the religious unions of the pagan world[5] and the synagogues among the Jews of the

[1] ἐκκλησίαι.

[2] ἡ ἐκκλησία, 1 Cor. x. 32; xii. 28; Col. i. 18, 24, etc.

[3] ἡ κατ' οἶκον ἐκκλησία, 1 Cor. xvi. 19; Col. iv. 15; Philem. 2; Rom. xvi. 5.

[4] Cf. especially 1 Cor. xii. 27 ff.; also Rom. xii. 4 ff.

[5] We are indebted to the works of Georg Heinrici for this valuable analogy.

Dispersion. These two analogies with their motley variety of offices and names of offices (very clearly illustrated by inscriptions) are a sufficient hint that we had better not look to find forms of 'constitution' and names of offices quite uniform in all St. Paul's churches. What held those scattered churches of St. Paul together all over the Mediterranean world was in the last resort not their 'constitution' but the personality behind them all, which 'burned'[1] with sympathy at their every trouble, the personality of the apostle. It was his prayer and self-sacrificing manual labour, his messages, letters and visits, and his sharing in the common work of love that kept the saints together.

His letters are a witness how wide and how manly his ethical ideal was; they are full of detached moral exhortations. Problems of the day came before this great pastor in plenty, and he settled them all from the certainty of his fellowship with Christ, and always in the light of the Gospel. But no one should make of these scattered detached sayings a Pauline 'system of ethics,' and we must most certainly avoid the mistake of saying that things which happen not to be mentioned in the letters lay 'beyond his ethical horizon.' Here too[2] we must repeat: the letters are fragments. Nor is St. Paul a professed ethical theorist; like other great spiritual guides, in important questions of ethical principle he felt no necessity to harmonise his principles with one another: everything comes from God, from Christ, through the Spirit, and yet St. Paul believes man is capable of everything.

[1] 2 Cor. xi. 29, *τίς σκανδαλίζεται, καὶ οὐκ ἐγὼ πυροῦμαι;*

[2] Cf. p. 172 n. 11 above.

Determinists and indeterminists can therefore both appeal to his authority; St. Paul himself was neither the one nor the other: to him the oar was as valuable as the sail:—

> 'So then, my beloved, even as ye have always obeyed, work out not in my presence only, but now much more in my absence, your own salvation with fear and trembling. For it is God which worketh in you both to will and to work, for His good pleasure." [1]

Perhaps the greatest thing about this highly practical ethical ideal is the fact that its energy was in no way paralysed by the mighty hopes that were at work in St. Paul's soul.

The 'hope in Christ,' [2] the 'hope of Christ' [3] which we find in St. Paul is not a comparatively outlying portion of the 'system,' like the section on eschatology which is crowded in or crowded out at the end of a term's lectures on dogmatics. It is one of the motive forces of his life in Christ. This could be demonstrated merely from the importance he attaches to the ideas of 'testament,' 'promise,' and 'inheritance,' which all point to the future. To St. Paul salvation is not a thing of the past but of the present and future.

[1] Phil. ii. 12, 13, *ὥστε, ἀγαπητοί μου, καθὼς πάντοτε ὑπηκούσατε, μὴ ὡς ἐν τῇ παρουσίᾳ μου μόνον ἀλλὰ νῦν πολλῷ μᾶλλον ἐν τῇ ἀπουσίᾳ μου, μετὰ φόβου καὶ τρόμου τὴν ἑαυτῶν σωτηρίαν κατεργάζεσθε. θεὸς γάρ ἐστιν ὁ ἐνεργῶν ἐν ὑμῖν καὶ τὸ θέλειν καὶ τὸ ἐνεργεῖν ὑπὲρ τῆς εὐδοκίας.* The difficult phrase *ὑπὲρ τῆς εὐδοκίας* is probably employed like the *ὑπὲρ εὐχαριστίας* which occurs frequently, like a formula, in Egyptian inscriptions of the imperial period at Tehnéh (Annales du Service des Antiquités, 1905, pp. 150 ff.), which are set up 'in gratitude' to the gods.

[2] 1 Cor. xv. 19, *ἐν Χριστῷ ἠλπικότες.*

[3] 'Christ-hope,' 1 Thess. i. 3, *ἡ ἐλπὶς τοῦ κυρίου ἡμῶν Ἰησοῦ Χριστοῦ.*

To represent the hope of St. Paul as 'eschatology' deprives it of its perennial freshness, and does not after all enable any one to reconstruct a uniform system from the statements in the letters, for they all point different ways and are strongly influenced by the writer's mood. St. Paul himself says of hope that it is not to be confused with seeing,[1] and although his own hope may possess a high degree of personal certainty ('we know,' says St. Paul, when he is hoping[2]) we observe on the whole a marked psychological polarity in his anticipation of the future. I am by no means confident to assume that instead of the polar relation there was a gradual 'evolution' from one to the other extreme.

There are two poles as it were to St. Paul's hope of Christ.

Relying implicitly on the prophetic words of Jesus, the apostle is certain that the 'coming' of Christ to complete the Kingdom of God on earth will soon take place—so certain that he himself hopes to witness that coming.[3] This lively hope that Christ will come to us is entirely native Jewish in its spirit. Contrasted with it, however, is the more tender longing that we may come to Christ[4]:—

> 'I have the desire to depart and be with Christ.'

This condition 'with Christ'[5] is the higher stage

[1] Rom. viii. 24, ἐλπὶς δὲ βλεπομένη οὐκ ἔστιν ἐλπίς.

[2] οἴδαμεν, 2 Cor. v. 1.

[3] 1 Thess. iv. 17; 1 Cor. xv. 51 f.

[4] Phil. i. 23, τὴν ἐπιθυμίαν ἔχων εἰς τὸ ἀναλῦσαι καὶ σὺν Χριστῷ εἶναι.

[5] σὺν Χριστῷ, 1 Thess. iv. 17, v. 10; 2 Cor. xiii. 4; Phil. i. 23; Rom. viii. 32.

of the 'in Christ' which can be experienced here on earth. He who is united 'with Christ,' 'face to face,'[1] will have put off all that is fleshly, and will possess a 'spiritual body'[2] similar to the lucent body of Christ Himself.[3] The apostle's hope did not, however, dogmatically determine the time of this metamorphosis. At one time it takes its direction from the conviction of 'the resurrection,' which is more Jewish and Pharisaic: the dead will rest for a time in the grave, and will be awakened at the coming of Christ, and with those that are then still alive will be 'changed' into the spiritual.[4] Another time his prophetic gaze is more Hellenistic, directed on the immortality of the soul:—

> 'For we know that if our earthly tent-house be dissolved, we have a building from God, a house not made with hands, eternal, in the heavens.'[5]

Thus in St. Paul there run side by side with each other Eastern, native Jewish, and Western, Hellenistic and cosmopolitan expressions of hope, and the great popular preacher feels no compulsion to harmonise them theoretically. The sacred stream which rolls its waters towards eternity shows for a long time the double colouring due to its two tributaries. The artless realism of the popular imagination is shown in the fact that St. Paul has incorporated in his 'mystery'[6] of hope, as something taken for granted,

1 1 Cor. xiii. 12, *πρόσωπον πρὸς πρόσωπον.*

2 *σῶμα πνευματικόν*, 1 Cor. xv. 35 ff.

3 Phil. iii. 21, *σύμμορφον τῷ σώματι τῆς δόξης αὐτοῦ.*

4 1 Cor. xv. 51 ff.

5 2 Cor. v. 1, *οἴδαμεν γὰρ ὅτι ἐὰν ἡ ἐπίγειος ἡμῶν οἰκία τοῦ σκήνους καταλυθῇ, οἰκοδομὴν ἐκ θεοῦ ἔχομεν, οἰκίαν ἀχειροποίητον αἰώνιον ἐν τοῖς οὐρανοῖς.* Cf. p. 62 above.

6 1 Cor. xv. 51, *ἰδοὺ μυστήριον ὑμῖν λέγω.*

features derived from the ancient popular beliefs of his fathers—the dramatic character of the events expected, the voice of the archangel,[1] the blast of the trumpet,[2] the 'descent' of Christ from heaven,[3] the ascent of the faithful 'into the air,' 'to the clouds,' to meet the Lord,[4] and the fiery glow of the Judgment Day lighting up the whole picture.[5]

The effectual certainties in it all are the Last Judgment by Christ[6] and His saints,[7] the annihilation of all the Satanic and daemonic powers hostile to God,[8] the defeat of the 'last' enemy, death,[9] the reign of Christ as King,[10] the final completion of the salvation already experienced on earth 'in Christ' at length 'with Christ,' *i.e.*, in personal fellowship face to face,[11] and finally the handing back of the Kingdom by the Son to the Father.[12] But at the remotest distance of the horizon of eternity swept by the apostle's prophetic vision we still see the flaming certainty[13]:—

'God is all in all.'

The eye that was privileged to take this last look was not blinded by the lightning[14] of the day of the Lord. St. Paul for his own part drew many practical inferences from the approaching end (*e.g.*, that it was

[1] 1 Thess. iv. 16.

[2] 1 Thess. iv. 16; 1 Cor. xv. 52.

[3] 1 Thess. iv. 16, *καταβήσεται ἀπ' οὐρανοῦ*.

[4] 1 Thess. iv. 17, *ἁρπαγησόμεθα ἐν νεφέλαις εἰς ἀπάντησιν τοῦ κυρίου εἰς ἀέρα*.

[5] 2 Thess. i. 8; 1 Cor. iii. 13 ff.

[6] 2 Cor. v. 10, etc.

[7] 1 Cor. vi. 2 f.

[8] 1 Cor. xv. 24 f.

[9] 1 Cor. xv. 26.

[10] 1 Cor. xv. 25, etc.

[11] Cf. p. 190.

[12] 1 Cor. xv. 24, 28.

[13] 1 Cor. xv. 28, *ὁ θεὸς τὰ πάντα ἐν πᾶσιν*.

[14] Matt. xxiv. 27 (Luke xvii. 24).

inexpedient for him to marry [1]), but his longing in Christ for the new world, though enthusiastic and ardent, does not degenerate to an unhealthy and barren chiliasm or quietism. On the contrary, it set free moral forces to act on this transitory [2] world. Certainly without the hope of Christ St. Paul would never have become famous in history as the man of practice, the apostle of Christ.

[1] 1 Cor. vii. 7, 8, 26.

[2] Cf. 1 Cor. vii. 31, παράγει γὰο τὸ σχῆμα τοῦ κόσμου τούτου.

ST. PAUL THE APOSTLE

CHAPTER VIII

ST. PAUL THE APOSTLE

Born in the borderland between the Hellenistic and the Semitic world, on one of the great international roads connecting the East and the West, Saul, the Semitic Hellenist who was also called Paul, felt a vast compelling impulse to traverse the world from its eastern to its western end:—

> 'Necessity is laid upon me; yea, woe is unto me, if I preach not the gospel.'[1]
>
> 'I must also see Rome.'[2]

The sick man, buffeted by the messenger of Satan,[3] was travelling from place to place throughout almost a whole generation.[4] The Jew who had come from Cilicia, Jerusalem, and Syria to Ephesus and Corinth, looks longingly beyond Rome to the end of the world, to Spain.[5] The mystic, full of the Spirit, who on the coast of Asia Minor hears in a vision the voice of the West,[6]

> 'Come over and help us,'

---

[1] 1 Cor. ix. 16, ἀνάγκη γάρ μοι ἐπίκειται· οὐαὶ γάρ μοί ἐστιν, ἐὰν μὴ εὐαγγελίζωμαι.

[2] Acts xix. 21, δεῖ με καὶ Ῥώμην ἰδεῖν.

[3] 2 Cor. xii. 7.

[4] 2 Cor. xi. 26, ὁδοιπορίαις πολλάκις.

[5] Rom. xv. 22 ff.

[6] Acts xvi. 9, διαβὰς . . . βοήθησον ἡμῖν.

is a man whose practical performance is almost unparalleled[1] :—

'I laboured more abundantly than they all.'

The seer who foresaw the coming Christ and the new heaven and the new earth sought to prepare the old world for the coming of the new, and spread over it a network of organisation which was destined to affect the history of the world for thousands of years.

The way in which St. Paul affected the history of the world is most clearly seen in his work as a missionary.[2]

This does not mean, of course, that the world contemporary with him observed or had the remotest conception of the mighty influence vouchsafed to the work of his life. The wandering tentmaker did not attract the attention of his age.[3] To the Roman official before whose tribunal he was placed by the denunciation of malicious adversaries, he was an obscure Jew, or perhaps a mad enthusiast.[4] Occasionally, it is true, as in Cyprus,[5] St. Paul impressed even distinguished Romans, and by the power of his personality he often made a great impression on

[1] 1 Cor. xv. 10, περισσότερον αὐτῶν πάντων ἐκοπίασα. We might take this literally and illustrate it with statistics. The map at the end of the volume shows about twenty places in which the primitive apostolic cult was established, and about thirty places connected with the Pauline cult of Christ.

[2] To supplement the following sketch cf. the excellent studies by Paul Wernle, *Paulus als Heidenmissionar*, 2nd ed., Tübingen, 1909, and by Georg Heinrici, *Paulus als Seelsorger*, Gross-Lichterfelde, 1910.

[3] Cf. pp. 58 and 77 above.

[4] Acts xxvi. 24.

[5] Acts xiii. 12.

simple folk. Once in the interior of Asia Minor they took him to be the god Hermes [1]; another time the Anatolians received him as an angel of God, or even as Jesus Christ Himself.[2] So, too, the natives of the island of Malta, who had at first suspected the prisoner Paul to be a murderer, afterwards, when they saw him throw into the fire a poisonous snake that hung on his hand, were very soon ready to pronounce Paul to be a god.[3] And before that, in the awful storm which ended with the shipwreck off Malta, Paul was the only one of the 276 persons on board the Alexandrian corn-ship who kept his self-possession, and by his exhortations saved the others from despair.[4]

But the leading men of his time, especially the literary leaders, took no notice of the wanderer on the whole, and if he does, as at Athens, come into contact with the philosophers, they either put him off with phrases of the worldly wise,[5] or they abuse him [6] and regard him as a ridiculous personage [7]:—

'What would this seed-pecker say?'

Paul himself felt the distance which separated him

1 Acts xiv. 12. 2 Gal. iv. 14.

3 Acts xxviii. 3–6.

4 Acts xxvii. 33 ff. There is a remarkable parallel to this scene in the life of Goethe. In May, 1787, off Capri, on the return voyage from Messina, his vessel got into a current during a calm and was in danger of being dashed to pieces on the rocks of the island. Then the worldling encouraged the despairing passengers and exhorted them to pray to the Mother of God. But the strength of spontaneity (and that means everything in religion) was on the side of the apostolic voyager in Mediterranean waters.

5 Acts xvii. 32. 6 Acts xvii. 32.

7 Acts xvii. 18, *τί ἂν θέλοι ὁ σπερμολόγος οὗτος λέγειν*

from the leading men of letters. It is not from any feeling of weakness, but with a strong consciousness of superiority, that he calls himself a layman and a person unknown.[1]

To the world at large Paul the missionary was one of the numerous wandering orators who then went up and down the world in the service of some philosophical or religious cause[2] :—

'A setter forth of strange daemons.'[3]

We know something more particularly about the preachers of popular philosophy who gathered the public around them in the great cities of antiquity. The disciples of the Stoa and of the Cynic philosophy were especially active in their itinerant propaganda.

But there was also no lack of religious emissaries. The age of St. Paul is a missionary age not only on his account, but also by reason of the great migration of pagan deities which transplanted eastern cults to the West and North and Graeco-Roman cults to the East.

We have important proofs of missionary work before St. Paul's in the immediate surroundings of St. Paul himself.

On the one hand the Pharisees in particular, like the Jews in general, made propaganda for their cause. Jesus says, in His controversial utterances against the Pharisees[4] :—

'Ye compass sea and land to make one proselyte.'

---

[1] Cf. p. 78 above.

[2] On this point cf. most recently E. von Dobschütz, *Die Thessalonicher-Briefe* (Meyer X[7]), Göttingen, 1909, pp. 2 ff.

[3] Acts xvii. 18, ξένων δαιμονίων . . . καταγγελεύς.

[4] Matt. xxiii. 15, περιάγετε τὴν θάλασσαν καὶ τὴν ξηρὰν ποιῆσαι ἕνα προσήλυτον.

Thus the very school of Judaism to which Paul attached himself as a young man had already given practical effect to the instinct of expansion, and the splendid stirring language used by St. Paul in writing to the Romans [1] reflects the Jewish feeling of religious superiority which psychologically impelled him and his countrymen to missionary enterprise.

On the other hand we find at Ephesus in the period of St. Paul's missionary work a church of twelve Baptists.[2] These Ephesian disciples of John the Baptist surely allow us to conclude with more or less certainty that there had been some sort of Baptist propaganda.

The whole religious world contemporary with St. Paul was thus in a state of decided movement even before he began his labours. The roads that Paul traversed as a missionary had been trodden before him by the emissaries of Isis, of the God of the Jews, and of the Great Mother of Phrygia.

Yet it would surely be impossible to mention any other missionary of that period whose journeys can have led him so far as did St. Paul's. St. Paul's journeys are lines drawn from the principal centres of culture in the East to the principal centres of intercourse in the West. Any one who, with the map of the Roman Empire before him, merely hears the names of St. Paul's stopping-places will be bound to wonder at the worldwide extent of his sphere of work. Tarsus, Jerusalem, Damascus, Antioch, Cyprus, Iconium, Galatia, Phrygia, Ephesus, Philippi, Thessalonica, Athens, Corinth, Illyricum, Rome, perhaps also Crete and Spain—the sower who ploughed the

[1] Rom. ii. 19 f.; cf. p. 96 above.

[2] Acts xix. 1 ff.

furrows and scattered the seed over this wide area deserves to have it said of him that his field was the world.

The cosmopolitan cities were his special sphere of work. Paul the city-resident evangelised in the cities; churches dedicated to St. Paul should therefore be built not 'before the walls' but in the forum, where in an ancient city stood the temple of Hermes,[1] the god whom the people of Lystra took St. Paul to be.[2] Amid the bustle and hurry of labour, where the waves of the human sea roar and break, while high in the air the wires of the talking giant-city vibrate as they link up church-tower with hospital, market, and Parliament House, it is fitting that there should be also in our country churches of St. Paul from whose pulpits the Crucified may be preached.

Maps of the Roman Empire, being generally on a small scale, can only show the most important places. The places connected with St. Paul are almost without exception places that are noted on even the smallest map. Names of villages and small towns, such as crop up from the mists of oblivion in the Gospel records and cause such terrible annoyance to philosophical fictionists and destructive critics who write about Jesus at the present day, because they are not mentioned by Tacitus or in the Talmud, are practically absent from the records of St. Paul. Appii Forum ('the Market of Appius') and 'The Three Taverns' are only mentioned as stations on the road from Puteoli to Rome.[3]

It is only another way of expressing the same observation when I add that, since the means of communication in the Mediterranean world have

[1] Vitruvius i. 7, 'Mercurio autem in foro.'

[2] Acts xiv. 12. [3] Acts xxviii. 15.

been modernised, it is possible to-day to reach almost all the important places connected with St. Paul by steamer or by railway, or by both. A glance at the map accompanying this volume, on which for this reason the modern lines of communication have been indicated, will certainly repay the trouble at this point. The following places connected with St. Paul, apart from those which he touched only in passing, are now on the railway: Tarsus, Jerusalem, Damascus and 'Arabia,' Iconium (Konieh), Phrygia, Galatia, Ephesus (Ayasoluk), Laodicea (Gonjeli) with Colossae and Hierapolis, Beroea (Verria), Rome. We find ports for steamers at Cyprus, Ptolemais (Acre), Neapolis in Macedonia (Kavalla), Nicopolis (Paleo Prevesa), Crete, Malta. There are approaches both by rail and steamer to Thessalonica (Saloniki), Athens (with its port at Piraeus), and Corinth. The only place of first-rate importance in St. Paul's life and wanting in these lists is Antioch on the Orontes; but its present port, Alexandretta, only a short day's journey distant, lies already within the district served by the Baghdad Railway.[1]

Of course the European companies whose capital is invested in these modern means of communication have not speculated on the few scholars who might wish to follow the footsteps of St. Paul. The steamship lines and the railroads have to obey the geographical conditions which determine human intercourse, and which are essentially the same as they were at the time when the ancient routes by water and by land were accommodated to them.

As I look at Paul the evangelist of the ancient city one thing alone strikes me as peculiar: that he should

[1] Cf. p. 30 n. above.

never have gone to Egypt, especially to Alexandria, the international headquarters of the Jews of the Dispersion. Apart from his voyages in Alexandrian ships[1]—one of them called 'The Dioscuri'[2]—the only connexion that we know of between Paul the Christian and Egypt is an indirect one. Apollos of Alexandria had laboured in the Corinthian church after St. Paul's departure,[3] and St. Paul gratefully refers to this as a continuation of his own work in the garden of the Lord.[4]

I have no certain explanation to offer why St. Paul, who on one occasion was taken for an Egyptian,[5] never went as a missionary to Egypt. Did he regard Alexandria, which would be 'Egypt' to him, just as in the main Corinth and its environs were 'Achaia,'[6] and Ephesus with its environs 'Asia'[7]—did he regard Alexandria, in consideration of its enormous Jewish population, as belonging not to pagan territory but to the 'circumcision,'[8] and therefore to St. Peter's mission field?[9] He is jealously concerned that every missionary shall have his own province and not go beyond it,[10] and we may be sure in particular that the agreement with Peter, James, and John, the 'pillars,'[11] was loyally observed by him. Or had there already been other Christian missionaries in Egypt at an early date? Unfortunately we are altogether in the dark as to the beginnings of Egyptian Christianity.

The most probable answer seems to me the follow-

[1] Acts xxvii. 6; xxviii. 11.
[2] Acts xxviii. 11.
[3] Acts xix. 1.
[4] 1 Cor. iii. 6.
[5] Acts xxi. 38.
[6] 2 Cor. ix. 2, etc.
[7] Rom. xvi. 5, R.V.
[8] Gal. ii. 9.
[9] Gal. ii. 9.
[10] 2 Cor. x. 13 ff.; Rom. xv. 20.
[11] Gal. ii. 9.

ing: The Jewish persecutions which broke out at Alexandria in 38 A.D., when St. Paul's missionary work was beginning, and which culminated in fearful massacres, made a mission to Egypt an actual impossibility to begin with, and drove St. Paul to the North and West, even if he had wished to undertake missionary work in the South. Afterwards, when Egypt was at rest, no doubt other persons did the work of evangelisation there.[1]

But even without Egypt St. Paul's sphere of work is of unparalleled extent.

What was it that drove this man forth into the world?

His experience on the road to Damascus was of fundamental importance to St. Paul in his missionary capacity, as in other things. His conversion was not only the transformation of an enemy of Christ into a friend of Christ, it was the transformation of an apostle of Pharisaic Judaism into an apostle of Christ. It was the revulsion of a religious consciousness, and especially of the consciousness of a mission, such as we see reflected in the proud words already referred to in St. Paul's letter to the Romans.[2]

St. Paul himself hints to the Galatians[3] that Damascus meant two things to him: the revelation of the living Christ, and the obligation to preach that Christ as a gospel among the nations.

Elsewhere, too, we have numerous proofs of a

[1] From 1 Cor. ix. 6 it may be concluded that Barnabas was still working as a missionary midway between 50 and 60 A.D. The later tradition of the Clementine Homilies makes Barnabas go to Alexandria. There was not much 'place' (Rom. xv. 23) left him anywhere else as a missionary to the heathen.

[2] Rom. ii. 19, 20; cf. pp. 96 and 199 n. 1 above.

[3] Gal. i. 16; cf. Eph. iii. 1–7; 1 Tim. i. 11 f.

powerful consciousness of his mission in St. Paul. His language becomes peculiarly solemn when he speaks of his mission. He is the 'slave'[1] who works in the service of his Master. Grace has been given him to be

> 'a minister of Christ Jesus unto the Gentiles, ministering the gospel of God, that the offering up of the Gentiles might be made acceptable.'[2]

He is one of the evangelists of good things spoken of by the prophet, whose footsteps are beautiful.[3] He is

> 'a herald and an apostle, . . . a teacher of the Gentiles.'[4]

He can even say[5]:—

> 'We are ambassadors therefore on behalf of Christ,
> As though God were intreating by us:
> We beseech you on behalf of Christ,
> Be ye reconciled to God.'

Against opponents who impugned his mission he was especially wont to defend himself as being no whit behind the other apostles.[6] Even the remorse-

[1] Rom. i. 1, etc.; 1 Cor. iv. 1; ix. 17; 2 Cor. v. 18; vi. 4; Col. i. 25.

[2] Rom. xv. 15 f., διὰ τὴν χάριν τὴν δοθεῖσάν μοι ἀπὸ τοῦ θεοῦ, εἰς τὸ εἶναί με λειτουργὸν Χριστοῦ Ἰησοῦ εἰς τὰ ἔθνη, ἱερουργοῦντα τὸ εὐαγγέλιον τοῦ θεοῦ, ἵνα γένηται ἡ προσφορὰ τῶν ἐθνῶν εὐπρόσδεκτος.

[3] Rom. x. 15 (LXX Isa. lii. 7), ὡς ὡραῖοι οἱ πόδες τῶν εὐαγγελιζομένων τὰ ἀγαθά.

[4] 1 Tim. ii. 7, ἐγὼ κήρυξ καὶ ἀπόστολος, . . . διδάσκαλος ἐθνῶν. Cf. 2 Tim. i. 11.

[5] 2 Cor. v. 20, ὑπὲρ Χριστοῦ οὖν πρεσβεύομεν, ὡς τοῦ θεοῦ παρακαλοῦντος δι' ἡμῶν. δεόμεθα ὑπὲρ Χριστοῦ· καταλλάγητε τῷ θεῷ.

[6] Especially in Galatians and 2 Corinthians.

ful thought that he was 'the least of the apostles,' 'not worthy to be called an apostle,' because he persecuted the church of God,[1] could be overcome by the certainty [2] :—

> 'by the grace of God I am what I am.'

Most touching of all, however, are his words to the Corinthians [3] :—

> 'Necessity is laid upon me.
> Woe is unto me if I preach not the gospel.'

The apostle's consciousness of his mission is strengthened by his hope of the end; the time is short,[4] salvation is at the doors: [5] it is time now to prepare the world for the coming change.

Nevertheless there are occasions when the

> 'Debtor both to Greeks and to Barbarians,
> Both to the wise and to the foolish,' [6]

confesses that he entered a new field of work with anxiety :—

> 'And I was with you in weakness, and in fear, and in much trembling.' [7]

---

[1] 1 Cor. xv. 9, ἐγὼ γάρ εἰμι ὁ ἐλάχιστος τῶν ἀποστόλων, ὃς οὐκ εἰμὶ ἱκανὸς καλεῖσθαι ἀπόστολος, διότι ἐδίωξα τὴν ἐκκλησίαν τοῦ θεοῦ.

[2] 1 Cor. xv. 10, χάριτι δὲ θεοῦ εἰμὶ ὅ εἰμι.

[3] 1 Cor. ix. 16; cf. p. 195 above.

[4] 1 Cor. vii. 29.

[5] Rom. xiii. 11 f.

[6] Rom. i. 14, Ἕλλησίν τε καὶ βαρβάροις, σοφοῖς τε καὶ ἀνοήτοις ὀφειλέτης εἰμί.

[7] 1 Cor. ii. 3, κἀγὼ ἐν ἀσθενείᾳ καὶ ἐν φόβῳ καὶ ἐν τρόμῳ πολλῷ ἐγενόμην πρὸς ὑμᾶς.

And what depth of feeling is expressed in the picture conjured up by the three words [1] :—

'At Athens alone.'

So that even St. Paul's consciousness of his mission had its ebb and flow.

By combining the occasional references in St. Paul's letters with the narrative in the Acts of the Apostles we are able to obtain a very incomplete,[2] but in the main trustworthy picture of the outward course of St. Paul's missionary work. Some of the gaps can be filled up from the materials for social history furnished by the world contemporary with him, things which we find to some extent unchanged at the present day if we travel in the footsteps of St. Paul. Even the apocryphal Acts of various apostles, worthless as they often are as biography, furnish useful material for social history in illustration of the manner and difficulty of travelling, adventures on the road and at inns—in short, the light and atmosphere of the ancient East. The excellent Acts of John, for instance, give a very unvarnished and lifelike picture of the wandering life of a Primitive Christian missionary, and enable the modern traveller, if he possesses a sense of humour, to smile even at the discomforts lurking in the worst night-quarters.

Our knowledge of the apostle's sea voyages is especially imperfect. The gospel which first was sounded on the Lake of Gennesareth for fishers and

[1] 1 Thess. iii. 1, ἐν Ἀθήναις μόνοι.

[2] Cf. the allusions in 2 Cor. xi. 23–33, only a small portion of which are recorded elsewhere.

boatmen continued to love the rhythm of oars and the wind-filled sail. And where formerly the rude religion of seamen confided in the protection of Asclepius and Serapis, or even the God of Abraham,[1] now the youthful Christ made hearts strong amid the howling rage of the Mediterranean storm,[2] and called for a blessing on the hard ship's bread.[3] St. Paul must often have been at sea; even before his last voyage to Jerusalem[4] he could look back upon three shipwrecks of which we know no further details. We appreciate all the more the one picture of the voyage to Rome in the last two chapters of the Acts of the Apostles. With its lively description even of what is purely nautical and of the wonderful adventures of the shipwrecked party it forms a little apostolic Odyssey, only it is not a fiction but the reflection of real experiences in the soul—an ancient, not a modern soul—of a companion of St. Paul, and for that reason a unique document of the social history of the Roman imperial period.

In describing the experiences of Paul the missionary on land, the writer of the Acts of the Apostles again shows a happy and as a rule trustworthy touch, although he is less fond of a sober white light than of the play of the seven colours. The popular demonstration in the theatre at

[1] Cf. for instance the fine inscriptions put up by sailors in the 'Harbour of Letters' in the island of Syros, beginning with the imperial period (*Inscriptiones Graecae* XII. 5, No. 712). The pagan inscriptions are succeeded by Jewish, and these by Christian inscriptions, a unique exhibition of the continuity of ancient piety in the Mediterranean. On Serapis as a rescuer from peril of the sea cf. the letter written by Apion, an Egyptian recruit, *Light from the Ancient East*, pp. 167–171.

[2] Acts xxvii. 21 ff.

[3] Acts xxvii. 35.

[4] 2 Cor. xi. 25.

Ephesus[1]—the events connected with the arrest of St. Paul at Jerusalem[2]—these and other scenes where the bloodthirsty passions of the multitude are aroused stand out in the sharpest relief when viewed from the religious position of the modern East. The same fanaticism which had once made St. Paul a persecutor, and which afterwards caused him to be stoned himself,[3] has smouldered on there till the present day, and still breaks out into bloody massacres under the eyes of the European consulates.

The financial basis of the missionary journeys was the simplest imaginable. Paul's wants were few, and the Master's divinely plain words of instruction respecting the equipment of His emissaries[4] were doubtless not unknown to him.

He probably travelled as a rule on foot; only once do our authorities speak of his riding, namely when he was conveyed from Jerusalem to Caesarea on the coast.[5] The painters, who love to give an aristocratic air to Primitive Christianity, have mounted him—quite wrongly, I think[6]—upon a proud steed for his journey to Damascus, in the same way that they

[1] Acts xix. 23 ff. [2] Acts xxi. 27 ff.

[3] Acts xiv. 19; 2 Cor. xi. 25.

[4] Mark vi. 8 ff. and parallels; cf., by way of contrast, the caravan of a begging apostle of the Syrian goddess, *Light from the Ancient East*, pp. 109, 110.

[5] Acts xxiii. 24, 31 f.

[6] The narratives in the Acts of the Apostles all speak against it.—The sound of horses' hoofs is heard all through the (aristocratic) Old Testament, but in the New Testament (apart from St. Paul's Roman escort, Acts xxiii. 23, 32, and the commonplace in James iii. 3) there are no horses except in the visions of the Revelation of St. John. Jesus rides on an ass.

delight to clothe him on Mars' Hill with classical drapery—as though that was necessary. The real St. Paul had a simple coat and the dusty sandals of a foot passenger. He even seems to have preferred walking to sailing: on his last journey to Jerusalem he left the ship at (Alexandria) Troas and travelled on foot to Assos, where his companions then took him on board again.[1] His baggage was no doubt of the smallest dimensions; once he left behind him with his friend Carpus at (Alexandria) Troas not only his Bible-rolls and papers, but even the cloak which is often very necessary even for summer nights in Anatolia.[2]

He also travelled without any family. While other apostles, for instance the brothers of our Lord and Peter, were accompanied on their journeys by their wives,[3] St. Paul for his part, without wishing to impose a command on others, had renounced marriage,[4] probably to some extent under the pressure of his hopes of the end of the world.[5] Moreover, he abstained of his own free will[6] from exercising a right that was generally admitted[7] and had the authority of Jesus[8] to commend it,[9] the right of a missionary to be supported by the churches.

What he required he earned by his own labour. He is the first artisan missionary, and he is proud of the fact.[10] His churches are poor, and he will not be a burden to them.[11] He is almost nervously

[1] Acts xx. 13, 14.
[2] 2 Tim. iv. 13.
[3] 1 Cor. ix. 5.
[4] 1 Cor. vii. 8.
[5] 1 Cor. vii. 26; cf. p. 191 f. above.
[6] 1 Cor. ix. 15.
[7] 1 Cor. ix. 4 ff.
[8] Matt. x. 10; Luke x. 7.
[9] 1 Cor. ix. 14.
[10] 1 Cor. ix. 15.
[11] 1 Thess. ii. 9; 2 Cor. xi. 9, etc.

proud when his opponents accuse him of basely seeking his own advantage.[1] Only in the case of those who stood very near to him did he make an exception and accept charitable gifts.[2]

His handicraft procured him at times, too, the first acquaintanceship and perhaps lodgings in a strange town. His association at Corinth and afterwards at Ephesus with the family of Aquila and Priscilla, tentmakers, is characteristic.[3] These two Christians, birds of passage like himself, were of the greatest possible service to St. Paul the missionary; once they rescued him from a most desperate situation at the risk of their own lives.[4]

From the house in which he had found lodging St. Paul no doubt went as a rule[5] on the Sabbath to the synagogue, in order to effect something by the spoken word. The writer of the Acts of the Apostles has much to report of such visits to synagogues,[6] and is here certainly not incredible. If St. Paul had not worked within the organisation of the synagogue, how otherwise could the frequent punishments[7] be explained which he had to suffer at the hands of the synagogue authorities?

In the synagogue Paul found the Septuagint and men whose piety had been influenced by the

[1] 2 Cor. xi. 7 ff.; xii. 13 ff., 16 ff.; cf. p. 71 above.

[2] 2 Cor. xi. 9; Phil. iv. 15, 18.

[3] Acts xviii. 2; cf. Appendix I.

[4] Rom. xvi. 3 f.; cf. *Light from the Ancient East*, pp. 119 f.

[5] Acts xvii. 2, 'as his custom was.'

[6] Acts xiii. 5 (Salamis in Cyprus); xiii. 14 (Antioch in Pisidia); xiv. 1 (Iconium); xvii. 2 (Thessalonica); xvii. 10 (Beroea); xvii. 17 (Athens); xviii. 4 (Corinth); xviii. 19 (Ephesus); xix. 8 (Ephesus).

[7] 2 Cor. xi. 24.

Septuagint, Jews, Gentiles, and proselytes. The 'Gentiles' whom St. Paul won over no doubt came largely from the ranks of the proselytes or semi-proselytes who had already been under Jewish influences. The alternative that has been often formulated in connexion with the question of the composition of his churches—'Jewish Christians or Gentile Christians?'—is too narrow. There were also Gentile Jewish Christians, who had been originally Gentiles, and who became first Jews and then Christians.

But it was not only in the synagogue that Paul pleaded his cause. In the streets, in the market-place,[1] in the lecture-rooms, for example 'in the school of Tyrannus' at Ephesus,[2] and even when he was in prison 'in bonds' he did successful missionary work at one time or another[3]:—

> 'The word of God is not bound.'[4]

In quiet times, of course, he was also at people's disposal in his own dwelling,[5] and often enough, no doubt, he was pressed by business and surrounded by visitors.[6] Where he worked for any length of time the news soon got about that the preacher of the Gospel could work miracles; cloths that he had touched were credited with healing powers and ability to compel daemons,[7] and he himself at times

[1] Acts xvii. 17.

[2] Acts xix. 9, *ἐν τῇ σχολῇ Τυράννου.*

[3] Philemon 10; Phil. i. 12 f.; cf. Acts xvi. 33, and pp. 18 f. above.

[4] 2 Tim. ii. 9, *ὁ λόγος τοῦ θεοῦ οὐ δέδεται.*

[5] Acts xxviii. 30 f.

[6] 2 Cor. xi. 28.

[7] Acts xix. 11 f.

can recall acts of power—'the signs of an apostle'[1] he calls them—which had accredited him as a genuine apostle.[2]

Gradually he gathered round him quite a number of assistants in his missionary work. His first companion, Barnabas,[3] was at least his equal in authority, but the later associates are decidedly subordinate to him. They shared in the work as fellow-travellers (St. Paul says pleasantly 'companions abroad'[4]), letter-writers,[5] letter-carriers,[6] personal representatives,[7] and of course as evangelists and teachers.[8] In delicate situations he was able to rely on them; the apostasy of John who was called Mark in Pamphylia,[9] or that of Demas, who once, evidently against the wishes of the apostle, went to Thessalonica,[10] was no doubt a rare exception. What an attractive personality is that of Titus, for instance, whose tact and firmness in a time of passionately strained relations restored order in the Corinthian church after it had been stirred up by agitators.[11]

St. Paul is fond of applying expressive titles full of personal feeling to these helpers — Timothy,

[1] 2 Cor. xii. 12, τὰ σημεῖα τοῦ ἀποστόλου.

[2] In Galatia, Gal. iii. 5; at Corinth, 2 Cor. xii. 12 and 1 Cor. ii. 4; in general, Rom. xv. 19.

[3] Acts ix.–xv.

[4] 2 Cor. viii. 19, συνέκδημος.

[5] As, for instance, Tertius did, Rom. xvi. 22.

[6] Titus, for instance, probably took a letter (now lost) to Corinth (2 Cor. vii. 6–9), and also probably our 2 Corinthians (2 Cor. viii. 6, 17).

[7] 1 Cor. xvi. 10; 2 Cor. viii. 23.

[8] 2 Cor. i. 19; Col. i. 7.

[9] Acts xiii. 13; xv. 37 ff.

[10] 2 Tim. iv. 10.

[11] The affair is alluded to throughout 2 Cor. ii., vii., viii.

Tychicus, Titus (who has just been mentioned), Silvanus, Aquila and Priscilla, Urbanus, Epaphroditus, Euodia, Syntyche, Clement, Philemon, Mark, Aristarchus, Demas, Luke the physician, and the rest. He calls them familiarly 'fellow-workers,' [1] a name borrowed from the workshop; in a spirit of comradeship the champion of Christ addresses them as 'fellow-soldiers,' [2] or still more vigorously, 'yokefellows' [3]—with a playful reference perhaps to the ox treading out the corn, which he interpreted to mean the apostles.[4] As they all looked up to one Master in common, his assistants are his 'fellow-slaves'; [5] but because they are in the service of that Master they are to the churches the reflected 'glory of Christ.' [6] Recollection of sufferings shared in common in prison makes him coin for Aristarchus [7] and Epaphras,[8] Andronicus and Junias,[9] the honourable title of 'fellow-prisoner.' [10] Phoebe, a Christian woman of Cenchreae, the port of Corinth, who had done much for his welfare, is singled out for distinction as his 'patroness,' [11] and the mother of his friend Rufus is even called 'mother,' [12] that being the plain, hearty way of showing his respect.

What a vast deal lies hidden behind these brief names! How many experiences, how much en-

[1] συνεργός, 1 Cor. iii. 9; 2 Cor. viii. 23; Rom. xvi. 3, 9, 21; Phil. ii. 25; iv. 3; Philemon 1, 24.

[2] συστρατιώτης, Phil. ii. 25; Philemon 2.

[3] σύζυγος, Phil. iv. 3.

[4] 1 Cor. ix. 9 f.; 1 Tim. v. 18; cf. p. 105 above.

[5] σύνδουλος, Col. i. 7; iv. 7.

[6] δόξα Χριστοῦ, 2 Cor. viii. 23.

[7] Col. iv. 10.

[8] Philemon 23.

[9] Rom. xvi. 7.

[10] συναιχμάλωτος.

[11] προστάτις, Rom. xvi. 2.

[12] Rom. xvi. 13.

durance, how much brotherhood! The strength more particularly of the emotional nature which speaks in these names was one of the magic charms wielded by St. Paul the leader of men. His influence on the common people depended not least on his ability to arouse the slumbering psychic forces even of the most simple by the hearty directness of his appeal as man to man.

All these associates in the apostle's work were, like himself, uncommonly active in their movements. If we were to mark on our map the routes of all their journeys that are known to us from the authorities, the lines would almost make a labyrinth, but we should feel all the more clearly how the Anatolian world was set thrilling at the trumpet blasts of the evangelists:—

'The word of the Lord runneth.' [1]

The people whose souls were moved by the mission of St. Paul and his faithful followers—the overwhelming majority of them at least—were men and women of the middle and lower classes:—

'Not many wise after the flesh,
Not many mighty,
Not many noble.
  But the foolish things of the world
God hath chosen, that He might put to shame the wise;
And the weak things of the world
God hath chosen, that He might put to shame the strong
    things.
  And the base things of the world,
And the things that are despised,
God hath chosen,
The things that are not,
That He might bring to nought the things that are.

---

[1] 2 Thess. iii. 1, ἵνα ὁ λόγος τοῦ κυρίου τρέχῃ.

In these lines,[1] ringing like a song of defiance, and inspired by the defensive pride which longs for the fray and rejoices in the strength of poverty despised, St. Paul has sufficiently well characterised the social structure of the church of Corinth. It has already been hinted[2] that even the holes and corners of the slums in this cosmopolitan city had witnessed conversions. It appears from the scenes at the Communion depicted by St. Paul[3] that some of the poor saints of Corinth occasionally 'had nothing'[4] whatever. Instead of sharing the food they had brought with them in a brotherly manner and waiting until all had been served before beginning to eat, many devoured their own supplies with greedy haste, and those who had nothing were obliged to hunger. The intense earnestness with which St. Paul treats this desecration of the Lord's Supper[5] enables us to divine that his sympathies were with the hungry.

St. Paul also speaks of the 'deep poverty'[6] of the Macedonian churches (Philippi, Thessalonica, Beroea). The advice which he gives to the assemblies of Galatian Christians to raise the collection for the brethren at Jerusalem gradually in small amounts every Sunday[7] (the touching

[1] 1 Cor. i. 26–28, *οὐ πολλοὶ σοφοὶ κατὰ σάρκα, οὐ πολλοὶ δυνατοι, οὐ πολλοὶ εὐγενεῖς· ἀλλὰ τὰ μωρὰ τοῦ κόσμου ἐξελέξατο ὁ θεός, ἵνα καταισχύνῃ τοὺς σοφούς· καὶ τὰ ἀσθενῆ τοῦ κόσμου ἐξελέξατο ὁ θεός, ἵνα καταισχύνῃ τὰ ἰσχυρά· καὶ τὰ ἀγενῆ τοῦ κόσμου καὶ τὰ ἐξουθενημένα ἐξελέξατο ὁ θεός, τὰ μὴ ὄντα, ἵνα τὰ ὄντα καταργήσῃ.*

[2] Page 71 above.

[3] 1 Cor. xi. 20–22, 33 f.

[4] 1 Cor. xi. 22, *τοὺς μὴ ἔχοντας.*

[5] 1 Cor. xi. 20–34.

[6] 2 Cor. viii. 2, *ἡ κατὰ βάθους πτωχεία αὐτῶν.*

[7] 1 Cor. xvi. 1 f.

prototype of the 'penny collections' for missionary purposes that have been so richly blessed among us) is a proof that in the interior of Asia Minor, where small change was still rarer than in the coast towns with their better earnings, the churches were also poor. Even in places where St. Paul had not personally conducted a mission it is probable that the slave element, for instance, was more strongly represented than the slave-holding freemen. At Colossae and Laodicea the 'masters' receive one single short exhortation,[1] the slaves, on the other hand, a whole string of commands and promises[2]—a fact which surely reflects the social structure of these churches.[3]

Yet St. Paul does mention certain fairly well-to-do Christians by name. Those who possessed a room so large that 'house churches' could assemble for edification there, as was the case with Aquila at Ephesus,[4] Nymphas and others at Laodicea,[5] Philemon at Colossae,[6] cannot have been poor. Gaius of Corinth, who offered the hospitality of his house to the whole body of the church,[7] belonged, no doubt, like his fellow-citizen Erastus, the city treasurer,[8] to the middle class. It is worth specially noticing that a few women whose names are honourably mentioned in the history of the Pauline mission were apparently persons of means: these are Chloe, probably at Corinth,[9] Phoebe at

[1] Col. iv. 1; Eph. vi. 9.
[2] Col. iii. 22–25; Eph. vi. 5–8.
[3] On the whole subject cf. my articles on 'Primitive Christianity and the Lower Classes' in The Expositor, February, March, and April, 1909.
[4] 1 Cor. xvi. 19; Rom. xvi. 5.
[5] Col. iv. 15.
[6] Philemon 2.
[7] Rom. xvi. 23.
[8] Rom. xvi. 23.
[9] 1 Cor. i. 11.

Cenchreae, the port of Corinth,[1] and Lydia at Philippi, though she came from Asia Minor.[2] Other women of the higher classes in Macedonia, considerable numbers of whom had been at first enthusiastic for the Gospel (at Thessalonica[3] women of the 'first' circles, and at Beroea[4] 'Greek women of honourable estate'), seem afterwards to have left their 'first love'[5]; otherwise it is difficult to understand the 'deep poverty' of the Macedonian churches later on.[6] In Antioch of Pisidia, it may be remarked, it was the women of honourable estate who allowed themselves to be degraded as the instruments of persecution against Paul and Barnabas.[7]

The subject matter of St. Paul's mission preaching is the living Christ, the Crucified,[8] with special stress on the near approach of the completed Kingdom of God and with strong moral demands.[9] Everything was presented at first with the greatest possible simplicity, in conscious regard of the educational necessities of mission work:—

> 'I fed you with milk, and not with meat; for ye were not yet able to bear it.'[10]

But gradually the treasures of the 'riches of Christ,'[11] of which we have spoken in earlier chapters, were more and more opened, and those unknown persons whom chance had brought together out of the

[1] Rom. xvi. 1 f.; cf. p. 213 above.
[2] Acts xvi. 14.
[3] Acts xvii. 4.
[4] Acts xvii. 12.
[5] Rev. ii. 4.
[6] 2 Cor. viii. 2.
[7] Acts xiii. 50.
[8] Gal. iii. 1, etc.
[9] Cf. Gal. v. 21, προεῖπον.
[10] 1 Cor. iii. 2, γάλα ὑμᾶς ἐπότισα, οὐ βρῶμα· οὔπω γὰρ ἐδύνασθε.
[11] Eph. iii. 8.

depths of the cosmopolitan city became the 'body of Christ,'[1]

'enriched in Him in all utterance and in all knowledge.'[2]

To some extent they appear to have been true revival churches, zealously held together by St. Paul, if necessary by sharp discipline,[3] but also by showing that he had great confidence in them.[4] A letter sent to Corinth and afterwards lost shows by its effects what an influence his personal authority was able to exert[5]:—

'For behold, this selfsame thing, that ye were made sorry[6] after a godly sort, what earnest care it wrought in you, yea, what clearing of yourselves, yea, what indignation, yea, what fear, yea, what longing, yea, what zeal, yea, what avenging!'

One reflects with astonishment, on hearing words like these, so delicate in their psychological discrimination, what extraordinary confidence St. Paul must have had in the receptiveness and responsiveness of soul belonging to the poor folk of Corinth.

[1] 1 Cor. xii. 27 (etc.), *ὑμεῖς δέ ἐστε σῶμα Χριστοῦ.*

[2] 1 Cor. i. 5, *ἐν παντὶ ἐπλουτίσθητε ἐν αὐτῷ, ἐν παντὶ λόγῳ καὶ πάσῃ γνώσει.*

[3] Cf. especially 1 Cor. v. 1 ff., where one who had committed incest is devoted to Satan, or 2 Cor. xiii. 2, or 1 Cor. xvi. 22. On the other hand, after he has been very severe, St. Paul counsels a return to the right path, 2 Cor. ii. 5–11.

[4] Cf. for instance 1 Thess. iv. 9 ff., the words addressed to those 'taught of God' at Thessalonica.

[5] 2 Cor. vii. 11, *ἰδοὺ γὰρ αὐτὸ τοῦτο τὸ κατὰ θεὸν λυπηθῆναι πόσην κατηργάσατο ὑμῖν σπουδήν, ἀλλὰ ἀπολογίαν, ἀλλὰ ἀγανάκτησιν, ἀλλὰ φόβον, ἀλλὰ ἐπιπόθησιν, ἀλλὰ ζῆλον, ἀλλὰ ἐκδίκησιν.* Cf. p. 69 above.

[6] By the letter he had sent.

In preaching Christ to Jews, no doubt appeal was made to the proof from Scripture (the Septuagint), just as in preaching to pagans there was occasional allusion to the divine wisdom to be found in the words of the poets. Of both these devices we have credible examples in the Acts of the Apostles.

The effect of these missionary addresses must have been powerful, and often no doubt sudden. St. Paul's own description of the powerful impression wrought on those who listened to Christian prophesying [1] undoubtedly reflects personal experiences of the prophet missionary and revivalist preacher. A stranger, perhaps an unbeliever, comes into the meeting and hears what is being said at the moment by the speaker who is prophesying in the Spirit. Straightway he sees his own inner self, the most secret thoughts of his heart, revealed by the inspired preacher's exhortation to repentance. Thunder-stricken he falls down before God, and confesses as he lies there :—

'God is in you of a truth.'

When St. Paul was detained by illness in Galatia, and began to preach there, his reception was nothing short of enthusiastic.[2]

On the other hand, St. Paul also encountered very serious obstacles, chiefly owing to the agitation of Judaeo-Christian apostles, zealous for the Law, who travelled in his wake and set the churches against him either by their own personal efforts or by letters.[3]

[1] 1 Cor. xiv. 24 f.

[2] Gal. iv. 13 ff.

[3] 2 Thess. ii. 2, 15 ; 2 Cor. iii. 1.

To these 'false brethren,'[1] these 'dogs and evil workers,'[2] who shrank from no manner of mischief, Paul was indebted for some of his most anxious hours. We are indebted to them for occasioning several of St. Paul's most valuable letters. He also suffered greatly at the hands of Jewish communities whose devotion to the Law led to denunciations and the infliction of chastisement by the synagogues; and even the business instincts of pagan religion were aroused against him, as shown by the riot provoked at Ephesus by Demetrius the silversmith.[3]

The missionary journeys were not anxiously planned out beforehand down to the smallest detail. It is true St. Paul did not travel at haphazard : he aimed naturally at the districts opened up by the ancient lines of communication, and particularly at cities with Jewish settlements. He had in his head a map of the scattered Jewish colonies, such as is imperfectly indicated by the blue markings on the map which accompanies this volume. In some cities no doubt he had family[4] or tribal[5] connexions, and availed himself of them. But he was fond of allowing himself to be turned aside from the regular route by a sudden inspiration[6] and to be drifted towards

[1] Gal. ii. 4, τοὺς ψευδαδέλφους.

[2] Phil. iii. 2, τοὺς κύνας, τοὺς κακοὺς ἐργάτας.

[3] Acts xix. 23 ff.

[4] A nephew of St. Paul was at Jerusalem, Acts xxiii. 16; cf. pp. 92, 111 above.

[5] Cf. his συγγενεῖς Andronicus, Junias, and Herodion at Ephesus (Rom. xvi. 7, 11), and the συγγενεῖς Lucius, Jason, and Sosipater who were with him at Corinth (Rom. xvi. 21).

[6] Gal. ii. 2; Acts xvi. 6, 7, 9 f.; (xvii. 15; xix. 1, Codex D).

new goals. No doubt he often experienced what he bade his faithful followers pray for[1]:—

> 'A great door and effectual is opened unto me.'[2]

The main lines of his missionary journeys are comparatively clear.

After his experience on the road to Damascus, he goes first of all to "Arabia.' It is not certain whether he began missionary work there at once. That he should have taken the opportunity to sketch out the system of Paulinism is as improbable as it is reasonable to suppose that he felt the desire for a period of quiet in which to collect himself. Then, after a short stay at Jerusalem, he labours as a missionary in Syria and Cilicia—that is to say, mainly in Antioch on the Orontes and in his native city of Tarsus, and after that with Barnabas in Cyprus, Pamphylia, Pisidia, and Lycaonia.

Next there follows, again after a short visit to Jerusalem, the journey which was most important in its effects, from Antioch on the Orontes viâ Tarsus through the Cilician Gates over the Taurus to Lycaonia, Phrygia, and Galatia. Here, in the old 'region of Galatia' we must, in my opinion, look for the churches to which the letter 'to the Galatians' was afterwards sent.[3] The intention of evangelising

[1] Col. iv. 3.

[2] 1 Cor. xvi. 9; cf. 2 Cor. ii. 12.

[3] The region of Galatia is marked in orange on the map accompanying this volume. The account of the origin of the Galatian churches in Gal. iv. 13–19 does not agree in the least with the statements in the Acts of the Apostles concerning the evangelisation done at Antioch in Pisidia, Iconium, Lystra and Derbe, in which cities many people would see the 'churches of Galatia.' The other statements in the Acts also do not agree

the west of Asia Minor and Bithynia, where there were plenty of Jewish communities, is overruled by the Spirit. The apostle feels guided across the sea, and goes by ship viâ (Alexandria) Troas to Macedonia, where churches are successfully founded at Philippi, Thessalonica, and Beroea. After an unavailing effort at Athens he reaches Corinth,[1] where he secures a success that is all the more significant.

A sea voyage brings him by way of Ephesus to Palestine, a land journey to the Syrian Antioch, and, again through the Cilician Gates, into the interior of Asia Minor, to Galatia and Phrygia, until at length Ephesus becomes for some time the centre of his work. Of this Ephesian period we know extremely little, but in it St. Paul must have experienced considerably more than what is recorded in our fragmentary authorities. At Ephesus several of his most important letters were written, some of them probably during an imprisonment. From Ephesus he made journeys by land and sea, as shown especially by his letters to Corinth. At Ephesus he underwent great suffering for the faith, and he met with the most loyal and self-sacrificing devotion.

After a journey which led him 'through' Macedonia[2] as far as Illyricum, there follows a peaceful sojourn at Corinth. St. Paul then makes up his mind to convey the funds collected by him for the

with this 'South Galatian' hypothesis. Were it true we should expect at Gal. i. 21 a mention of the foundation of the churches in 'South Galatia.'

[1] This arrival of St. Paul at Corinth can now, I think, be fixed chronologically with great probability. Cf. Appendix I.

[2] When St. Paul speaks of a journey 'through' Macedonia (1 Cor. xvi. 5) we naturally imagine it as a journey from east to west, that is to say probably along the Via Egnatia.

saints at Jerusalem to the Holy City and then to start for Rome and Spain. He journeys by land and by water through Macedonia and Asia Minor to Palestine, but at Jerusalem he is arrested and is brought by sea from Caesarea to Rome. The question whether St. Paul, after his two years of work there,[1] actually carried out his projected[2] journey to Spain is to me still an open one, but I reckon with the possibility of an affirmative answer.

These, of course, are no more than hints. The map will show my conception of the routes of the missionary journeys in detail. The missionary's own letters and the Acts of the Apostles enable us to illustrate the missionary work of St. Paul from a series of bright and lively pictures familiar to us all, the church that stands out most realistically being that of Corinth.

I should like at least to call attention to three pictures which are comparatively little noticed in the long series.

In the first place, the collection for the poor saints of the mother church at Jerusalem. Being a cause specially dear to the apostle, it is mentioned again and again throughout several of his letters,[3] and its characteristics become clearer when viewed against the background afforded by the practice of religious collections in the contemporary world.[4] The warmth of St. Paul's brotherly affection, his prudence as a man of business, his loyal observance

[1] Acts xxviii. 30 f.

[2] Rom. xv. 24, 28.

[3] 1 and 2 Corinthians and Romans.

[4] Cf. *Light from the Ancient East*, pp. 103–106, 109 f.

of an agreement,[1] and his delicate tact, are all revealed in his treatment of this one matter, and so too the readiness of his infant churches to take action even at a sacrifice to themselves appears in the best possible light.

Next, there is the case of the runaway slave Onesimus, which is treated in the letter to Philemon[2] —a typical case of St. Paul's attention to an individual soul. This one case teaches us better than long investigations could do what the secret of this missionary's influence was. It was the suggestive power of his entirely trustful and entirely brotherly personality which bound people to him.[3]

Finally, in the little letter to the Christians of Ephesus which is preserved in the sixteenth chapter of Romans, we see what St. Paul the missionary made of these people. There he stands amidst his faithful followers, united with them in the faith of Christ and in the sufferings of Christ, knowing each one, and exchanging with all of them a pressure of the hand or a friendly look—with men and women—from Prisca and her husband Aquila to Rufus and his mother, whom the apostle himself gratefully calls by the same loving name.[4] In all those unpretentious greetings we feel what is implied though not spoken. In those lines the unknown and forgotten inhabitants of the great city of antiquity, some by their names recognisable as slaves, are striving upward from the dull vegetating mass, upward to the light, having become personalities, saints in Christ through Paul the missionary. The strength of such souls is hallowed and unimpaired; the future will be theirs.

[1] Gal. ii. 10.
[2] Cf. pp. 17 ff. above.
[3] Cf. p. 213 f. above.
[4] Cf. p. 213 n. 12 above.

A peculiarly kindly fate has preserved to us in the record a relic of one of these unknown persons. St. Paul had dictated the little letter to his associate Tertius, and then gave him permission to add a line from himself; the privilege is as characteristic of St. Paul as of Tertius. And just as we find such lines added by some one who is not the sender in other letters that have come down to us from the ancient world—as, for example, in a letter from an Egyptian woman, Helena, to her brother Petechon,[1] this postscript by her father:—

'I also, Alexander your father, salute you much . . ."

so Tertius writes[2]:—

'I salute you, I Tertius, who have written the letter, in the Lord.'

In whatever way we take the expression 'in the Lord,' which is appended here like a seal—whether we construe it with 'I salute you'[3] or with 'have written'—in any case this line from Tertius contains the phrase which may be described as the most fundamental in St. Paul's vocabulary[4]—

'in the Lord.'

Others may call it a formula repeated by the pupil —I am disposed to attach a higher value to the con-

[1] The Oxyrhynchus Papyri, No. 1067, 3rd cent. A.D., κἀγὼ Ἀλέξανδρος ὁ π[α]τὴρ ὑμῶν ἀσπάζομαι ὑμᾶς πολλά . . . .

[2] Rom. xvi. 22, ἀσπάζομαι ὑμᾶς ἐγὼ Τέρτιος ὁ γράψας τὴν ἐπιστολὴν ἐν κυρίῳ.

[3] This is no doubt the more likely to be correct.

[4] Cf. p. 128 above.

tribution which Tertius all unknowingly made to the New Testament. I see behind this line as it were the impress of the great man's creative soul on the soul which the great man had awakened in the insignificant brother. Tertius stands before us as a type of the people who were elevated by Paul the missionary from their dull existence in the mass to the sphere of new-creative grace, to the hallowing fellowship with Jesus Christ the Lord.

It is certain that St. Paul did his missionary work with the prospect of martyrdom before his eyes. Once he suffered his most trusted friends, the Christians of Philippi, to have a glimpse of his thoughts [1] :—

> 'Yea, and if I am poured out as a drink-offering at the sacrifice which I minister as a priest [2] by work on your faith, I joy and rejoice with you all.'

The presentiment was fulfilled. At Rome it was vouchsafed him to 'give his body,' and to experience in a martyr's death the literal completion of his fellowship of suffering and death with the Crucified.

[1] Phil. ii. 17, *ἀλλὰ εἰ καὶ σπένδομαι ἐπὶ τῇ θυσίᾳ καὶ λειτουργίᾳ τῆς πίστεως ὑμῶν, χαίρω καὶ συγχαίρω πᾶσιν ὑμῖν.* Cf. 2 Tim. iv. 6, and Rom. xv. 30 f.

[2] Cf. Rom. xv. 16 (p. 204 above).

ST. PAUL IN THE WORLD'S RELIGIOUS HISTORY

CHAPTER IX

ST. PAUL IN THE WORLD'S RELIGIOUS HISTORY

St. Paul the apostle's 'work of Christ'[1] culminates in a martyrdom like Christ's.

Recorded with blood in the annals of Christianity and mirrored to the historian in but a few pages of letters, his life-work irradiates the thought of the patristic and scholastic writers whose folios fill the libraries.

How are we to determine (what he never himself anticipated) his importance in the history of the world ?

Besides his great work in extending and organising the cult of Christ, which is specially obvious, the following are facts of world-wide importance in the history of religion.

Though not himself the founder of the new cult—the origin of the cult of Christ is the secret of the primitive mother church of Palestine—St. Paul underwent with elemental vehemence the experience of Christ which is the psychological preliminary to the cult of Christ, and he practically created the greater part of its classical forms of expression.

He made the religion of Christ world-wide by going beyond the Messianic, that is to say, specifically Jewish and national appreciation of the Person of

[1] Phil. ii. 30, τὸ ἔργον Χριστοῦ.

Jesus. Christ the Lord, Christ the Spirit—St. Paul having made these the centre of the faith, the ancient and Aramaic cult of the Messiah struggles forward to the position of a religion of all nations and of all times.

This Lord, this Spiritual Christ, however, bears also the features of the Man Jesus, the poor, humiliated Jesus of the Gospel tradition, who ministered lovingly and at last obediently was crucified. Thus Pauline Christianity, and through Paul Christianity at large, was saved from the excesses of mythological and theosophical imaginings. During well-nigh two thousand years of Christian speculation concerning Christ, the cross of Golgotha has ever remained a towering landmark to prevent all-too-subtle Christologists from losing their way completely. The identity insisted on by St. Paul of the Crucified with the Living and of the Living with the Crucified, of the Earthly with the Heavenly and the Heavenly with the Earthly, secures to the religion and cult of Christ two things: ethical sobriety and enthusiastic sincerity.

The mere Spiritual Christ, so easily liable to become attenuated to a mental conception about Christ, would have created neither a religion of the people nor a religion of the peoples, but would have remained a rapidly worn-out thesis for discussion by a narrow circle of Christologists. The mere historical Jesus would certainly have had greater carrying-power as the foundation of the new church, but would have made Christianity retrospective, bound by the Law like Judaism, rigid like Islam. The Pauline religion of Christ, with its outspoken confession of the Christ, present and to come, who is Jesus the Crucified, was able to create a communion of worship which was both popular and of world-wide historic effect, full of ethical power, not a book-religion looking backward to the Law, but a spiritual religion with face set forward.

The greatest of St. Paul's achievements, however, was this, that he connected Christian piety inseparably with the Person of Jesus Christ.

Jesus of Nazareth stood, with His experience of God and His mighty confidence in the nearness of the Kingdom of God, entirely self-supported. St. Paul placed himself and mankind with all their hopes and troubles in Christ. Where Jesus in lonely consciousness of His mission stands face to face with the Father, St. Paul stands before God, and with him stand the others, 'in Christ' and 'through Christ.'

Was St. Paul tampering with the old Gospel of Jesus concerning God and the nearness of His Kingdom when he thus incorporated with it religious faith in Christ?

No! He secured to the many the experience of God which had been the possession of One.

For the great mass of the weary and heavy-laden it is impossible to emulate the religious experience of Jesus, so heroic is its isolated independence. Immediacy in their experience of God is the privilege of the few religious geniuses who appear perhaps once in a thousand years. Even a St. Paul found grace not in the wild transport of ecstasy, but in the peace resulting from Christ's proximity; and if that was so, then of the poor dryasdust souls who sit down in their studies to write books about God, how many dare venture to wing their flight so as to behold Him?

The multitude most certainly who dwell below the altitude of learning—the insignificant many whose existence under God's sun and whose divine destiny are after all not annulled by the weary scoffing of the supposed superman [1]—these require the Paraclete and Mediator. Painfully they climb rung by rung the ladder which is set up to heaven, holding the hand of their Helper; but at each uncertain step there is more joy in heaven than over the titanic knowledge which thinketh to take the firmament by storm.

St. Paul's Christianity founded on Christ is the necessary form in which alone the Master's revelation of God could be assimilated by mankind, in which alone it could fashion a perennial religion for the people, and for the peoples a religion powerful enough to mould the history of the world. St. Paul did not invent a Christology for intellectual people to adopt intellectually. What he did was to draw on the depths of his own mystical and spiritual experience of Christ and to display before the eyes of the poor and humble, and such as feel themselves to be inwardly poor and humble, the Divine yet human Redeemer, in whose fellowship union with the Divine is vouchsafed even to the poorest and most helpless soul.

St. Paul's Christianity founded on Christ is therefore neither a breach with the Gospel of Jesus nor a sophistication of the Gospel of Jesus. It secures for the souls of the many the Gospel experience of God which had been the possession of One, and it does so by anchoring these many souls in the Soul of the One.

[1] 1 Cor. i 28.

APPENDICES

APPENDIX I

THE PROCONSULATE OF L. JUNIUS GALLIO

An Epigraphical Study towards the Absolute Chronology of St. Paul's Life.

(*See the phototyped facsimile facing title-page.*)

IN my book, "Light from the Ancient East," written only a few years ago, I used the following words [1] :—

> 'No tablets have yet been found to enable us to date exactly the years of office of the Procurators Felix and Festus or of the Proconsul Gallio, which would settle an important problem of early Christian history.'

The important problem of early Christian history which I hoped might be solved by tablets still resting beneath the accumulated rubbish of centuries, is the chronology of the apostolic age, particularly that of the Apostle Paul. We were not in a position to name one tolerably certain date that would place the relative chronology of St. Paul, which is in the main determinable, on a firm basis and thus bring us nearer to the absolute chronology.[2] There always

[1] *Light from the Ancient East*, p. 5.

[2] The fact is explainable from the character of the Primitive Christian tradition concerning St. Paul, to which attention has

remained a margin of uncertainty amounting to at least five years.

From the historians of the Imperial period, unless surprising fresh discoveries of lost texts should be made, there is scarcely anything new to be expected. Even such ingenious combinations of data as Eduard Schwartz [1] recently published concerning the years of office of Felix and Festus are not so convincing as to meet with general acceptance. Any real advance is to be expected rather from non-literary texts. Should it prove possible, for instance, to fix the proconsulship of Gallio in Achaia, which is mentioned in Acts xviii. 12, we should obtain a starting-point of special importance, because the clear statements of the narrator enable us to make further calculations backwards and forwards from this point.

Let us glance rapidly at the facts narrated in Acts xviii. St. Paul comes from Athens to Corinth.[2] There he finds Aquila the Jewish tentmaker, the husband of Priscilla, who had 'lately'[3] come to Corinth from Italy, having been banished with the other Jews from Rome by an edict of Claudius.[4] St. Paul is given lodging and employment in the house of his fellow-craftsman.[5] Every Sabbath he

been called more than once in the preceding pages of this book. Being tradition of a popular kind it had no interest in fixing facts chronologically; it is not calculated for the interests of scholars. As a whole it is the more trustworthy historically because so artless.

[1] 'Zur Chronologie des Paulus,' Nachrichten von der Kgl Gesellschaft der Wissenschaften zu Göttingen, philol.-histor. Klasse, 1907, pp. 264 ff. I mistrust Schwartz's paper partly on exegetical grounds.

[2] xviii. 1.

[3] προσφάτως, xviii. 2.

[4] xviii. 2.

[5] xviii. 3.

goes out evangelising, first in the Jewish synagogue before Jews and Greeks,[1] and then, after strong opposition from the Jews,[2] in the house of a proselyte named Titius Justus, hard by the synagogue,[3] with the highly successful result that Crispus, the ruler of the synagogue, with his family, and afterwards many of the Corinthians, came over to the faith and were baptized.[4] This whole period of missionary activity lasted a year and a half.[5]

> 'And he dwelt there a year and six months, teaching the word of God among them.'

After this clear statement of time the narrator continues[6]:—

> 'But when Gallio was proconsul of Achaia, the Jews with one accord rose up against Paul, and brought him before the judgment-seat, saying: "This man seduces men to an unlawful religion."'

The proconsul, however, refuses to be drawn into a trial; he declares that the dispute is an internal quarrel within the Jewish community, and orders the Jews away from his tribunal.[7] Enraged at their failure, the disappointed Jews fall upon

[1] xviii. 4 f.

[2] xviii. 6. It is probably this opposition that St. Paul himself alludes to in letters written at Corinth, 1 Thess. ii. 15 f., and 2 Thess. iii. 2.

[3] xviii. 7.

[4] xviii. 8 ff.

[5] xviii. 11.

[6] xviii. 12 f., Γαλλίωνος δὲ ἀνθυπάτου ὄντος τῆς Ἀχαΐας κατεπέστησαν ὁμοθυμαδὸν οἱ Ἰουδαῖοι τῷ Παύλῳ.—It is well known that Gallio was the brother of the philosopher Seneca.

[7] xviii. 14 ff.

the ruler of their own synagogue, Sosthenes, and maltreat him in the presence of the proconsul, who declines to interfere.[1] St. Paul, however, remains a considerable number of days[2] longer in Corinth after these events, and then sails for Syria by way of Ephesus.[3]

Any one reading this account for the first time, and knowing that the governors of the senatorial provinces, the proconsuls, held office normally for a period of one year,[4] would arrange the succession of events as follows:—

1. Edict of Claudius against the Jews: emigration of Aquila and Priscilla from Rome to Corinth.
2. Very soon afterwards,[5] arrival of St. Paul at Corinth.
3. A year and a half of missionary work at Corinth.
4. Arrival of the proconsul Gallio at Corinth.
5. The Jews accuse St. Paul before Gallio without success.
6. St. Paul remains still a considerable number of days at Corinth.
7. Departure of St. Paul for Ephesus and Syria.

The salient point in the series is No. 4. The phrase

'But when Gallio was proconsul of Achaia'

can only mean that, as St. Luke understood, after St. Paul had evangelised for a year and a half at Corinth, a new proconsul arrived in the person of Gallio, with whom the Jews then proceeded to

[1] xviii. 17.
[2] ἡμέρας ἱκανάς.
[3] xviii. 18 f.
[4] Cf. p. 252 below.
[5] Cf. προσφάτως, xviii. 2.

try their luck.[1] The passage has been thus, and rightly I think, explained by H. Lehmann[2] and Oskar Holtzmann,[3] not to mention other authorities.

If Gallio entered on his proconsulship in the month m of the year y, the arrival of St. Paul at Corinth would have to be dated approximately eighteen months earlier;[4] the arrival of Aquila and Priscilla at Corinth and the edict of Claudius against the Jews would be somewhat (but not much) earlier still. In the same way we should be able with some certainty to reconstruct the later chronology of St. Paul's life by starting from the year y.

Now what do we know about this year y? With the aid of a stone found at Delphi we can now calculate it with greater probability than has been possible hitherto.

For my first knowledge of this stone I was indebted to P. Thomsen, who in a bibliography[5]

[1] The case is exactly the same as in Acts xxiv. 27–xxv. 2, where St. Luke tells us that after two years a new procurator came and the Jews then renewed proceedings against St. Paul before him.

[2] *Claudius und Nero und ihre Zeit*, vol. i., Claudius und seine Zeit, Gotha, 1858, p. 354: when Gallio 'arrived at Corinth, the Jews immediately brought an accusation against St. Paul, who had been working for eighteen months in the city.'

[3] *Neutestamentliche Zeitgeschichte*,[2] Tübingen, 1906, p. 132: 'St. Paul's first residence at Corinth lasted a year and a half (Acts xviii. 11). Towards the end if not after the expiry of this time (Acts xviii. 12 f., 18) Gallio became proconsul of Achaia.'

[4] In making the calculation of course we must be generous enough not to insist on the 'eighteen months' down to the last minute; but we may employ that number as a clear approximate determination, requiring at utmost but a small amount of adjustment.

[5] Mitteilungen und Nachrichten des Deutschen Palästina-Vereins, 1909, p. 31.

of the year 1909 referred to Joseph Offord's account [1] of the four fragments of a Delphic inscription published by Émile Bourguet.[2] I may as well add at once the other references to the inscription which are known to me. Alexander Nikitsky,[3] I believe, was the first to publish a fragment of the stone; he gave a drawing of it, but, as far as I can see, without any detailed discussion and without causing anybody to take further notice of the fragment. H. Pomtow, however, had already among his papers, which he kindly allowed me to examine in December, 1910, for the purposes of the present work, a copy of the main portion of the inscription, with which he has been acquainted for more than twenty years. In the autumn of 1910 he obtained for me, through the kind offices of his collaborator in epigraphy, Dr. Rüsch, an accurate photograph of the published fragments together with a paper squeeze.[4] Before this A. J.-Reinach, in reviewing Bourguet's work, had pointed out the importance of the inscription in

[1] 'St. Paul at Corinth,' Palestine Exploration Fund, Quarterly Statement, April, 1908, p. 163 (cf. also January, 1908, p. 5).

[2] *De rebus Delphicis* imperatoriae aetatis capita duo [a Paris thesis], Montepessulano, 1905, p. 63 f. Bourguet did not go into the chronology of St. Paul; he contented himself with stating Gallio's year of office as A.D. 52, on the authority of the *Prosopographia*. Cf. p. 255 n. 2 below.

[3] In his Russian work, brought to my notice by H. Pomtow, on 'Epigraphical Studies at Delphi,' I.–VI., Odessa, 1894–95, Plate VII., No. xlvii. It is the large fragment which stands second in our facsimile.

[4] From which the phototyped facsimile to accompany the present volume was made by Albert Frisch, Royal Art Printing Works, Berlin W. 35. In order to secure a sharper reproduction of what has been preserved, the under surface of the squeeze was photographed.

determining St. Paul's chronology, and as far as I can see he was the first to do so[1] :—

> 'ce texte fixe définitivement à 52 le séjour de saint Paul à Corinthe.'

Offord then in the article already mentioned[2] placed the beginning of Gallio's proconsulship in the year 52, the arrival of St. Paul at Corinth in the autumn of the year 52, and his departure from Corinth in the beginning of the year 53.

Sir W. M. Ramsay[3] calculated on the authority of the inscription that Gallio's proconsulship ran from April, 52, to April, 53, and that St. Paul arrived at Corinth in October, 51.

H. Coppieters[4] did not himself offer any figures, but merely remarked that the inscription would make it possible to fix the date of the proconsulship, while Louis Jalabert[5] described Bourguet's statement (Gallio's year of office A.D. 52) as important for the calculation of St. Paul's chronology.

Carl Clemen,[6] also accepting Bourguet's date of A.D. 52 for Gallio's proconsulship,[7] considered it to be a confirmation of his own earlier calculation.[8]

The Delphic inscription had occupied my attention

[1] Revue des Études grecques, 20 (1907), p. 49. I am indebted to Louis Jalabert for the reference.

[2] *Loc. cit.*, p. 164.

[3] The Expositor, May, 1909, p. 468 f.

[4] *Dictionnaire apologétique de la Foi catholique*, Tome I. (Paris, 1910), col. 268.

[5] *Ibid.*, col. 1428 (article 'Épigraphie').

[6] Theologische Literaturzeitung, 35 (1910), col. 656.

[7] '... that Gallio was proconsul of Achaia in the year 52.'

[8] *Paulus*, I. p. 396, '... that Gallio arrived at Corinth in the spring of 52.'

for a considerable time when, in a short notice[1] of Jalabert's *Épigraphie*, I announced my intention of publishing a closer investigation of the text.[2]

A few months later there appeared an article written by E. C. Babut and Alfred Loisy,[3] who had no knowledge of the preceding stages of the discussion.[4] Babut calculated that the proconsulship of Gallio extended from the first third of the year 52 to the first third of 53,[5] and accordingly Loisy, whose hypertrophied critical mistrust of the above analysed report in the Acts of the Apostles makes him very suspicious, was of opinion that the accusation of St. Paul before Gallio, if historical, must be placed in the year 52 or the beginning of the year 53.[6]

Finally, William P. Armstrong,[7] who refers to a portion at least of the preceding discussion, including Jalabert's note and my own, reprinted Bourguet's text and calculated Gallio's period of office as from the spring or early summer of 51 to that of 52, or (which he thought more probable) from 52 to 53.

To me the most important fact in the whole discussion, apart from Bourguet's original publica-

[1] Theologische Literaturzeitung, 35 (1910), col. 796.

[2] My investigation was finished in all but a few particulars in March, 1911; on 2 May, 1911, I offered some remarks on the subject in the Archaeological Society at Berlin.

[3] 'Le proconsul Gallion et saint Paul,' Revue d'Histoire et de Littérature réligieuses, 2 (1911), pp. 139-144 of the number for March and April.

[4] Cf. their expression of astonishment (p. 139) that no student of St. Paul had noticed the document although it had been published for five years.

[5] *Loc. cit.*, p. 142.

[6] *Ibid.*, p. 144.

[7] The Princeton Theological Review, April, 1911, pp. 293–298.

tion, was the statement by Babut[1] that meanwhile, in addition to the four fragments already published, three new fragments of the Delphic inscription had been discovered. Just as I was about to send my own manuscript to the printer I received from Babut a photograph of these fragments,[2] which he very kindly sent me at my request, and soon afterwards Bourguet sent me with the same scholarly courtesy, also at my request, the squeeze of two of these fragments and a copy of all three.[3]

On the 30th April, 1911, Pomtow had very kindly given me a squeeze which he took in 1887 of the middle fragment of the three.[4] This had already been published by Nikitsky.[5] Even in 1887 Pomtow, as is clear from his MS. papers, had been led by the similarity of the lettering to compare this fragment with those which Bourguet afterwards published, so far as they were then accessible. He decided, however, from differences in the spaces between the lines, that it could not be united with them. Even to-day Pomtow is of opinion that the 'new' fragments, though carved by the same stonemason as the old ones, did not form part of the text of the same rescript, but were probably the conclusion of another rescript. In further proof of this he refers to differences in the height of the letters in the two groups of fragments.

[1] *Loc. cit.*, p. 139.

[2] With letter dated Montpellier, 23 April, 1911.

[3] With letter dated Athens, 8 May, 1911. These were the two Delphi fragments Nos. 728 and 500. Bourguet very kindly added a new squeeze of the greater part of the old fragments already published by him.

[4] This is fragment No. 2311. I have thus seen squeezes of all three of the 'new' fragments.

[5] Plate VII., No. xlvi.

I am unable at present to decide the question whether the 'new' fragments really belong to the old ones or not; to do so I should be obliged in the first place to examine the tablets myself at Delphi. Pomtow's argument from the spacing of the lines and the size of the letters does not seem to me absolutely convincing, because in both these respects even the old fragments are not quite uniform in their workmanship. Here, however, I may be quite content to leave the question open. Valuable as the 'new' fragments are in reconstructing the text of the rescript of Claudius, if they do belong to the others, they seem to me to throw no new light so far on our particular chronological problem.[1]

I may therefore, I think, confine my attention here to the old fragments.

I proceed first to the description and text of the four old fragments. For the details of the description I am indebted to Pomtow's MS. papers.

The material is whitish grey limestone from the Hagios Elias quarries near Delphi. The four fragments are now preserved in the Museum at Delphi, their numbers in the collection[2] being 3883, 2178, 2271,[3] 4001.

[1] Two of these fragments have not yet been published; the third may be read in Nikitsky's book (see p. 243 n. 5 above). I of course respect the wish expressed to me by Bourguet that I should use the unpublished fragments he sent me with discretion, and therefore refrain from giving their text or a facsimile of them. It is to be hoped that we shall soon be indebted to the approved scholarship of Bourguet for an edition of the text and a settlement of the special question touched on above.

[2] The numbers are here given in the order in which the fragments stand in the text.

[3] Bourguet p. 63 gives the old number, 59.

Our facsimile [1] gives these four fragments in what is supposed to be their original positions,[2] on a reduced scale of about 1 : 3·4. The height of the letters amounts to 18–20 millimetres (*i.e.*, about three-quarters of an inch). Pomtow is confident that the inscription was originally set up on an outer wall of the south side of the temple of Apollo at Delphi.

The text seems to be horribly mutilated, and it really is so. But, nevertheless, as regards those portions which concern our problem, we may say that chance has for once behaved reasonably and benevolently. Just those passages which are of the most importance to us are clearly legible and quite usable.

The length of the lines in the inscription is, I think, certainly underestimated by Bourguet, who by restoration brought the first line up to a total of 54 letters. The title of *pontifex maximus* forms part of the full style of Claudius,[3] and I have therefore inserted ἀρχιερεὺς μέγιστος, thus making a line of 71 letters. The original line of the inscription must have been about 1·40 metre long (*i.e.*, 55 inches). In

[1] Facing the title-page of this book.

[2] In the opinion of the archaeologists who have examined the originals (Pomtow, Bourguet, and Rüsch) there can be no doubt that the fragments really do all belong together.

[3] Gaheis in Pauly-Wissowa, *Real-Encyclopädie* der klassischen Altertumswissenschaft, 3 (Stuttgart, 1899), col. 2787.—Occasionally ἀρχιερεύς occurs alone as equivalent to *pontifex maximus* (David Magie, De Romanorum iuris publici sacrique vocabulis sollemnibus in Graecum sermonem conversis, Lipsiae, 1905, p. 64); I have preferred the longer formula because that seems to me to predominate in the other known rescripts of Claudius. But we must of course reckon with the possibility that ἀρχιερεύς, the shorter expression, may be the right reading.

the first line the letters seem to be somewhat farther apart than in the following lines.

The text with probable restorations is given opposite.[1]

In ordinary script, with a few additional restorations which I have essayed for the sake of illustration, and for which I must refer to the commentary, the text would be as follows :—

Τιβέρ[ιος Κλαύδιος Κ]αῖσ[αρ Σεβαστ]ὸς Γ[ερμανικός, ἀρχιερεὺς μέγιστος, δημαρχικῆς ἐξου-]
σίας [τὸ ιβ′, αὐτοκράτωρ τ]ὸ κϛ′, π[ατὴρ π]ατρί[δος, ὕπατος
τὸ ε′, τιμητής, Δελφῶν τῆι πόλει χαίρειν].
Πάλ[αι μὲν] τῆι π[όλει] τῶν Δελφ[ῶν πρόθ]υμο[ς γενόμενος
. . . . εὐτύ-]
χησα. Ἐπετήρη[σα δὲ τὴ]ν θρησκεί[αν τ]οῦ Ἀπό[λλωνος
τοῦ Πυθίου . . . .
νῦν λέγεται καὶ [πολ]ειτῶν ερι . . [ἐ]κεῖναι ω . . . .
. . . . [καθὼς Λούκιος Ἰού-]
νιος Γαλλίων ὁ φ[ίλος] μου κα[ὶ ἀνθύ]πατος [τῆς Ἀχαΐας
ἔγραψεν. . . . . διὰ τοῦτο συγχωρῶ ὑμᾶς]
ἔτι ἕξειν τὸν πρό[τερ]ο[ν . . . . . .]ε[. . . . .
. . . . τῶν ἄλ-]
λων πόλεων κα — — — (about 60 letters)
αὐτοῖς ἐπιτρέ[πω — — (about 58 letters)
φῶν ὡς πολε— — — — (about 62 letters)
ται μετῴκι[σα — — — (about 62 letters)
[το]ύτου — — — — — (about 65 letters)
— — — — — — — — — — — — — — — — — — — —
— — — — — — — — — — — — — — — — — — — —

In commenting on this text we may start from the undoubted fact that we have here before us one of the Imperial letters such as have been preserved by ancient authors, and especially by inscriptions.[2] It

[1] The imperfect letters are restored by means of dotted lines; probable restorations of lacunae are printed in small type.

[2] Cf. *Light from the Ancient East*, pp. 379 f.

ΤΙΒΕΡ ιος κλαυδιος ΚΑΙΣ αρσεβαστΟΣ Γερμανικος αρχιερευς μεγιστος δημαρχικης εξου
ΣΙΑΣ το ·ιβ| αυτοκρατωρ τΟ·ΚΣΙΠ ατηρ πΑΤΡΙ δος υπατος το ·ε| τιμητης δελφων τηι πολει χαιρειν
ΠΑΛαι μεν ΤΗΙΠ ολει ΤΩΝ ΔΕΛΦων προθΥΜΟς γενομενος .... ευτυ
ΧΗΣΑΕΠΕΤΗΡΗσα δε τη ΝΘΡΗΣΚΕΙαν τΟΥΑΠΟλλωνος του πυθιου ....
ΝΥΝΛΕΓΕΤΑΙΚΑΙ πολ ΕΙΤΩΝΕΡΙ .. εΚΕΙΝΑΙΩ .... λουκιος ιου
ΝΙΟΣΓΑΛΛΙΩΝΟΦ ιλος ΜΟΥΚΑ ιανθυ ΠΑΤΟΣ της αχαιας ....
ΕΤΙΕΞΕΙΝΤΟΝΠΡΟ τερΟν .... ΙΙΕ ....
ΛΩΝΠΟΛΕΩΝΚΑ
ΑΥΤΟΙΣΕΠΙΤΡΕ πω
ΦΩΝΩΣΠΟΛΕ
ΤΑΙΜΕΤΩΚΙ σα
τοΥΤΟΥ

THE GALLIO INSCRIPTION TRANSCRIBED AND RESTORED.

is no less evident that it is a letter from the Emperor Claudius to the city of Delphi, although the name of the addressee in the praescript has been lost. We may assume from the first—and this is of importance in attempting the restoration of the mutilated text—that the contents of the letter must have been something favourable to Delphi.[1] The Emperor Claudius perhaps guaranteed anew some old privileges of the sacred city, just as he confirmed to the Jews of Alexandria their old privileges by letter,[2] and in a letter to the authorities of Jerusalem graciously settled a question that strongly excited the religious sensibilities of the Jews.[3] Other inscriptions, some of them newly published by Bourguet,[4] prove that the relations of this very Emperor Claudius to Delphi were of long standing and friendly. Excellent analogies are also furnished by numerous letters from other emperors to the city of Delphi. Recorded, like the letter of Claudius, in the form of an inscription, they were public documents, and a good proportion of them have come down to us in considerable fragments.[5]

We come now to details. Line 1 has already been discussed as regards the probable number of letters it contained. The restoration of the name of Claudius is quite certain.

Line 2 is the most important as bearing on our problem, because it contains the decisive date. The

[1] Otherwise the document would hardly have been recorded on stone and set up on the temple of Apollo.

[2] Josephus, *Antt.* xix. 5, 2, has preserved the text of this letter of Claudius.

[3] This letter of Claudius has also been handed down by Josephus, *Antt.* xx. 1, 2.

[4] *De rebus Delphicis*, pp. 62 f.

[5] Cf. Bourguet, pp. 59–93.

12 denoting the number of times Claudius had been invested with the tribunician power (δημαρχικὴ ἐξουσία) is only restored, but the 26 (κϛ) denoting the number of times he had been acclaimed imperator (αὐτοκράτωρ), which is of far greater importance to us, is above all doubt. At my request Hermann Dessau most obligingly put together for me in January, 1911, the available materials for calculating the 26th acclamation of Claudius as imperator [1] :—

"Altogether Claudius was acclaimed imperator 27 times. As *imperator XXVII.* he appears for the first time on a monument of the 12th year of his tribunician power (which ran from 25 January, A.D. 52, till the same date in 53), viz. a monumental arch [2] of the Aqua Claudia at Rome inscribed:—

> Ti. Claudius Drusi f. Caisar Augustus Germanicus pontif. maxim., tribunicia potestate XII., cos. V., imperator XXVII., pater patriae.

"As the aqueduct was dedicated [3] on 1 August, 52, the inscription should give the style of Claudius as it was on 1 August, 52.

"Claudius appears as *imperator XXVI.* in several inscriptions besides the one from Delphi. To begin with there is C.I.L. VIII. suppl. No. 14727 (Africa)

[1] Cf., moreover, Gaheis, *loc. cit.*, col. 2812 f. I give the data *in extenso*, because erroneous statements have been made more than once in previous discussions of the question. Some writers especially have partly misunderstood the statements of Cagnat, *Cours d'épigraphie latine*, Supplément à la troisième édition, Paris, 1904, p. 478.

[2] *Corpus Inscriptionum Latinarum*, VI., No. 1256 = Dessau, *Inscriptiones selectae*, No. 218. Only the beginning of the inscription is quoted above.

[3] Frontinus, *De aquis*, i. 13.

and XIII. No. 254 (Aquitania).[1] The year of his tribunician power, wanting in both these instances, is given in an inscription from the Carian city of Cys[2]:—

Τιβέριον Κλαύδιον Καίσαρα Γερμανικὸν αὐτοκράτορα θεὸν Σεβαστόν, ἀρχιερέα μέγιστον, δημαρχικῆς ἐξουσίας τὸ δωδέκατον, ὕπατον τὸ πέμπτον, αὐτοκράτορα τὸ εἰκοστὸν καὶ ἕκτον, πατέρα πατρίδος.

"This inscription certainly belongs to the period between the beginning of the 12th tribunician power and the first appearance of the 27th imperatorial acclamation, *i.e.*, between 25 January and 1 August, 52.

"It is highly probable that the imperial letter contained in the Delphi inscription is also to be placed in this period, although it is not altogether impossible that Claudius received his 26th imperatorial acclamation during his 11th tribunician power.[3] He certainly received his 22nd and 24th imperatorial acclamations during his 11th tribunician year,[4] and, of course, also the 23rd, though that has not yet been found recorded. The 25th has also not yet been found, but it might fall likewise in the 11th tribunician year, *i.e.*, before 25 January, 52. If the 26th also occurred in the 11th year it could only be towards the end of that year, *i.e.*, at the end of 51 or in January, 52. But this assumption cannot be regarded as at all probable."

[1] For this passage, which is not mentioned in Dessau's note, I am indebted to Lehmann (*Claudius*, Book IV., p. 43), who quoted it from Muratori.

[2] Bulletin de Correspondance Hellénique, 11 (1887), p. 306 f.

[3] We should then have to read τὸ ιαʹ instead of τὸ ιβʹ in line 2 of the Gallio inscription.

[4] References are given by Gaheis, *loc. cit.*, col. 2812.

The small margin of uncertainty in dating the 26th imperatorial acclamation does not matter as far as our question is concerned. *Claudius addressed his letter to Delphi at some time between (the end of 51, or more probably) the beginning of 52 and 1 August, 52.*

In line 2 I have supplied conjecturally the titles of consul (ὕπατος) and censor (τιμητής). The formula Δελφῶν τῆι πόλει χαίρειν agrees in the order of its words with the usage of the praescripts in other imperial letters.

Bourguet in 1905 took line 3 as part of the praescript,[1] restoring it thus: πάλ[ιν ? τ]ῆι π[όλει τ]ῶν Δελφ[ῶν προθ]υμό[τατα χαίρειν]. As regards both form and contents this restoration seems to me to be open to grave objection; προθυμότατα χαίρειν would, I think, be quite unusual. Bourguet now, however, as he informed me in the letter mentioned above, proposes a different restoration: . . . τῇ] παλ[αιοτά]τηι π[όλει τ]ῶν Δελφ[ῶν, which Baron Hiller von Gaertringen[2] had also conjectured independently. Attractive as this restoration is, it seems unusual to me if it is to form part of the praescript of the letter; cf. the remark on line 2 above. For my conjecture πάλαι . . ., which would be the beginning of the Emperor's reference to his old feelings of friendly interest in Delphi, cf., for instance, the beginning of the edict of Gn. Vergilius Capito[3] (48 A.D.), καὶ πάλαι μὲν ἤκουον.

In line 4, to judge from the squeeze taken by Rüsch, χησα is, I think, more probable than Bourguet's χ . . ισα. We might then conjecture

[1] *De rebus Delphicis*, p. 63.

[2] Letter dated Westend, 29 April, 1911.

[3] In the inscription given by Dittenberger, *Orientis Graeci Inscriptiones Selectae*, No. 665_{15}.

[εὐτύ]χησα, which fits in not badly, I think, with what we should expect the thought to be: the Emperor says with condescending hyperbole that it has been his happiness hitherto to give the city of Delphi signs of his favour. An exact parallel to the following sentence,[1] 'I have observed the worshipping of Apollo,'[2] is furnished by a letter of Hadrian's to Delphi[3]: καὶ εἰς τὴν ἀρ[χαιότητα τῆ]ς πόλεως καὶ εἰς τὴν τοῦ κατέχοντος α[ὐτὴν θεοῦ θρησ]κείαν[4] ἀφορῶν. So, too, Claudius speaks of the πάτριος θρησκεία in his letter to the Jews of Alexandria,[5] and similarly in his letter to the authorities at Jerusalem.[6]

In lines 5 and 6 the restored reading ['Ιού]νιος is beyond doubt; Λούκιος is probable.[7]

In line 6 ὁ φ[ίλος] μου κα[ὶ ἀνθύ]πατος is also unexceptionable. 'My dearest friends'[8] is the term applied to King Agrippa and King Herod by Claudius in his edict of toleration for the Jews.[9] The expression 'friend' seems to have been in official use with special reference to provincial governors. Trajan in a letter to the town of Delphi speaks of [ἀ]νθυπάτῳ καὶ φίλῳ μου 'Ερενν[ί]ῳ Σατορνείνῳ;[10] and in a

[1] Hiller von Gaertringen attempts a quite different restoration: ἀπ' ἀρ]χῆς ἀεί [τ' or γ'] ἐτηρή[σατε τὴ]ν, etc. I prefer the restoration given above for the sake of the parallel from the letter of Hadrian; in the main it is Bourguet's.

[2] Instead of τ]οῦ 'Από[λλωνος] we might also conjecture θε]οῦ 'Από[λλωνος].

[3] Bourguet, p. 78.

[4] For the genitive after θρησκεία cf. also Col. ii. 18, θρησκεία τῶν ἀγγέλων.

[5] Cf. p. 247 n. 2 above. [6] Cf. p. 247 n. 3 above.

[7] Cf. p. 259 below, the Gallio inscription from Plataea.

[8] On the expression 'friend of the Emperor' cf. *Light from the Ancient East*, p. 383.

[9] Josephus, *Antt.* xix. 5, 3, τῶν φιλτάτων μοι.

[10] Bourguet, p. 70.

letter from Marcus Aurelius to the Synodus of Smyrna the Proconsul T. Atilius Maximus is called ὁ κράτιστος ἀνθύπατος καὶ φίλος ἡμῶν.[1] The whole form of expression tends to show that Gallio was the Proconsul in office at the time of the letter.[2]

We may here at once discuss the question of the dating of his proconsulship.[3] The governors of the senatorial provinces, the *proconsules* (ἀνθύπατοι), whom the Senate as a rule appointed by lot, held office for a year.[4] It was an exception for a proconsul to remain longer in office. It is on record that the exception of a proconsulship lasting for two years occurred in some cases under Claudius,[5] but I consider it very probable that in this particular case of the proconsuls of Achaia the rule was observed.

In the year 44 the province of Achaia, which had previously for some time been combined with Macedonia and had been under a *legatus Augusti pro praetore* was given back to the Senate by Claudius.[6] Was he likely, in this special case of a province restored to the Senate, so soon afterwards to disregard the privilege of the Senate, which lay in the

[1] Dittenberger, *Sylloge*,[2] No. 406.

[2] Numerous examples of the mention of the proconsul in office in imperial letters will be found in Léon Lafoscade, *De epistulis* (aliisque titulis) imperatorum magistratuumque Romanorum . . . (a Paris thesis), Insulis, 1902, p. 127, under ἀνθύπατος.

[3] Here, too, I am indebted for kind assistance to Dessau.

[4] Theodor Mommsen, *Römisches Staatsrecht*, I.,[3] p. 255.

[5] Dio Cassius, lx. 25, 6, καίτοι καὶ ἐπὶ δύο ἔτη τινὰς ἐῶν αὐτῶν ἄρχειν (44–45 A.D.).

[6] Dio Cassius, lx. 24, 1, τήν τε Ἀχαΐαν καὶ τὴν Μακεδονίαν αἱρετοῖς ἄρχουσιν, ἐξ οὗπερ ὁ Τιβέριος ἦρξε, διδομένας ἀπέδωκεν ὁ Κλαύδιος τότε τῷ κλήρῳ.

annual nomination of the governors of its provinces? Moreover, there is the fact that Gallio fell ill with fever in Achaia, and himself attributed the disease to the climate;[1] it is therefore not exactly credible that he should have remained there any longer than necessary. In any case, however, it seems to me that in chronological calculations what we have to do is to take the normal condition of things as our basis, not the remotely possible exception.[2] We must assume that the proconsulship of Gallio lasted one year until it has been proved to have lasted longer.

Now if Gallio, on the evidence of the Delphi inscription, was in office in the period of the 26th imperatorial acclamation of Claudius, it is possible to calculate with great probability the date of his entry upon his duties. Gallio's *entry* upon office is the salient point of the problem.

The mistaken notion occurs not infrequently that the date in the calendar year at which a proconsulship began was somewhere about 1 April.[3]

A more inconvenient date, however, could hardly

[1] Seneca, *Ep. Mor.*, 104, 1: 'Illud mihi in ore erat domini mei Gallionis, qui cum in Achaia febrim habere coepisset, protinus navem adscendit clamitans non corporis esse sed loci morbum.'

[2] This is rightly insisted on by Sir W. M. Ramsay, The Expositor, May, 1909, p. 469.

[3] For instance, Carl Clemen in his excellent *Paulus*, i., Giessen, 1904, p. 396, says that the office had 'to be entered on before the beginning of April by a law of Claudius,' and refers to Dio Cassius, lx. 13, 17. But there is no such passage; the reference probably comes from Gustav Hoennicke, *Die Chronologie des Lebens des Apostels Paulus*, Leipzig, 1903, p. 28, where, however, it is said more correctly that by a law of Claudius the new proconsuls had to leave Rome before the beginning of April. The intended reference is Dio Cassius, lx. 17, 3.

be imagined, because it would compel the proconsuls, if their province was at a great distance from Rome, to travel at the most unfavourable time of the year. We possess, moreover, positive information. Tiberius in 15 A.D. had decreed that the officials should leave Rome 'within' the new moon of the month of June;[1] this would point to 1 July as the day of entry upon office, a date that would in many respects be a favourably chosen one. Obviously, however, the time was not exactly ample for reaching some provinces, and it must have been recognised that the date had not been happily chosen. Claudius therefore—no doubt also because he was annoyed by the length of time that the new dignitaries hung about the capital—gave orders in A.D. 42 that they must start before the April new moon.[2] In the following year he reduced this very early date to the time before the middle of April.[3]

We may therefore say that the date of the *entry* upon office was about the middle of the calendar year—at any rate some time in summer.[4]

The account in the Acts of the Apostles seems to me to harmonise with this conjecture. If, as seems to me beyond doubt, Acts xviii. 12 speaks of the *new* proconsul, we obtain for St. Paul's voyage to

[1] Dio Cassius, lvii. 14, 5, ἐκέλευσέ σφισιν ἐντὸς τῆς τοῦ Ἰουνίου νουμηνίας ἀφορμᾶσθαι. That is, of course, to be understood as the last possible date of departure.

[2] Dio Cassius, lx. 11, 6, κατέδειξε δὲ καὶ τάδε, τούς τε κληρωτοὺς ἄρχοντας πρὸ τῆς τοῦ Ἀπριλίου νουμηνίας, ἐπειδήπερ ἐπὶ πολὺ ἐν τῷ ἄστει ἐνεχρόνιζον, ἀφορμᾶσθαι.

[3] Dio Cassius, lx. 17, 3, πρὸς δ' ἔτι τοῖς ἄρχουσι τοῖς κληρωτοῖς, βραδέως ἔτι καὶ τότε ἐκ τῆς πόλεως ἐξορμωμένοις, προεῖπε πρὶν μεσοῦν τὸν Ἀπρίλιον ἀπαίρειν.

[4] Mommsen, *Staatsrecht*, II.,[3] p. 256, assumes 1 July as the normal date.

Syria (Acts xviii. 18 ff.) the very best time of the year :—

about July beginning of the new proconsulship,

soon afterwards unsuccessful accusation brought by the Jews,

further residence of St. Paul at Corinth,

departure for Syria (say) in August or September of the same year.[1]

If then the letter of Claudius to Delphi was written between (the end of 51 or, more probably) the beginning of 52 and 1 August, 52, and Gallio was then[2] in office, *he entered on his proconsulship in the summer* (nominally 1 July ?) *of 51 A.D.*[3]

Line 6 f. The restoration of the end of line 6 is

[1] There is an interesting parallel in the date at which Festus, the imperial procurator, happened to enter on his office. Harnack (*Die Chronologie der altchristlichen Litteratur bis Eusebius*, vol. i., Leipzig, 1897, p. 237) very rightly conjectures, from the statement in the Acts of the Apostles concerning St. Paul's departure for Rome, that Festus entered on his duties in summer. Of course, no decisive weight is to be attached to this parallel, because it is not concerned with a proconsulship lasting for one year.

[2] In the *Prosopographia Imperii Romani*, II., Berolini, 1897, p. 238, Dessau gave 52 as the date of Gallio's proconsulship, and Bourguet (p. 64) obviously regarded it as an established fact. In 1897, however, it was only a conjecture, though a happy one. 'The fact that the date now proves to be right is no justification for having assumed it then,' Dessau wrote to me on 20 January, 1911.

[3] The purely logical possibility that he entered on his official duties on 1 July, 52, and that the letter of Claudius was written between 1 July and 1 August, 52, suggests itself for a moment, but only to be rejected as altogether improbable. The 1 August, 52, is not the day on which Claudius received his 27th imperatorial acclamation, but only the *terminus ante quem* for this title.

of course not certain; συγχωρῶ at any rate is the technical expression for the conferring of imperial favours.[1] The words ἔτι ἕξειν τὸν πρό[τερ]ο[ν] suggest, what was *a priori* probable, that some earlier privileges of Delphi were to be confirmed.

Line 7 f. might of course be restored as [πολ]λῶν πόλεων.[2]

In line 9 f. I should conjecture with Pomtow [Δελ]φῶν ὡς. Bourguet's [συμ]φώνως is, however, just as well possible.

In line 12 considerations of space make [το]ύτου more probable than Bourguet's [ἀ]υτοῦ.

The conclusions as regards the chronology of St. Paul are easily drawn. If Gallio entered on his office approximately in the middle of the summer of 51, and if the accusation of St. Paul by the Jews took place soon afterwards, then, since he had already been working for approximately eighteen months in Corinth, *St. Paul must have come to Corinth in the first months of the year 50, and left Corinth late in the summer of the year 51.*

I refrain from comparing this calculation with the more or less divergent results obtained by others above named who have made use of the Gallio inscription. I have given all the materials, and every one can make this examination for himself. Still less is there any need for me to show seriatim the incorrectness of earlier attempts to find a merely hypothetically possible date, varying from A.D. 48

[1] Cf. the letter of Claudius in Josephus, *Antt.*, xix. 5, 3, Trajan's letter to Delphi in Bourguet, p. 70 (which I suppose is rightly restored), and Lafoscade, p. 110 f.

[2] But cf. ταῖ[ς] ἄλ[λαις] πόλεσιν in a letter of Hadrian's, Bourguet, p. 79.

to A.D. 54, for Gallio's proconsulship. I would rather note that as early as 1858 H. Lehmann,[1] whose knowledge of the sources for the time of Claudius was very exact, got at the truth (and at the same time stated the problem in the true way) when he placed Gallio's *entry* on office in the summer of 51.

I should like, however, at least to refer to the confirmation which my calculation of the time of St. Paul's stay at Corinth receives from a statement which has often been noted in Orosius. On the authority of 'Josephus' Orosius says that Claudius in the ninth year of his reign expelled the Jews from Rome.[2] That would mean the year which ran from 25 January, 49, to the same date in 50. And since St. Paul on arriving at Corinth met Aquila the tentmaker there, Aquila having 'lately'[3] arrived from Italy after his expulsion from Rome by the edict of Claudius, from this also we could conclude that, if the apostle reached Corinth at the beginning of the year 50, the year 49 would be approximately the year of the edict of Claudius against the Jews.

Sir W. M. Ramsay,[4] it is true, maintains that Orosius is always a year behind in his chronology of

[1] *Claudius*, p. 354. It is true, he places the arrival of St. Paul at Corinth as early as the end of the year 49 (p. 332); but even this is not impossible.

[2] Orosius, vii. 6, 15, 'Anno eiusdem nono expulsos per Claudium urbe Iudaeos Iosephus refert.' The same statement in Bede, *De temporum ratione*, a. 4007, is certainly taken from Orosius.

[3] Acts xviii. 2, προσφάτως ἐληλυθότα ἀπὸ τῆς Ἰταλίας . . . διὰ τὸ τεταχέναι Κλαύδιον χωρίζεσθαι πάντας τοὺς Ἰουδαίους ἀπὸ τῆς Ῥώμης.

[4] *St. Paul the Traveller and the Roman Citizen*,[11] pp. 254 and 68; The Expositor, May, 1909, p. 468. He therefore places the expulsion of the Jews 'according to Orosius' in the year 50.

Claudius; but that does not dispose of the remarkable coincidence between our calculation and Orosius, for in this case Orosius is giving not his own chronology but that of his authority, 'Josephus,' and (this is very important to observe) without attaching much value to Josephus.[1] In our texts of Flavius Josephus the statement, it must be admitted, is wanting. It is possible that Orosius means some other 'Josephus,'[2] or that he has made a mistake in the name of his authority; but the statement itself, for which he does not profess any particular respect, 'cannot be his own invention.'[3] That I take to be obvious,[4] though I do not wish to attach decisive weight to the coincidence with Orosius.

[1] In vii. 6, 15, he continues: 'Sed me magis Suetonius movet qui ait hoc modo: Claudius Iudaeos impulsore Christo adsidue tumultuantes Roma expulit.'

[2] This conjecture is not so remote as it may seem at first sight. In the ancient Church there was current a collection of facts to be committed to memory, probably chiefly for catechetical purposes, large portions of which are preserved in the *Hypomnesticon* of the so-called 'Christian Josephus' (Joseppus Christianus), and which is to some extent much older than the *Hypomnesticon*. In the list of high priests in this 'Josephus' (ii. 80, Migne, Patrologia Graeca, 106), which still awaits investigation, the beginning of the war of the Jews against the Romans is dated *ἔτους ὀγδόου Κλαυδίου*, the reference perhaps being to the Jewish rebellion under Ventidius Cumanus (Schürer, I.,[3] p. 568 f.; in the English translation, *History of the Jewish People*, First Division, trs. by Rev. John Macpherson, vol. ii., Edinburgh, 1890, pp. 171–3). Here, it seems, is a 'Josephus' who gives us a date in the reign of Claudius similar to the one found in Orosius.

[3] Schürer, III.,[4] p. 62 (a passage which is not to be found in the English translation, Second Division, trs. by Sophia Taylor and Rev. Peter Christie, vol. ii., Edinburgh, 1885, p. 237). Earlier in his text he dates the edict 'probably 49 A.D.'

[4] Harnack, *Chronologie*, i. p. 236, also considers the statement worthy of notice.

The inscription at Delphi does not exhaust the epigraphical material referring to Gallio. There is a tablet from Pompeii,[1] inscribed with a receipt, which bears on the question of his consulship, and has been often made use of,[2] though it still unfortunately offers some puzzles. Besides this there is a Boeotian inscription[3] which certainly mentions Gallio, perhaps as Proconsul, but without a date. The inscription was found on a pedestal in an abandoned chapel of Hagios Taxiarches, not far from Plataea[4]:—

ΗΠΟΛΙϹΠΛΑΤΑΙΕΩΝΛΟΥΚ /////
ΝΙΟΝΓΑΛΛΙΩΝΑΑΝΙΑΝΟΝ ///
ΠΑΤΟΝΤΟΝΕΑΥΤΗϹΕΥΕΡ ///
ΕΙ ///

It was published by Dittenberger, who thus restored it:—

ἡ πόλις Πλαταιέων Λούκ(ιον) [Ἰού]
νιον Γαλλίωνα Ἀνιανόν,[5] [ὕ]
πατον, τὸν ἑαυτῆς εὐερ[γ]
έτ[ην]

and referred it to the consulship of Gallio. There is no material impossibility in this view, but is it probable? When a Greek city erects a statue in honour of Gallio its benefactor, our first thoughts

[1] *Corpus Inscriptionum Latinarum*, IV., Suppl. No. 45.

[2] *E.g.*, by Hoennicke, *Die Chronologie des Lebens des Apostels Paulus*, p. 26.

[3] I am indebted to Dessau for referring me to this inscription.

[4] *Inscriptiones Graecae*, VII., No. 1676.

[5] See Dittenberger's note on this remarkable form of the name.

are of the Proconsul of Greece. I should therefore prefer this restoration:—

> ἡ πόλις τῶν Πλαταιέων Λούκ[ιον Ἰού-]
> νιον Γαλλίωνα Ἀνιανὸν [ἀνθύ-]
> πατον, τὸν ἑαυτῆς εὐερ[γ-]
> ἑτ[ην].

But I will not deny that Plataea may have shown her gratitude to Gallio after he had been Proconsul and had become Consul.

The question can be solved by an inspection of the stone itself. Even a squeeze would enlighten us as to the length of the lines and the size, etc., of the letters. As M. Keramopoulos, the Director of the Epigraphical Museum at Athens, holds out hopes of procuring me one, I may be able to return some day to this open question.

APPENDIX II

ON THE ALTAR OF THE UNKNOWN GOD

(*See the two autotypes.*)

The Greek inscription which St. Paul read on an altar at Athens,[1]

'To an unknown god,'

and which he viewed and interpreted with the eyes of a monotheistic missionary, has often been illustrated by literary evidence culled from Pausanias, Philostratus, and Diogenes Laertes.[2] We must conclude from this that in Greek antiquity cases were not altogether rare in which 'anonymous' altars[3]

'To unknown gods'[4]

or

'To the god whom it may concern'[5]

were erected, when people were convinced, *e.g.*, after experiencing some deliverance, that a deity had been gracious to them, but were not certain

[1] Acts xvii. 23, ἀγνώστῳ θεῷ. Cf. p. 81 above.

[2] The best presentment of the material will be found in the *Encyclopaedia Biblica*, vol. iv., London, 1902, cols. 5229 f.

[3] βωμοὺς ἀνωνύμους.

[4] ἀγνώστοις θεοῖς.

[5] τῷ προσήκοντι θεῷ (Diogenes Laertes, i. 110).

of the deity's name. Altars to 'unknown gods' on the way from Phalerum to Athens,[1] at Athens,[2] and at Olympia[3] are specially mentioned by Pausanias (second century A.D.) and Philostratus (third century A.D.).

Hitherto there has been no epigraphical evidence forthcoming to confirm these statements of ancient writers, and I have not infrequently heard the view expressed that their testimony counts for little. A recently discovered inscription, however, enables us to say with considerable probability that Pausanias and Philostratus are deserving of belief.

On 1 February, 1910, Wilhelm Dörpfeld and two of his collaborators gave a report before the Berlin Archæological Society of the excavations at Pergamum during the autumn of 1909. The most valuable result of a campaign rich in brilliant discoveries was the clearing of the sacred precinct and temple of Demeter, which from about the end of the fourth century B.C. until late in the imperial period must have been an important shrine, as shown by the architectural remains and the inscribed stones. The most remarkable epigraphical discovery, next to the inscription recording the foundation of the building, was brought forward at the meeting by Hugo Hepding, and has since been published by him in the Report of the excavations,[4] viz., the

[1] Pausanias, i. 1, 4.

[2] Philostratus, *Vita Apollonii*, vi. 3.

[3] Pausanias, v. 14, 8.

[4] Athenische Mitteilungen, 35 (1910), pp. 454–457. Hepding had before that very kindly allowed me to call attention to the inscription in a provisional notice in Die Christliche Welt, 24 (1910), cols. 218 ff., of which I have availed myself here.

ALTAR FROM THE SACRED PRECINCT OF DEMETER AT PERGAMUM—LEFT SIDE.

THE SAME—FRONT SIDE.

altar which is here reproduced in autotype facsimile.

The text of the older votive inscription on the altar, which is probably of the second century A.D., is unfortunately mutilated. Hepding thinks it should be thus restored, in what appears to me also the most probable form:—

θεοῖς ἁγν[ώστοις]
Καπίτω[ν]
δᾳδοῦχο[ς].

Symmetry requires that about six letters should be restored at the end of line 1; therefore ἀγγ[έλοις] is not probable, although shown to be a material possibility by a Latin inscription, *diis angelis*,[1] of the second or third century A.D. from Viminacium in Servia. ἁγί[οις], ἁγι[ωτάτοις], ἁγν[οῖς] are improbable restorations for material and partly for formal reasons. Hepding now[2] considers it possible that ἁγι[ωτάταις] must be read, because in a Peloponnesian inscription[3] there is mention of Demeter and Persephone as τοῖν ἁγιωτάτοιν θεοῖν, and ἡ θεός is often found at Pergamum. But on the other hand he points out that it would be hardly in keeping with Greek religious feeling

I am also indebted to Hepding for his courtesy in supplying a fellow-student with the photograph of the two sides of the stone. For a detailed description of the altar I refer to the Report of the excavations. The most important fact is that the altar was inscribed with a dedication first on the front and then on the left side. The second dedication [τοῖς Ἀ]νέμοις Κασίγνητος ἐπιβώμιος, for which I refer to Hepding, is also reproduced here in autotype.

[1] Jahreshefte des Österr. Archäol. Instituts, 8 (1905), Supplement, col. 5.

[2] Athenische Mitteilungen, 35 (1910), p. 456.

[3] *Corpus Inscriptionum Graecarum*, I., No. 1449.

to change after a short time the dedication of an altar sacred to the two chief deities of the holy precinct—and we know from the inscription on the left side of the stone,[1] also reproduced here, that the dedication of this altar was so changed. It would be less remarkable that an altar to unknown gods should receive no particular attention and then should be annexed for another cult. We should also expect to find on the stone some trace still remaining of the horizontal beginning[2] of the Ω if ἀγιωτάταις were the original reading. Moreover the adoration of 'unknown' gods harmonises well with the religious thought of the priests of the mysteries of Demeter at Pergamum in the second century A.D. as known to us from other inscriptions.[3]

These arguments of Hepding's are of a convincing nature, even if absolute certainty remains unattainable. I may add, however, that if Demeter and Persephone were intended we should expect the definite article, and perhaps the dual, as in the Peloponnesian inscription. The mere fact that a 'torchbearer' of Demeter dedicates the altar does not entitle us to conclude that he must have dedicated it to Demeter. We have at Pergamum undoubted examples to the contrary,[4] and this very Capito of our inscription is perhaps identical with

[1] Cf. p. 262 n. 4 above.

[2] Cf. in line 2 of the autotype the beginning of the Ω after the T.

[3] *E.g.*, a dedication to the Pantheion by M. Aurelius Menogenes, a hierophant and prytanis [*i.e.* chief priest of Demeter], Hepding, p. 454, and Hepding's remarks on pp. 454 ff.

[4] *E.g.*, a dedication to Helios by Cl. Nicomedes, a torchbearer (Hepding, p. 453).

the man who dedicated another altar at Pergamum to Zeus Megistos Soter.[1]

If rightly restored, the inscription

'To unknown gods
Capito,
torchbearer'

tells us that about a century after the foundation of the Christian church at Pergamum,[2] Capito, a priest of Demeter of Pergamum, who officiated as 'torchbearer' at her mysteries, dedicated the altar to 'unknown' gods. In some way or another—it may be easily imagined from many analogous dedications that a hint had been received in a dream—Capito had become convinced that he was under obligation to gods whose names were not revealed to him. He showed his appreciation by giving them an 'anonymous' altar.

No doubt the Athenian altar which made so deep an impression on the Apostle Paul also originated in the same sort of way—in gratitude to 'an' unknown god, the gift of an Athenian whose name stood perhaps beneath the line that St. Paul quoted. The missionary of the ancient world does not of course interpret the words as a modern epigraphist would.[3] He interprets them, as he does the Greek Old Testament,[4] with a strong interest

[1] Hepding, p. 457.

[2] The earliest evidence of Christianity at Pergamum is the letter of Christ in Rev. ii. 12 ff. The foundation of the church might, of course, very well go back to the time of St. Paul.

[3] St. Paul, however, himself hints that the sense he extracts from the inscription was not present to the consciousness of the person (or persons) who had dedicated the altar (Acts xvii. 23b).

[4] Cf. p. 104 f. above.

in their deeper meaning, the same that he afterwards extracts from the poet's words,

'For we are also his offspring.'

That which according to the letter applied to 'an' unknown god thus becomes to the apostle an unconscious[1] anticipation of 'the' unknown God.

[1] ἀγνοοῦντες, Acts xvii. 23.

APPENDIX III

EXPLANATORY REMARKS ON THE MAP—'THE WORLD AS KNOWN TO ST. PAUL'

The map at the end of this volume was drawn according to my instructions by H. Wehlmann and printed in seven colours by the firm of Dietrich Reimer (Ernst Vohsen), of Berlin. As regards the main features it is designed from the ancient, that is Pauline, point of view. Everything therefore is marked on it which the letters of St. Paul and the Acts of the Apostles show to have come within the range of Christianity as it struggled forward from East to West, or which, in the absence of authorities, might be assumed to have been within range.

It therefore seemed to me indispensable to include the whole Mediterranean world, instead of cutting it short at Rome as most Pauline maps do. It thus became necessary to make the map of a larger size than usual,[1] though even now the scale is much too small to please me. Nevertheless it is hoped that the map will give a clear and complete picture of the world of St. Paul, to which Spain certainly belonged, whether St. Paul ever really reached that extreme point or not.[2]

[1] If the map is to be frequently used it is advisable to have it mounted on linen or cardboard.

[2] Cf. p. 35 above.

The nomenclature of the map has also been, roughly speaking, determined from the ancient point of view. In the East it is Greek, in the West Latin; and where the two languages most markedly overlap it is Greek and Latin. It would be very misleading to furnish the whole Mediterranean world with Latin names. Rather than that it would be better to put everywhere the forms now current amongst us, which have been used in the text of this book; but in that case the map would be more likely to lose its ancient character, and we want it to be as accurate as possible. On the other hand there was no need to note Semitic names of places, except so far as they have become naturalised among us in their original form, because St. Paul (like the writer of the Acts of the Apostles) generally employed Hellenised forms. Where it was feasible, the topographical designations found in our New Testament authorities have been entered, *e.g.*, the popular names of parts of the Mediterranean Sea which are recorded in Acts xxvii. 5 and 27.

So far as it seemed desirable in the interest of readers of the book and users of the map who might be unfamiliar with the classical languages, the few ancient words that would perhaps not be immediately intelligible to them have been explained below in the footnote.[1] Everything else will, I think, be clear.

[1] Barbaroi = Barbarians. Basileia Kommagene = Kingdom of Commagene. Basileia Polemonos = Kingdom of King Polemo. Eparcheia (Provincia) = Province. Haimos = Balkan Mountains. He Asphaltitis Limne = The Asphalt Lake, the Dead Sea. He entos Thalassa (Mare internum) = The Inner Sea, Mediterranean. He [megale] Syrtis = The [Great] Syrtis, Syrtis Major. He mikra Syrtis = The Little Syrtis, Syrtis Minor. 'Ho Adrias' = Adria, popular name for the sea between Greece and Sicily.

For the sake of greater distinctness the mountains are only shown in a light grey tint, but the heights of the most important places in the primitive history of Christianity are noted in metres.[1]

The zone of the olive-tree, which is typical of Mediterranean culture and therefore of St. Paul's world, is tinted green after Theobald Fischer.[2]

In the extremely difficult and often very venturesome attempt to ascertain the provincial and other political boundaries about the year 50 A.D. I have chiefly followed Sir W. M. Ramsay's map.[3] For the boundary between 'the region of Galatia' and the province of Galatia, which is desirable on account of the Galatian problem, I have followed the map in the Encyclopædia Biblica.[4]

The problem of the ancient roads has not yet been solved with such certainty as might appear from some maps. In particular, the system of roads which existed between 30 and 60 A.D. cannot yet be reconstructed with complete confidence.

Hodos Egnatia = Via Egnatia, The Egnatian Way. kai = and. Kilikia Pedias = The plain of Cilicia. Kilikia Tracheia = Cilicia Trachea, the rugged, uneven part of Western Cilicia. Kyklades = The Cyclades. Kypros = Cyprus. Limne Gennesareth = Lake of Gennesaret, Sea of Galilee. Maiotis = Sea of Azov. Palaistine = Palestine. Phoinike = Phoenicia. Pontos Euxeinos = The Euxine or Black Sea. Propontis = Sea of Marmara. Pylai Kilikiai = The Cilician Gates. Pylai Syriai = The Syrian Gates. Sina Oros = Mount Sinai. To Aigaion Pelagos = The Aegean Sea. To Pelagos to kata ten Kilikian = The Sea of Cilicia. To Pelagos to kata ten Pamphylian = The Sea of Pamphylia. Via Appia = The Appian Way.

[1] Cf. p. 36 n. 2 above. [2] Cf. pp. 38–41 above.

[3] *St. Paul the Traveller and the Roman Citizen*,[11] London, n.d., map in pocket at end.

[4] Vol. ii., London, 1901, between cols. 1592 and 1593; cf. p. 221 above.

Being myself incompetent to pronounce on this important question, I have been very reserved in marking the ancient roads. The stages mentioned in St. Paul's journeys are themselves valuable contributions to the elucidation of the problem, and the modern routes allow of instructive conclusions being drawn as to the lines of ancient intercourse.[1] That was one of the reasons for marking the modern lines of communication on the map. In constructing the map I was chiefly guided by the endeavour to show my readers as clearly as possible (*e.g.*, by giving also the modern names)[2] that the world of St. Paul has not completely disappeared, but can still be viewed over wide stretches. Any one to whom this is already obvious may neglect the modern names; it was not thoroughly brought home to me until after my two journeys.

I attach special importance to the markings which illustrate religious and missionary history. They will be found explained under the title of the map itself.[3] Here again[4] we must beware of the argument from silence, which under the conscious or unconscious tyranny of the theory of mechanical inspiration is often applied with disastrous results. I am convinced, for example, that the Jews of the Dispersion were considerably more numerous and widely distributed than the present state of our knowledge indicates, and that the number of places

[1] Cf. p. 201 above.

[2] The modern names in the East, excepting those of a few important places, are collected in a special table in the top left-hand corner, so as not to overload the map.

[3] See also the information at pp. 88, 196 n. 1, 199 f., 220–223.

[4] Cf. pp. 172 n. 11 and 187 above.

influenced more or less strongly, directly or indirectly, by St. Paul was greater than we are able to ascertain from our fragmentary authorities. Here again therefore I repeat in the words of St. Paul,

'We know in part.'

In numbering the journeys of St. Paul, which also are certainly not all known to us, I have departed from the ordinary arrangement of 'four' journeys. Instead of counting four journeys it would surely be more correct to attempt to regard the whole youth and manhood of St. Paul as one long expedition. It would be easier moreover to establish this view of his life than to define what is meant by a single 'journey.' I regard as a 'journey' deserving of separate enumeration every portion of the apostle's voyage through life which is distinguished from the preceding portion by a sojourn somewhere which proved of peculiar importance in his history. Examples of such sojourns would be, in my opinion, the time at Damascus after his conversion, the years in Arabia, the fifteen days at Jerusalem after his return from Damascus, his visit to Jerusalem for the conference with the apostles, and the time before and after his arrest at Jerusalem. I should not so regard his second short visit to Corinth, which can only be established hypothetically.

I admit that from this point of view it would be possible to make two journeys of the one which I have numbered 11. The first visit to Corinth, which lasted more than a year and a half, seems to furnish a terminating point similar to that which is formed later on by the important three years of work at Ephesus.

INDICES

I

PLACES, PERSONS, SUBJECTS

II

GREEK WORDS

Only a few are noted here; any one familiar with the Greek New Testament will easily be able with the help of the other Indices to find most of the characteristic words used by St. Paul.

III

PASSAGES CITED

A. THE GREEK BIBLE

B. PAPYRI.

C. INSCRIPTIONS

D. AUTHORS

IV

INDEX TO THE MAP

"THE WORLD AS KNOWN TO ST. PAUL"

This Index contains (1) the names printed on the map itself, including such variants as are likely to occur in English works, (2) modern names from the list (already anglicised) in the left-hand corner of the map, and (3) a considerable number of the other modern equivalents which are not given by Professor Deissmann.

For readier reference certain of the more crowded squares of the map are supposed to be divided into quarters numbered respectively *a*, *b*, *c*, *d* in this order :—

a	*c*
b	*d*

Any one likely to make frequent use of the Index may be advised to carry out this division by means of actual lines in squares $G—K_3$, K_4.

Modern names are in *italics*.

The coloured markings of the map are indicated by the following symbols prefixed to names :—

* * Places with Jewish residents (marked blue on the map).
* † Primitive Gospel of Jesus (printed red on the map).
* ‡ Primitive apostolic cult of Christ (double red line and double cross).
* ¶ Pauline cult of Christ (single red line and cross).
* § Christian cult of unknown (possibly also Pauline) origin before Trajan (single red cross).

For statistical reasons these symbols are given only once for each case, and are not repeated when a place-name reappears in the Index under various forms. The system of cross-references calls attention to the marked form, no matter which of the possible forms of a name may be looked up. A cross-reference to another name or form always implies that a little extra information will be found there besides the mere position of the place on the map.

The sign = placed between two names is to be read "spelt on the map." It indicates that the second of the two names is the form which will be found on the map. *E.g.*, "Caria = Karia," or "*Adalia* = Attaleia." "Karia" is the spelling on the map. The modern name *Adalia* is not given on the map, but its ancient equivalent will be found there, spelt "Attaleia."

The heights above sea-level, which are given in metres on the map, have been entered in the Index and converted into feet.

ABBREVIATIONS.

F. = Fluvius, river.
ft. = feet.
L. = Lake.
m. = metres.
mt. = mountain.
q.v. = *quod vide*, "which see."

Alexandr(e)ia (Syria) *Alexandretta*, *Iskanderūn*, *Skanderūn* K_{3b}
¶Alexandr(e)ia Troas *Eski Stambul* H_{3a}
Alexandretta = Alexandreia (Syria) q.v.
Algeciras Carteia A_3
Alger, *Algiers* Icosium C_3
Alicante Lucentum B_3
Aligora. See Soloi
Alpes *Alps* (mts.) $D_{1,2}$, E_1
Alti Kara = Tauion q.v.
Amanos, -us, *Giaour Dagh* (mt.) K_{3b}
Amara = Amastris I_2
Amas(e)ia *Amasia* K_2
Amastris *Amara* I_2
Amblada *Selki* I_{3a}
*(§?) Amisos, -us, *Kara Samsun* K_2
Amorgos *Amorgo* H_{3b}
Amorion, -ium, *Hergan Kale* I_{3a}
Amphipolis *Neochori* G_2
Anamur = Anemurion q.v.
Anas F. *Guadiana* A_3
Ancona *Ancona* E_2
Ancyra = Ankyra q.v.
Andrapa *Iskelib* I_2
Andros *Andros* G_3
*Anemurion, -ium, *Anamur* I_{3d}
*?) *Angora* = Ankyra, 870 m. = 2,853 ft. I_{3c}
Anṭāki(y)eh = Antiocheia Syria q.v.
Antarados, -us, *Ṭarṭūs* K_{4a}
Antiocheia, Antioch in Cilicia, Antiochia ad Cragum I_{3b}
*¶Antioch(e)ia Pisidia, Antioch in Pisidia *Yalovatch*, 1,200 m. = 3,936 ft. I_{3a}
*‡Antioch(e)ia Syria, Antioch in Syria *Anṭāki(y)eh*, 80 m. = 262 ft. K_{3b}
*Antipatris *Ḳal'at Rās el-'Ain* I_{4d}
Antitauros, -us, *Binboa Dagh, &c.* (mt.) K_{3a}
Antivari F_2
Anthios, -ius, F. (Pisidia) I_{3a}
*Apame(i)a *Dineir* or *Geyiklar*, 932 m. = 3,056 ft. I_{3a}
Appia Via E_2
Appii Forum, Appiu Phoron (Ἀππίου Φόρον) E_2
Apollonia (in Cyrenaica) *Sūza Ḥamām* G_4
Apollonia (Illyricum) *Polighero* F_{2d}
*Apollonia (in Pisidia) *Olu-borlu* or *Olukman* I_{3a}
Apollonia *Polina? Klisali?* G_{2d}
Apollonia (Sozopolis) in Thrace *Sizeboli* H_2
Aquae Sextiae *Aix* D_2
*Aquileia *Aquileia* E_1
Aquincum *Budapest* F_1
*Arabia I_5, K_4
Arabissos, -us, *Yarpuz* K_{3a}
*Arelate *Arles* C_2
Aresli = Lysias I_{3a}
Arezzo Arretium E_2
*Argos *Argos* G_{3c}
Argostólion, *Argostoli* G_{3a}
Ariarath(e)ia *Azizieh* K_{3a}
Ariminum *Rimini* E_2
Arles. See Arelate
Arretium *Arezzo* E_2
Arsinoë (in Cyrenaica) *Tokra* G_4
*Arsinoë (in Egypt), Krokodilopolis, Crocodilopolis *Medinet el-Fayūm* 23 m. = 77 ft. I_5
Lake Moeris *Birket el-Karn*, in the Fayūm, is 44 m. = 144 ft. below sea-level.
Arsinoë *Famagusta* I_{3d}
*Arsinoites Nomos, Arsinoïte nome *Fayūm* I_5
Ascalon, Ashkelon = Askalon q.v.
"Asia" (Acts ii. 9, &c.) H_{3ac}

Asia Eparchela (province) H_{3c}
Asin Kalesi = Iasos q.v.
*'*Askalān* = Askalon I_{4d}
Asphaltitis Limne, He, ἡ ἀσφαλτῖτις λίμνη, *Bahr Lûṭ*, *Dead Sea*, 394 m. = 1,282 ft. below sea K_{4b}
Assos *Behram Keui* H_{3a}
*¶Athenae = Athenai *Athens* G_{3c}
Athos (mt.) 1,935 m. = 6,346 ft. G_{2d}
*Athribis *Atrîb* I_{4b}
Attal(e)ia *Adalia* I_{3b}
Augusta Taurinorum *Torino*, *Turin* D_1
Aulon *Valona* F_2
*Auzia *Aumale*, *Sūr Ghozlan* C_3
Avenio *Avignon* C_2
Ayas(h) = Aigai K_{3b}
Ayash Kaleh = Korykos q.v.
Ayasoluk = Ephesos q.v.
Azani = Aizanoi q.v.
Azizieh = Ariaratheia K_{3a}
*‡Azotos, -us *Esdūd* I_{4d}
Azov, *Sea of* = Maiotis K_1

Baalbec = *Ba'albek* Heliopolis q.v.
Babylon (in Egypt) *Maṣr el-'Atîḳa* $I_{4,5}$
Baetis F. *Guadalquivir* A_3
Baffa = Paphos Nea q.v.
Baghdad-Bahn, *Baghdad Railway* KL_3
Bahr Lûṭ. See Asphaltitis
Bahr Ṭabarīyeh = Gennesareth Limne q.v.
Bailân, *Pass v[on]*. See Pylai Syriai
Bala Hissar = Pessinus q.v.
Balanaia, -aea, *Bāni(y)ās* K_{3b}
Bâle = *Basel* D_1
Baleares I[nsul]ae *Balearic Isles* $C_{2,3}$
Balkan Mountains = Haimos H_2
Bāni(y)ās = Balanaia K_{3b}
Bāniyās = Kaisareia Philippu q.v.
Barata = *Bin Bir Kilis(s)e* or *Maden Sheh(e)r* I_{3d}
Barbar(o)i, Barbarians GH_1, KL_1, E_3
Barcelona Barcino C_2
Baretun. See Paraetonium
Bari Barium F_2
Basel D_1
Basileia Kommagene, Kingdom of Commagene I_{3d}, K_{3ac}
Basileia Polemonos, Kingdom of King Polemo KL_2
Bastia D_2
Bathys Limen *Batum* L_2
Bazarji Kalesi = Selinus q.v.
Behnesa Oxyrhynchus I_5
Behram Keui = Assos H_{3a}
Beilan Pass. See Pylai Syriai
Beirūt = Berytos q.v.
Beisān = Skythopolis q.v.
Belgrad(e) G_2
Benacus L. *Lago di Garda* E_1
**Benghazi* = Berenike, Berenice F_4
Bergama Pergamon q.v.
*¶Berea, Beroea = Beroia *Verria* 188 m. = 616 ft. G_2
Beroea = Beroia *Haleb*, *Aleppo* 370 m. = 1,213 ft. K_{3b}
*Berytos, -us, *Beirūt* K_{4a}
Bescera *Biskra* D_4
†Bethsaida Julias *Et-Tell* K_{4a}
Beyrout = Berytos q.v.
Bin Bir Kilis(s)e = Barata I_{3d}
Binboa Dagh = Antitaurus (mts.) K_{3a}
Birket el-Karn Moeris (lake, not named on map) 44 m. = 144 ft. below sea I_5
Bisanthe *Rodosto*, *Tekirdagh* H_2
Biskra Bescera D_4
*§Bithynia I_2
Bitolia = Herakleia q.v.
Bizerta = *Bizerte* D_3

*Bizya = Bizye *Viza* H_2
Black Sea = Pontos Euxeinos IK_2
*Boeotia = Boiotia G_3
Boghaz Keui = *Boghaz Köi* Pteria q.v.
Bologna. See Bononia
Bolos, *Volo* Iolcos G_{3c}
Bona = *Bône* D_3
*Bononia *Bologna* E_2
*Boreion, Boreum *Tabilbe* F_4
Borysthenes F. *Dnieper* I_1
Boṣrā = Bostra 881 m. = 2,889 ft. K_{4b}
Bozanti Khan = Podandos q.v.
Bregenz D_1
Brescia. See Brixia
Brigantium *Bregenz* D_1
Brindisi F_2
*Brixia *Brescia* E_1
Brundisium *Brindisi* F_2
Brūsa = *Brussa* Prusa H_2
Bucharest = *Bucuresci* H_2
Budapest Aquincum F_1
Budrūm = Halikarnassos q.v.
Budrūm = Kastabala q.v.
Bukarest, *Bucharest* H_2
Buldur 1,000 m. = 3,280 ft. I_{3a}
Bulgurlu(k) I_{3c}
Burg(h)as H_2
Byzantion, -ium, *Constantinople* H_2

Cabes = *Gabès* Tacapae D_3
Cabes, *Gulf of*. See Syrtis
Cádiz Gades A_3
Caesarea (in Cappadocia) = Kaisareia q.v.
*Caesarea (in Mauretania) *Shershel* C_3
Caesarea Philippi = Kaisareia Philippu q.v.
Caesarea Stratonis = Kaisareia Stratonos q.v.
Cagliari Carales D_3
Cairo = *Kairo* I_{4b}
Calpe *Gibraltar* A_3
Calycadnus F. = Kalykadnos q.v.
Candia = Herakleion (in Crete) q.v.
Candia = Krete q.v.
Canea = Kydonia q.v.
Cannes D_2
Capernaum = Kapharnaum q.v.
Cappadocia = Kappadokia q.v.
*Capua *Capua* E_2
Carales *Cagliari* D_3
Caria = Karia H_{3d}
Carnuntum *Petronell* F_1
Carpathos = Karpathos *Scarpanto* H_{3b}
Cartagena Nova Carthago B_3
Carteia *Algeciras* A_3
Cartenna *Tenez* C_3
*Carthago, Carthage E_3
Carthago Nova *Cartagena* B_3
Casos = Kasos *Kaso* H_{3b}
Castabala = Kastabala q.v.
Castri = Delphoi G_3
Castro, *Kastro* = Chios (town) H_{3a}
Castro, *Kastro* = Mitylene q.v.
Catana *Catania* F_3
Cattaro F_2
Cauda = Kauda *Gavdhos* or *Gozzo* G_{4b}
Celenderis = Kelenderis *Kilindria* I_{3d}
Cenchrea(e) = Kenchreai q.v.
Centumcellae *Civitavecchia* E_2
Cephallenia *Cephalonia* = Kephallenia G_3
Cerasus = Kerasos q.v.
Cestrus F. = Kestros *Ak Su* I_{3ab}
Cette Setius C_2
Chai = Ipsos q.v.
Chalcis = Chalkis (in Aetolia) *Varassova* G_{3a}
Chalcis = Chalkis (in Euboea) *Chalcis*, *Chalkis*, *Egripo* G_{3c}
Changra = Gangra q.v.
Chania = Kydonia q.v.

Dekapolis, Decapolis K_{4b}
Delminium *D(o)uvno? Gardun?* F_2
*Delos (position marked by arrow) *Mikra D(h)ilos*, *Mikro Dhili* H_{3b}
*Delph(o)i *Castri* G_3
Demas = Thapsus E_3
Dembre = Myra q.v.
Der'āt = *Adraha* q.v.
§Derbe *Gudelissin* I_{3d}
*Dertona *Tortona* D_2
*Dertosa *Tortosa* C_2
Didjle = Tigris F. L_3
Didyma H_{3b}
Dineir = Apameia q.v.
*Diokleia *Doghla?* H_{3c} (30° E.)
Dion, Dium *Malathria* G_2
Dnieper = Borysthenes F. I_1
Dniester = Tyras F. H_1
Docimium = Dokimaion *Istcha* (*Ichje*) *Kara Hissar* I_{3a}
Doghla? = Diokleia q.v.
Dokuz Keui = Mopsukrene I_{3d}
Dorylaeum = Dorylaion *'Shahr Eyuk* I_{3a}
D(o)uvno? = Delminium q.v.
Drave = Dravus F. EF_1
Drepanon, Drepanum *Trapani* E_3
Drina = Drinus F. F_2
Dulcigno = Uljcin F_2
Durazzo = Dyrrhachion, -ium F_2
Duver = Tlos q.v.
Duvno? = Delminium q.v.

Ebro = Iberus F. BC_2
Edessa *Vodhena* G_2
Edessa *Orfa*, *Urfa* K_{3d}
Edirné, *Adrianople* H_2
Edre'i = *Adraha* q.v.
Edrenos Chai = Rhyndakos F. H_{3c}
Egerdir Geul = Limnai q.v.
Egnatia Hodos, Egnatia Via G_2
Egripo = Chalkis and Euboea G_3
*Elaia, Elaea *Kaz Keui* H_{3a}
Elate(i)a *Lefta* G_3
Elba Ilva E_2
El-Baretun. See Paraetonium
Eleusis *Levsina* G_3
El-'Āṣi = Orontes F. K_{4a}
El-Helif L_3
**El-Hībeh* I_5
El-Jīsh = Gischala K_{4a}
El-Kabūsīyeh = Seleukeia Pieria K_{3b}
El-Ḳāhirah, *Kairo* I_{4b}
El-Ḳuds = Jerusalem q.v.
El-Mismieh = Phaina q.v.
Elymbo = Olympos q.v.
Emesa *Homs*, *Hums* K_{4a}
Emerita-Augusta *Mérida* A_3
Enevre = Neapolis (in Pisidia) q.v.
En-Nāṣira = Nazareth q.v.
Entos thalassa, he, *Mediterranean Sea* B_3–K_4
Eparcheia. See Provincia
Eparcheia Achaia G_3
„ Asia H_{3c}
„ Bithynia (q.v.) kai (= and) Pontus q.v. I_2
Eparcheia Galatia I_{3ac}
„ Kappadokia q.v. K_{3a}
„ Kilikia I_{3d}, K_{3b}
„ Kypros q.v. $I_{3d,4}$
„ Lykia H_{3d}
„ Makedonia G_2
„ Pamphylia I_{3b}
„ Syria q.v. $K_{3bd,4}$
„ Thrakia H_2
Epeiros, Epirus G_3
*¶Ephesos, -us *Ayasoluk* H_{3a}
Epidaurus *Ragusa vecchia* F_2
Eregli Heraclea Pontica = Herakleia I_2
Eregli = Kybistra q.v.
Eregli Perinthos H_2
Erīḥā = Jericho q.v.
Ermenek = Germanikeia q.v.
Esdūd = Azotus q.v.
Esh-Shām = Damaskos q.v.

Govdo, *Gozzo* = Klauda q.v.
Graz F_1
Grenna(h) = Kyrene q.v.
Gudelissin = Derbe q.v.
Gulek Boghaz = Pylai Kilikiai q.v.
Gumenek = Komana q.v.
Gureina = Kyrene q.v.

*Hadrumetum *Susa* E_3
Haemus = Haimos q.v.
Hagii D(h)eka. See Gortyna
Haifa IK_4
Haimos, Haemus *Balkan* (mts.) H_2
Haleb. See Beroia
*Halicarnassus = Halikarnassos *Budrūm* H_{3d}
Halys F. *Kizil Irmak* I_2K_{3a}
Hammâm Lîf Naro q.v.
Hassan Pasha. See Olbasa
He Asphaltitis Limne. See Asphaltitis
Hedschâz Bahn nach Mekka, *He(d)jaz Railway to Mecca* K_5
He entos thalassa *Mediterranean Sea* B_3–K_4
Heliopolis (in Syria) *Ba'albek* 1,170 m. = 3,837 ft. K_{4a}
*Heliopolis=Heliupolis *Maṭarîje*, *Matarieh* I_{4b}
Heluan, *Helwan* I_5
He [megale] Syrtis. See Syrtis
He mikra Syrtis. See Syrtis
Henchir Fuara = Theveste q.v.
Heraclea = Herakleia (in Macedonia) *Monastir*, *Bitolia* 610 m. = 2,000 ft. G_2
Heraclea Pontica = Herakleia *Eregli* I_2
Heracleum = Herakleion *Platamona?* G_{3c}
Heracleum = Herakleion (in Crete) *Megalokastron*, *Candia* H_{3b}
Hergan Kale = Amorion I_{3a}
Hermos, -us, F. *Gediz Chai* H_{3ac}
Hîbeh = *El-Hîbeh* q.v.
*¶Hierapolis *Tambuk Kalesi* (not "Pambuk") 360 m. = 1,180 ft. H_3
Hieropolis-Castabala = Kastabala *Budrūm* K_{3b}
Hierosolyma = Jerusalem q.v.
*Hippo Regius *Bône*, *Bona* D_3
Hippo Zarytus *Bizerte*, *Bizerta* D_3
Hispalis *Sevilla*, *Seville* A_3
*(¶?) Hispania *Spain* AB_2
Hissarlik = Troia H_{3a}
"Ho Adrias." See Adrias
Hodos Egnatia, Via Egnatia G_2
Ḥömṣ, *Homs*, *Hums*, Emesa K_{4a}
*Hypaepa = Hypaipa *Tapae* H_{3c}

Iader, Jadera *Zara* F_2
*Iasos, Iassus *Asin Kalesi* H_{3d}
Iberus F. *Ebro* BC_2
Icaria, Icaros = Ikaria q.v.
Ichje Kara Hissar = Dokimaion q.v.
Iconium = Ikonion q.v.
Icosium *Alger*, *Algiers* C_3
Ida (mt. in Crete) *Psiloriti* 2,497 m. = 8,190 ft. G_3
Ikaria, Icaria, Icaros *Nicaria* H_{3ab}
*¶Ikonion, Iconium, *Konia*, *Konieh* 1,027 m. = 3,368 ft. I_{3c}
Ilg(h)in = Tyriaion q.v.
Ilisra = Ilistra I_{3d}
¶Illyricum = Illyrikon F_2
Ilva *Elba* E_2
Imbros, *Imbro*, *Imrūz* H_2
Ineboli = Ionopolis I_2
Inn = Aenus F. E_1
Innsbruck Veldidena E_1
Iolcos = *Bolos*, *Volo* G_{3c}
Ionian Sea = "Ho Adrias" F_3
Ionopolis *Ineboli* I_2
Ios *Nio* H_{3b}
Iotapa I_{3b}
Ipsos, -us *Chai*, *Tchai* 1,020 m. = 3,345 ft. I_{3a}

Kephallenia, Cephallenia *Cephalonia* G_3
Kerasos, Cerasus *Kerasund* K_2
Kerāzeh = Chorazin q.v.
Kereli. See Misthia
Kérkyra = Korkyra q.v.
Kert(s)ch. See Pantikapaion
Kestros, Cestrus F. *Ak Su* I_{3ab}
**Kesur el-Ghennaia* D_3
Keupri Su = Eurymedon F. I_{3ab}
Kharadran = Charadra I_{3d}
Khatyn Serai = Lystra q.v.
Khavsa = Therma q.v.
Kherson = *Chersson* I_1
Khio = Chios q.v.
Khonas. See Kolossai
Kibris = Kypros q.v.
Kibyra, Cibyra Minor I_{3b}
Kilikia Ep[archeia], province of Cilicia $I_{3d}K_{3b}$
*¶Kilikia Pedias, Cilician Plain K_{3b}
*¶Kilikia Tracheia, Cilicia Trachea I_{3d}
Kilindria = Kelenderis I_{3d}
Kilis(s)e Hissar = Tyana q.v.
Kirid = Krete q.v.
Kirili Kassaba (?) = Misthia q.v.
Kition, Citium *Larnaka* I_{4b}
Kizil Irmak = Halys F. I_2
Klagenfurt Virunum E_1
Klauda, Kauda, Clauda, Cauda, *Gavdhos*, *Govdo*, *Gozzo* G_{4b}
Klaudiopolis, Claudiopolis *Eski Hissar* I_2
Klisali (?) = Apollonia q.v. G_{2d}
*Knidos, Cnidus *Kavo Krio* H_{3b}
Knossos, Cnossus H_{3b}
Kokussos, Cocusus *Geuksun* K_{3a}
¶Kolossai, Colossae (3 miles N. of *Khonas*) H_{3c}
Komama, Comama I_{3b}
Komana, Comana Cappadociae *Shahr* K_{3a}
Komana, Comana Pontica *Gumenek* K_2
Kommagene Basileia, kingdom of Commagene $I_{3d}K_{3ac}$
Konia, *Konieh.* See Ikonion
Konope, Conopa, *Conopina* G_3
Konstantinopel, *Constantinople* H_2
Korakesion, Coracesium *Alaya* I_{3b}
*Korasion, Corasium I_{3d}
Korghoz = Korykos q.v. I_{3d}
*¶Korinthos *Corinth* G_3
Korkyra, Corcyra, *Kérkyra*, *Corfù* (town and island) F_3
*Korykos, Corycus (in Cilicia) *Korghoz* or *Ayash Kaleh* I_{3d}
*Korykos, Corycus (in Lycia) I_{3b}
*Kos (island), Cos *Cos*, *Stanchio*, *Stanko*, *Istan Keui* H_{3b}
Kos (town) *Kos* H_{3b}
Kotiaion, Cotyaeum *Kutaya* 980 m. = 3,214 ft. H_{3c}
Kovella Panormos (harbour near Miletus) H_{3b}
Krateia, Crateia *Geredeh* I_2
Kremna, Cremna *Girme* I_{3b}
*¶Krete *Crete*, *Candia*, *Kirid* GH_3
Krokodilopolis. See Arsinoë
Kroton, Croto *Cotrone* F_3
Kustendji = Tomoi H_2
Kutaya = Kotiaion q.v.
Kybistra, Cybistra *Eregli* 1,050 m. = 3,444 ft. I_{3d}
Kydnos, Cydnus F. *Tersus Chai* I_{3d}
Kydonia, Cydonia *Canea*, *Chania* G_3
Kyklades, Cyclades GH_3
*‡Kypros Eparch[eia], Province of Cyprus *Cyprus*, *Kibris* $I_{3d,4}$
Kyrenaïke, Cyrenaica G_4
*Kyrene, Cyrene *Grenna(h)*, *Gureina* G_4
Kyzikos, Cyzicus H_2

Ladik = Laodikeia Katakekaumene I_{3c}
Lādiḳīyeh = Laodikeia (Syria) K_{3b}
Laerte(s) I_{3b}

Lamia *Lamia*, *Zeitouni*, *Zituni* G_{3a}
*¶Laodicea ad Lycum = Laodikeia (province of Asia) *Gonjeli*, *Eski Hissar*. H_{3c}
Laodicea Combusta = Laodikeia Katakekaumene *Yorg(h)an Ladik*, *Ladik* I_{3c}
Laodicea ad Mare = Laodikeia *Lādiḳīyeh*, *Latakia* K_{3b}
La Punta. See Aktion.
Laranda *Karaman* 990 m. = 3,247 ft. I_{3d}
*Laris(s)a *Larissa*, *Yeni Sheh(e)r* 74 m. = 242 ft. G_3
Larius L. *Lago di Como* D_1
Larnaka = Kition I_{4b}
Lasaea = Lasaia G_{4b}
Latakia = Laodikeia (Syria) K_{3b}
Lebda = Leptis E_4
Lechaeum = Lechaion (ancient port of Corinth) G_3
Lefta = Elateia G_3
Leghorn = *Livorno* E_2
Lemanus L. *Lake of Geneva* D_1
Lemnos *Limni*, *Stalimene* H_{3a}
*Leontopolis *Tell el-Jehûdije*, *-ieh* I_{4b}
Leptis, Leptis Magna *Lebda* E_4
Leucas = Leukas *Santa Maura* G_{3a}
Levsina = Eleusis G_{3c}
Liakhura = Parnassos q.v.
Libanos, -us *Lebanon* K_{4a}
Libya GH_4
Ligeris F. *Loire* C_1
Liguria D_2
Lilybaeum, Lilybaion *Marsala* E_3
Limas(s)ol (in Cyprus) I_{4b}
Limnai, -ae *Egerdir Geul* (lake) 870 m. = 2,853 ft. I_{3a}
Limne Asphaltitis. See Asphaltitis
Limne Gennesareth. See Gennesareth
Limni = Lemnos H_{3a}
*Limyra I_{3b}
Lisbóa, *Lisbon* Olisipo A_3
Lissa = Issa F_2
Livadia = *Liwadia* I_2
Livorno, *Leghorn* E_2
Lixus A_3
Loire = Ligeris F. C_1
Lopadion, -ium *Ulubad* H_2
L(o)utro (?) = Phoinix (in Crete) q.v. G_{3d}
Lucentum *Alicante* B_3
Ludd = Lydda q.v.
Lugano D_1
*Lugdunum *Lyon(s)* C_1
Lycaonia = Lykaonia q.v.
Lycia = Lykia q.v.
Lycus F. = Lykos q.v.
*‡Lydda *Ludd* I_{4d}
Lydia H_{3c}
*¶Lykaonia, Lycaonia I_{3c}
Lykia Eparcheia, province of Lycia H_{3d}
Lykos F., Lycus *Kelkit Irmak* K_2
Lykos F., Lycus *Churuk Su* H_{3c}
Lykostomo = Tempe (valley) G_3
Lyon(s). See Lugdunum
Lysias *Aresli* I_{3a}
*¶Lystra *Khatyn Serai* ca. 1,230 m. = about 4,034 ft. I_{3a}

Macedonia, Province = Eparcheia Makedonia G_2
Macestus F. = Makestos, q.v.
Machan = Matiane I_{3c}
Maden Sheh(e)r = Barata q.v.
Madrid B_2
Maeander F. = Maiandros q.v.
Maeotis = Maiotis, *Sea of Azov* K_1
Maggiore Lacus Verbanus D_1
*Magnesia (on the Hermos) *Manisa* 80 m. = 262 ft. H_{3c}
§Magnesia (on the Maiandros) *Morali* H_{3c}
Mago *Mahón* C_3
Maiandros, Maeander, Scamander F. *Mendere Chai* H_{3c}

Maiotis, Maeotis *Sea of Azov* K_1
Major *Majorca*, *Mallorca* C_3
Makedonia Eparcheia, Province of Macedonia G_2
Makestos, Macestus F. *Simav Chai*, *Susurlu Chai*, *Susigirli Chai* H_{3c}
Malaca *Málaga* B_3
Malathria = Dion G_2
Malatia, *Old*, *Eski Sheh(e)r* = Melitene K_{3c}
Mallorca, *Majorca* Major C_3
Malta Melite E_3
Manisa = Magnesia q.v.
*Mantine(i)a *Pal(a)eopoli(s)* G_{3a}
Marash = Germanikeia q.v.
Mare Adriaticum, *Adriatic Sea* EF_2
Mare Internum, *Mediterranean Sea* B_3–K_4
Mare Tuscum, *Tyrrhenian Sea* $E_{2,3}$
Maris F. *Maros* G_1
Marmara, *Sea of* = Propontis H_2
Maros(h) = Maris F. G_1
Marsala Lilybaion, -aeum E_3
Marseille(s). See Massilia
Maṣr el-ʿAtîḳa Babylon (Egypt) $I_{4,5}$
*Massilia *Marseille(s)* D_2
Matarieh = *Maṭarîje* Heliupolis q.v.
Matiane *Machan* I_{3c}
Mauretania A_4–D_3
Medînet el-Faijûm. See Arsinoë
*Mediolanum *Milan(o)* D_1
Megali D(h)ilos = Rheneia q.v.
Megalokastron = Herakleion q.v.
Megara *Megara* G_{3c}
Melilla = Rusaddir B_3
Melite, -a *Malta* E_3
Melitene *Eski Sheh(e)r* q.v. K_{3c}
*Melos *Milos* G_3
Memphis *Mitrahīna* I_5
Menorca, *Minorca* Minor C_3
Mérida Emerita-Augusta A_3
Mersin, *Mersina* I_{3d}
Mesolóngion, *Missolonghi* G_{3a}
Messana, Messene *Messina* F_3
Midilli, *Midüllü* = Mitylene q.v.
Mikra D(h)ilos = Delos q.v.
Milan(o). See Mediolanum
*¶Miletos, Miletus *Palatia* H_{3b}
Milos = Melos q.v.
Minor *Menorca*, *Minorca* C_3
Missis = Mopsuhestia K_{3b}
Missolonghi = *Mesolóngion* G_{3a}
Misthia *Monastir?* (*Kirili Kassaba*) I_{3a}
Mitrahīna = Memphis I_5
Mitrovitza G_2
Mitrowicz. See Sirmium
Mitylene (island), Lesbos *Mitylene*, *Midilli* H_{3a}
Mitylene (town) *Castro*, *Kastro* H_{3a}
Mocissus = Mokissos q.v.
Moeris *Birket el-Karn* (lake, but not named on map) 44 m. = 144 ft. below sea I_5
Moesia Provincia G_2
Mokissos, Mocissus *Kir-shehr* I_{3c}
Monastir = Herakleion (Macedonia) q.v.
Monastir ? = Misthia q.v.
Mopsu(h)estia *Missis* K_{3b}
Mopsucrene = Mopsukrene *Dokuz Keui* I_{3d}
Morali = Magnesia (on Maiandros) q.v.
Mukeis = Gadara q.v.
Mulai Idrīs Zarhōn. See Volubilis
München, *Munich* E_1
Murtana = Perge q.v.
Murviedro = Saguntum B_3
Myconos = Mykonos (position marked by arrow) *Myconus*, *Miconi* H_{3b}
*Myndos, -us *Yemishlu* H_{3b}
Myra *Dembre* I_{3b}
Mysia H_{3ac}

Pambuk Kalesi. See Hierapolis
Pamphylia Eparch[eia], province of Pamphylia I_{3b}
*Panormos, Panormus *Palermo* E_3
Panormos (harbour near Miletus) *Kovella* H_{3b}
Pantellaria = *Pantelleria* E_3
*Panticapaeum = Pantikapaion *Kert(s)ch* K_1
Paphlagonia I_2
*¶Paphos Nea *Baffa* I_{4a}
Pappa *Tcharyk Serai* I_{3a}
Paraetonium = Paraitonion *El-Baretun* H_4
Parlasan = Parnassos, -us I_{3c}
Parnassos, -us *Liakhura* (mt.) 2,500 m. = 8,200 ft. G_{3ac}
*Paros *Paros* H_{3b}
Pass v[on] Bailân, Beilan Pass 670 m. = 2,197 ft. K_{3b}
Patara *Gelemish* H_{3d}
Patavium, *Padova*, *Padua* E_1
Patino = Patmos H_{3b}
*Patrai, -ae *Patras* G_{3a}
Pelion (mt.) *Plessidi* 1,630 m. = 5,346 ft G_{3a}
Pella (Macedonia) G_2
‡Pella (Palestine) *Fahil* K_{4b}
Pelusion, -ium *Tineh* I_{4b}
*§Pergamon, -um *Bergama* 60 m. = 196 ft. H_{3a}
¶Perga = Perge *Murtana* I_{3b}
Perinthos, -us *Eregli* H_2
Perugia Perusia E_2
Pesaro Pisaurum E_2
Pessinus *Bala Hissar* 850 m. = 2,788 ft. I_{3a}
Petronell = Carnuntum F_1
*Phaena = Phaina, *El-Mismieh* 620 m. = 2,033 ft. K_{4a}
*Phanagoria near *Taman* K_1
Pharsalos *Phersala* 140 m. = 459 ft. G_{3a}
Pharus *Lesina* F_2
*Phaselis *Tekir-ova* I_{3b}
Phasis *Poti* L_2
Phazemon-Neapolis. See Neapolis
Phenice (Acts xxvii. 12) = Phoinix q.v.
Phenice (Acts xi. 19, &c.), Phenicia = Phoinike q.v.
Phersala = Pharsalos q.v.
*§Philadelph(e)ia *Ala Sheh(e)r* 190 m. = 623 ft.
Philaenorum arae F_4
Philippeville Rusicade D_3
*¶Philipp(o)i *Filibedjik* G_2
Philomelion, -ium *Ak-Sheh(e)r* 1,020 m. = 3,345 ft. I_{3a}
Phiva = Thebai q.v.
Phocaea = Phokaia q.v.
†‡Phoenicia = Phoinike (should be doubly underlined in red on map) K_{4a}
Phoenix = Phoinix *L(o)utro?* G_{3d}
*Phokaia, Phocaea *Eski Focha* H_{3a}
*¶Phrygia $H_{3c}I_{3a}$
Piali = Tegea q.v.
Pindos, -us *Pindus* (mts.) G_{3a}
Pisa Pisae E_2
Pisaurum *Pesaro* E_2
Pisidia I_{3a}
Pityussae I[nsul]ae, *Pithyusae Isles*, *Iviza* and *Formentera* C_3
Platamona. See Herakleion
Plessidi. See Pelion
Po = Padus F. DE_1
Podandos, -us *Bozanti Khan* 860 m. = 2,820 ft. I_{3d}
*Pola *Pola* E_2
Polemonos Basileia, kingdom of King Polemo KL_2
Polighero. See Apollonia
Polina (?) See Apollonia
*(‡?)Pompeii E_2
Pompeiopolis (Paphlagonia) *Tash Keupri* I_2
Pompeiopolis or Sol(o)i I_{3d}
*§Pontos, -us I_2
Pontos Euxeinos, Pontus Euxinus *Black Sea* IK_2

*§Sardes, -is = Sardeis *Sart* 104 m. = 341 ft. H_{3c}
Sardinia, *Sardinia* D_2
Sarepta *Sar(a)fend*, *Surafend* K_{4a}
‡Saron, Sharon (plain) I_{4d}
Saros, -us F. *Sihūn* K_{3ab}
Sart = Sardeis q.v.
Savaria, Sabaria *Stein am Anger* F_1
Save = Savus F. F_1
Scamander F. = Maiandros q.v.
Scardona *Scardona* F_2
Scarpanto = Karpathos H_{3b}
*Schedia I_{4b}
Scio = Chios q.v.
Scodra = Skodra *Skútari*, *Scutari* F_2
Scutari = Chrysopolis H_2
Scythae, Scythians = Skythai HI_1
Scythopolis = Skythopolis q.v.
Sebaste(i)a *Sivas* K_{3a}
Sebasṭīyeh = Samareia Sebaste q.v.
Sebastopol = *Sewastopol* Cherronesos I_2
Sebastopolis *Sulu Serai* K_{3a}
Sebenico F_2
Seleucia = Seleukeia (in Cilicia) *Selefke* I_{3d}
Seleucia = Seleukeia Pieria *El-Kabūsīyeh* K_{3b}
Selinus *Selinti* (*Bazarji Kalesi*) I_{3b}
Selki = Amblada I_{3a}
Senia *Zeng* $EF_{1,2}$
Sestos, -us *Yalova* H_2
Setif = Sitifis q.v.
Setius *Cette* C_2
Seulun = Prymnessos I_{3a}
Sevilla, Seville *Hispalis* A_3
Sfax E_4
Shahr = Komana q.v.
Shahr Eyuk = Dorylaion I_{3a}
Sharon = Saron q.v.
Shershel = Caesarea C_3
Sicilia = *Sicily* E_3
Sicyon = Sikyon q.v.
*Side *Eski Adalia* I_{3b}
Sidhero, Cape = Salmone H_{3b}
Sidi Bu Shater, *Marabout oj*. See Utica
*‡Sidon *Ṣaidā* K_{4a}
Sidra, G. of. See Syrtis
Siga B_3
Sighajik = Teos q.v.
Sihūn = Saros F. K_{3ab}
Sikelia, Sicilia *Sicily* E_3
*Sikyon, Sicyon *Vasiliko* G_{3c}
Silvium E_1
Simav Chai = Makestos F. q.v.
Sina Oros, Mount Sinai, *Jebel Musa* I_5
Sinope *Sinūb* K_2
Siracusa = Syrakusai q.v.
Sirmium near *Mitrowicz* $F_{1,2}$
Siscia *Siszek* F_1
*Sitifis *Setif* D_3
Sivas = Sebasteia K_{3a}
Sizeboli = Apollonia q.v.
Skanderūn = Alexandreia q.v.
Skodra, Scodra, *Skútari*, *Scutari* F_2
Skythai, Scythae, Scythians HI_1
*Skythopolis, Scythopolis *Beisān* K_{4b}
*§Smyrna *Smyrna*, *Ismīr* H_{3a}
Sofia G_2
Sol(o)i (in Cyprus) *Aligora* I_{3d}
Sol(o)i, Pompeiopolis (in Cilicia) I_{3d}
Sousse. See Hadrumetum
Sozopolis. See Apollonia
Spain = (Hi)spania q.v.
Spalato F_2
Spania (Σπανία, Rom. xv. 24, 28). See Hispania
*Sparta *Sparta* G_{3b}
Sporades H_{3ab}
Stalimene = Lemnos H_{3a}
Stambul, *Constantinople* Byzantion H_2
Stein am Anger = Savaria q.v.

†Tiberias *Ṭabarīyeh* K_{4a}
Tiberias, Sea of. See Gennesareth
Tiberis F. *Tiber* E_2
Tibessa = Tipasa q.v.
Ticino = Ticinus F. D_1
Tifesh = Tipasa q.v.
Tigani = Samos (town) H_{3a}
Tigris F. *Tigris*, *Didjle* L_3
Tineh = Pelusion I_{4b}
Tingis *Tanger*, *Tangier* A_3
*Tipasa *Tibessa*, *Tifesh* C_3
Tisia F. *Theiss* G_1
Tlos *Duver* 460 m. = 1,508 ft. H_{3d}
To Aigaion Pelagos *Aegean Sea* GH_3
Tokra = Arsinoë (in Cyrenaica) q.v.
Tolm(e)ita = Ptolemaïs (in Cyrenaica) q.v.
Tolosa *Toulouse* C_2
Tom(o)i *Constantza* H_2
To Pelagos to kata ten Kilikian, "the sea which is off Cilicia" (Acts xxvii. 5) I_{3d}
To Pelagos to kata ten Pamphylian, "the sea which is off Pamphylia" (*ibid.*) I_{3b}
Torino, *Turin* Augusta Taurinorum D_1
Tortona. See Dertona
Tortosa. See Dertosa
Toulon Telo Martius D_2
Toulouse Tolosa C_2
*§Tralle(i)s *Aidin* H_{3c}
Trapani Drepanon, -um E_3
Trapezus *Trebizond* K_2
Treis Tabernai (Τρεῖς Ταβέρναι), Tres Tabernae, Three Taverns E_2
Triest(e) Tergeste E_1
Tripoli. See Oea, Tripolis
Tripoli vecchio = Sabrata E_4
Tripolis EF_4
Tripolis *Tripoli*, *Ṭarābulus* K_{4a}
Troas. See Alexandreia
Trogylion, Trogyllium *Kanapitza* (cape) H_{3a}
Troia, Troja, Troy *Hissarlik* H_{3a}
Tunis E_3
Turicum *Zürich* D_1
Turin = *Torino* Augusta Taurinorum D_1
Turris Libisonis *Porto-Torres* D_2
Tuz Geul = Tatta q.v.
Tyana *Kilis(s)e Hissar* 1,120 m. = 3,673 ft. I_{3c}
Tyras *Akkerman* I_1
Tyras F. *Dniester* H_1
Tyriaeum = Tyriaion *Ilg(h)in* 1,028 m. = 3,371 ft. I_{3a}
*‡Tyros, -us, Tyre *Ṣūr*
Tyrrhenian Sea = Mare Tuscum $E_{2,3}$

Uljcin, *Dulcigno* F_2
Ulubad = Lopadion H_1
Urfa, *Orfa* Edessa K_{3d}
Ushak. See Temenothyrai
*Utica *Marabout of Sidi Bu Shater* DE_3
Uzunjaburj = Olba q.v.

Valence Valentia CD_2
Valencia Valentia B_3
Valetta E_{3b}
Valona = Aulon F_2
Varassova = Chalkis (in Aetolia) G_{3c}
Varna Odessos, -us H_2
Vasada *Yonuslar* I_{3a}
Vasiliko = Sikyon q.v.
Veldidena *Innsbruck* E_1
Venetus L. *Lake of Constance* D_1
Venezia, *Venice* E_1
* *Venosa* Venusia F_2
Verbanus Lacus *Lago Maggiore* D_1
Verona *Verona* E_1
Verria = Beroia q.v.
Via Appia E_2
Via Egnatia = Hodos Egnatia G_2
* *Vicenza* Vicetia E_1
Vido = Narona F_2

Vienna *Vienne* CD_1
Vienna = Vindobona *Wien* F_1
Virunum *Klagenfurt* E_1
Viza = Bizye q.v.
Vizir Keupri = Neapolis q.v.
Vodhena = Edessa G_2
Volo, *Bolos* Iolcos G_{3c}
*Volubilis near *Mulai Idrīs Zarhōn* A_4

Wien, *Vienna*, Vindobona F_1

Yāfā = Joppe q.v.
Yalova = Sestos H_2
Yalovatch = Antiocheia Pisidia q.v.
Yarpuz = Arabissos K_{3a}
Yemishlu = Myndos q.v.
Yenije Kahveh = Termessos q.v.
Yeni Sheh(e)r = Larisa q.v.
Yeshil Irmak = Iris F. K_2
Yonuslar = Vasada I_{3a}
Yorg(h)an Ladik = Laodikeia Katakekaumene q.v.

Zacynthus = Zakynthos *Zante* G_{3a}
Zara. See Iader
Z(e)it(o)uni = Lamia q.v.
Zela *Zilleh* K_2
Zeng = Senia $EF_{1,2}$
Zengibar Kalesi = Isaura q.v.
Zürich Turicum D_1